The Kingdom and the Power

THE KINGDOM AND THE POWER

The Theology of Jürgen Moltmann

Geiko Müller-Fahrenholz

SCM PRESS

Translated by John Bowden from the German *Phantasie
für das Reich Gottes. Die Theologie Jürgen Moltmanns.
Eine Einführung,* published 2000 by Christian Kaiser
Verlag/Gütersloher Verlagshaus, Gütersloh.

0 334 02801 9

This edition first published 2000 by
SCM Press
9–17 St Albans Place London N1 0NX

SCM Press is a division of
SCM-Canterbury Press Ltd

Typeset by Regent Typesetting, London
Printed in Great Britain by
Biddles Ltd, Guildford and King's Lynn

For Helga

Contents

Preface   11

1. In the Prison Camp: Liberation   15
   1. A success story?   15
   2. 'Operation Gomorrah'   16
   3. The quest for God begins near to death   18
   4. The Bible boy: conversion to and with the Bible   20
   5. Friendship in a foreign land   21
   6. After Auschwitz: only the suffering God can help   23
   7. Imprisoned yet free   24

2. Community against the Horizon of the Rule of Christ   26
   1. The context: steps towards independence   26
   2. The focus of the programme: the horizon
      of the rule of Christ   30
   3. A programmatic writing without an echo   36

3. Hope, or In the Undertow of the Kingdom   40
   1. Bonn 1964   40
   2. *Theology of Hope*: the most important arguments   42
      (a) Bloch's *Principle of Hope* baptized?   42
      (b) *Theology of Hope*: basic content   44
   3. A retrospect   57

4. Everything is Decided by the Cross   62
   1. *El Dios Crucificado*   62
   2. *The Crucified God*   63
      (a) Who is God on the cross of the Godforsaken One?   64

(b) Who is this man?   67
(c) The cross – the suffering God   71
(d) Following the Crucified One – the compassionate   74
3. Summary: the programmatic element
in *The Crucified God*   77

5. In the Fellowship of the Spirit of God   80
1. Convergences   80
(a) The trinitarian dynamic   80
(b) The 'oppressed Christians throughout the world' 81
(c) The messianic Spirit of God in a time of uncertainty 83
2. *The Church in the Power of the Spirit*
– a sketch of the content   84
(a) 'The church of Jesus Christ'   85
(b) 'The church of the kingdom of God'   90
(c) 'The church as a community
of messianic service to the kingdom of God'   94
3. Unclear signals? Notes on a programmatic
writing which is not one   100
(a) Comparisons with 'The Community against
the Horizon of the Rule of Christ'   100
(b) Universalism and the church   102
(c) Church and community   103
(d) Ecclesiology and ethics   105

6. On Being a Christian – The Messianic Fragment   107
1. Introduction: Why there is no 'ethic'   107
2. The passion for the kingdom – ethical approaches   111
3. Friendship in a messianic light   116
4. The quest for the subject: community –
people – humankind   118
5. Fragment as chance   121

7. Liberation Theology for the First World?
The 1977 Turning Point   123
1. Where is nowhere?   123
2. Liberation theology for the First World   126
(a) The first step: separation   128

(b) The second step: identity   131
(c) The third step: integration   133

8. On Unification – The Theology of the Trinity as a
    Retelling of God's History of Love   137
    1. Convergences   137
        (a) 'Unification of God' – An argument for
             trinitarian thinking from Jewish belief in God   138
        (b) The Abba mystery   140
    2. Developments   142
        (a) God's passion narrative   142
        (b) The salvation of the world in
             the passion of God   144
        (c) Perichoresis and movement   146
    3. The practical relevance of trinitarian thinking   147
    4. Is trinitarian thinking a form of mysticism?   150

9. Creation: The Wonder of Existence   153
    1. Creation as indwelling   153
    2. The crown of creation: God's sabbath   156
    3. Human beings as the image of the Trinity   160
    4. The partners and the opponents   163
    5. For a habitable world   164

10. Under Way on the Way of the Messiah   167
    1. The messianic   167
    2. The 'way' of Jesus Christ   170
    3. A 'postmodern' christology   172
    4. In conclusion: two impressions of a reader   177

11. The Superabundance of the Power of God   182
    1. God's *ruach* – creative power and power of life   184
    2. Experience – the medium of *ruach*   186
    3. Living in the Spirit – the dynamic of grace   188
        (a) Liberation   189
        (b) Justification   190
        (c) Rebirth   192
        (d) Sanctification   194

(e) Charismatic power   195
     4. The Holy Spirit as person   196

12. What Remains is Expectation: *The Coming of God*   200
     1. 'He who comes' – time in the advent of God   201
     2. What will become of me?   204
         (a) Resurrection of the flesh   205
         (b) Death and sin   206
         (c) Where are the dead?   207
     3. Time itself becomes different   207
     4. When God is all in all – the restoration
         of all things   213
     5. *Soli Deo gloria* – in the realm of glory   215

13. Contemporary and Comrade of the Kingdom   219
     1. The contemporary   219
     2. The comrade of the kingdom   221
     3. Comrade and friend   223
     4. Comradely theology   224

14. Discovering the Inviting Mystery – Messianism and
     Mysticism in Moltmann's Theology   230
     1. The central theme: history in the advent of God   230
     2. World history as 'anonymous' kingdom of
         God history?   232
     3. A speculative theology?   235
     4. Talking about God is talking to God   237
     5. The mystical ground of theology   240
     6. Kingdom of God – kingdom of freedom   242

A Select Bibliography of the Works of Jürgen Moltmann   245

Notes   249

Preface

The work of Jürgen Moltmann is now so extensive that it is difficult to get an overall view of it. First there are the three great 'programmatic writings' from the years 1964 to 1975 which made Moltmann famous. The most notable of these is *Theology of Hope*. Then there are the 'Contributions to Systematic Theology', six important volumes which have appeared between 1980 and 1999. Before them and alongside them are many sermons and essays, articles and reviews. There are already 528 titles in a list of publications up to 1985.

How can we find our bearings here? Where has Moltmann's theology changed, and how? What basic features have remained the same?

This book is an 'aid to reading', a descriptive and explanatory way through Moltmann's work. In it my aim has been to sketch out the personal, ecumenical and political background to his books, which they also investigate. This attention to the contemporary contexts makes it easier to get at the programmatic focal points and theological leitmotifs developed in the books; for Jürgen Moltmann has always attempted to do his theological work in deliberate and committed dialogue with his contemporaries.

I have concentrated on the major works and only occasionally referred to shorter books or articles. I have not been concerned to give an encyclopaedically precise account of all the writings. Moreover it would have gone beyond the bounds of this book for me to have looked at the many investigations of Moltmann's work or particular complexes of themes in it. By now the secondary literature on Moltmann has become so extensive that to describe it would amount to an independent research project.

I should also emphasize quite specifically that this book is not an academic 'evaluation' or 'critique' of Moltmann's work. First, it is still too early for that. Who knows with what new directions Moltmann will yet surprise us? Secondly, I am not sufficient of an expert to be able to examine the academic 'correctness' of the references to the history of theology or the analyses and the conclusions for systematic theology which are drawn from them. Others must and will do that.

For me, Moltmann is the most important German-speaking Protestant theologian since the Second World War. His books reflect the problems which have left their stamp on the second half of the twentieth century. At the same time they contain critical discussions with the great theologians of the first half of the twentieth century. Here in particular I would mention Karl Barth, Rudolf Bultmann, Dietrich Bonhoeffer, Ernst Bloch, Martin Buber, Franz Rosenzweig and Karl Rahner. To this degree preoccupation with Moltmann's work has also helped me once again to consider the most important themes in twentieth-century theology, and to define and examine my own standpoint.

In addition to this, the basic positions of Reformation theology also play a major role for Moltmann. His Reformed positions can be recognized most clearly in his understanding of community. But this stamp does not prevent him from investigating Orthodox theology in detail. It is characteristic of the range of Moltmann's thought that Jewish traditions are combined with Orthodox, Catholic and Reformation insights in a theological project which markedly bears the stamp of liberation theology. To this degree the great themes of theology from two millennia are reflected in his work. Therefore it also represents a legacy that we must take to heart at the beginning of the third millennium.

My concern has been to express the basic features of Jürgen Moltmann's theology as evocatively as possible. Of course here I have also come to ask some critical questions. I have noted them in individual sections and summed them up in the two concluding chapters in the hope of thus opening up some perspectives which will facilitate dealing with Moltmann's work.

Time and again Jürgen Moltmann has been ready in a most

friendly way to satisfy my curiosity and to provide me with information which would not otherwise have been accessible to me. I am very grateful to him for that. I would be glad if he felt that my account was an appropriate reflection of his thought. I am also grateful to Christian Kaiser Verlag/ Gütersloher Verlagshaus and particularly to its theological editor, Herr Diedrich Steen, for friendly and expert support in this enterprise. A profound word of thanks goes to John Bowden for his thoughtful translation.

My deepest thanks go to my wife, who has shared my work on this book in a most intimate way and tolerated my 'absences' with much patience. Therefore the book is dedicated to her.

Autumn 1999   Geiko Müller-Fahrenholz

I

In the Prison Camp: Liberation

1. A success story?

A copy-book professorial career. Jürgen Moltmann's academic
rise looks just like a professional 'success story'. He studied and
gained his doctorate in Göttingen, and then spent five years as a
pastor (in Bremen-Wasserhorst), at the same time qualifying as a
university teacher. After that came a call to the Kirchliche
Hochschule in Wuppertal in 1959. Four years later, in 1963, he
moved to Bonn and then another four years later was called to
Tübingen. There Moltmann taught systematic theology for more
than twenty years until his retirement. And although a man born
in Hamburg has never really felt at home among the Swabians
(and this is also true of his wife, Elisabeth Moltmann-Wendel,
who comes from Potsdam), the two of them could not bring
themselves to move north. In venerable and busy Tübingen, high
above the Neckar, with its view over to the Jura, probably the
most famous theological couple in Germany have worked on
various projects. Nothing like 'retirement' seems to have been
provided for in their lives.

This is a rare professorial career. At a stroke *Theology of Hope*
brought Moltmann international fame. But many more of his
books sold in large numbers and have been translated into many
European and Asian languages. It is certainly no exaggeration to
say that Moltmann is the best-known German-speaking academic theologian at the end of the twentieth century.

But how has it come about that this scholar who is so used
to success has become the treasured and revered conversation-
partner of people who have to work in radically different conditions, which as a rule are also incomparably more burdensome,

for example in Latin America or Korea? The stages of his career –
Hamburg, Bremen, Wuppertal, Bonn, Tübingen – betray nothing
of the sources of the theological passion on which Moltmann's
manifold and extensive work draws and which finds an echo in
all parts of the world.

2. 'Operation Gomorrah'

The essential element cannot be recognized at first glance. So we
must look again, more closely. We need to examine the inner
developments in the life of this man to be able to understand the
elementary decisions and impressions which govern his work. So
the question to ask is: what are the key experiences which have
given this life its unique direction?

Here I must make it clear that this book is not concerned
to provide a complete biography, far less a psychologizing
'analysis', of the events and developments which have shaped
Moltmann. But it is important to seek out the decisive crossroads
in his life, the points and times which prefigure what will only
develop much later. These key experiences are not only
important for understanding Moltmann's work; they also indicate the elementary levels at which Moltmann's experiences of
life and work touch on the work and experiences of many other
people.

In 1995 Moltmann said in a service in London: 'In July 1943 I
was an air force auxiliary in a battery in the centre of Hamburg,
and barely survived the fire storm which the Royal Air Force's
"Operation Gomorrah" let loose on the eastern part of the city.
The friend standing next to me at the firing predictor was torn to
pieces by the bomb that left me unscathed. That night I cried out
to God for the first time: "My God, where are you?" And the
question "Why am I not dead too?" has haunted me ever since.
Why are you alive? What gives your life meaning? Life is good,
but to be a survivor is hard. One has to bear the weight of grief.
It was probably in that night that my theology began, for I came
from a secular family and knew nothing of faith.'[1] A single night
can completely change a life.

Moltmann had really wanted to study mathematics and physics. Einstein, Planck and Heisenberg had been the heroes of his youth. He had gone to war with Goethe's poems and the soldier's edition of *Faust*, but in the prisoner-of-war camp, in Mass Camp 2226 in Zedelgam near Ostend, then in Labour Camp 22 in Kilmarnock, and finally, from June 1946, in Norton Camp, Goethe's fine verses lost their meaning. 'Cold horror' seized the nineteen-year-old soldier over the total defeat, the destroyed cities of Germany, the millions of refugees. He had escaped with his life, but was confronted with nothing. Even 'colder' was the horror which seized the young man when in the Scottish camp he was confronted with photographs of Bergen-Belsen and Auschwitz, namely the horror that he had not only fought in vain but had suffered for criminals and had been sacrificed by criminals. So not only was the war for Germany, the 'holy Fatherland', lost, but Germany itself seemed to be lost. Horror and shame changed into a deep, desperate weariness with life. 'In the Scottish labour camp, together with some other astonished prisoners, I was for the first time given a Bible by a well-meaning army chaplain . . . I read it without much comprehension, until I stumbled on the psalms of lament: . . ."I was dumb with silence . . . my lifetime is as nothing in thy sight . . . for I am a stranger . . ." They were the words of my own heart and they called my soul to God. Then I came to the story of the passion, and when I read Jesus' death cry, "My God, why have you forsaken me?" I knew with certainty: this is someone who understands you . . . the divine brother in distress, who takes the prisoners with him on his way to resurrection. I began to summon up the courage to live again, seized by *a great hope* . . . This early fellowship with Jesus, the brother in suffering and the redeemer from guilt, has never left me since.'[2]

Half a century later Moltmann still spoke with deep emotion of the two years that he spent in Norton Camp. This re-education camp had turned into a little university and there the young man began to study theology. The involvement of the YMCA had produced a rich library for the German prisoners. A course of lectures was organized involving such famous theologians as the

Swede Anders Nygren and the Dane Soe, the Dutchman Visser't
Hooft, the young General Secretary of the World Council of
Churches at that time in the process of formation, or the great
John R.Mott, the founder of the International Missionary Council
and ecumenical godfather. In these personalities the ecumenical
movement entered the camp, but Moltmann had already experienced its transforming power earlier, above all during a visit
from Dutch students.

These students 'told us that Christ was the bridge on which
they could cross to us, and that without Christ they would not be
talking to us at all. They told of the Gestapo terror, the loss of
their Jewish friends, and the destruction of their homes. We too
could step on to this bridge which Christ had built from them
to us, and could confess the guilt of our people and ask for reconciliation. At the end we all embraced. For me that was *an
hour of liberation*.'[3]

In imprisonment, liberation. During the war and in the prisoner-
of-war camp Moltmann had the revolutionary experiences which
opened him up to faith in Christ and a lifelong pre-occupation
with questions of Christian belief. In these early experiences we
recognize the leitmotifs which still stamp his theology.

3. *The quest for God begins near to death*

Moltmann's theology begins in the night when the fire storm
destroyed great parts of his home city of Hamburg and killed his
best friend, standing next to him. It begins with a cry from the
fear of death, more precisely with a question, 'My God, where
are you?'

Christian faith had played no role in his secular home. There
were no prayers, no religious education. The confirmation classes
under Provost Hansen, who was tainted with National Socialism,
had been more of a repulsive experience. God played no role for
the young man.

In the night when a world perished, the question of God and
thus of the sense of living on among so many dead was wrenched
from the young man.

The situation is paradigmatic: Moltmann's theology arises out of a question. And it remains a questioning theology, a theology of curiosity. It comes into being in the night of an immediate and cruel proximity to death, and therefore in the end it is never about learned intellectual games but about questions of life and death. It does not arise out of the peaceful and cheerful awareness of an unshakeable certainty in God but out of the abysmal experience of the remoteness of God. Therefore it does not have any apologetic interest either, and does not assert that it should or could develop something like a closed 'system' of learning about God. No 'Dogmatics' has come from Moltmann's pen, no 'Summa' of theology. Moltmann's first great books are 'programmatic writings'. In their resolute 'one-sidedness' they are fundamentally always meant as invitations to conversation; they are 'indications of a quest' aimed at dialogue with others. They are exclamation-marks which are to be read as question-marks.[4]

Moreover the great cycle of systematic theology which Moltmann has presented since 1980, and which now is complete in six volumes, explicitly understands itself as 'contributions'. So we read in the preface to the first volume, *The Trinity and the Kingdom of God*: 'By using the word "contributions", the writer recognizes the conditions and limitations of his own position, and the relativity of his own particular environment. He makes no claim to say everything, or to cover the whole of theology. He rather understands his own 'whole' as part of a whole that is much greater. He cannot therefore aim to say what is valid for everyone, at all times and in all places. But he will set himself, with his own time and his own place, within the greater community of theology.'[5]

It is one of the hallmarks of a seeking and questioning theology that it brings into intellectual play its own existential involvement and the conditions which are given by history and context. It remains experimental, incomplete, fragmentary: 'For me, *from the start* theology has been an adventure with an uncertain outcome, a voyage of discovery into an inviting mystery. My theological virtue has not been humility, but only curiosity and imagination for the kingdom of God.'[6]

It is also part of this experimental approach that Moltmann has sought a variety of different forms of expression for his theology. Alongside the academic treatises there are books with sermons and articles. It is not least through the influence of his wife and the feminist theology she represents that in his later works he occasionally relates very personal experiences.

4. *The Bible boy: conversion to and with the Bible*

An army chaplain gives a Bible, and a twenty-year-old begins to read. In the midst of desperation, shame, loneliness and homelessness the young man hears a new voice. It comes from an old book, but at the same time it speaks to him from the soul and calls his soul to God.

It was only later that the theological teachers came, above all Karl Barth, and then Hans Joachim Iwand, Ernst Wolf, Otto Weber and then the Dutchman A.A. van Ruler. Then inspiring companions entered his field of view, above all the philosopher Ernst Bloch and then the great Jewish scholars Rosenzweig, Scholem and Benjamin. But the way to faith was not prepared by a spiritual father or a comparable spiritual director. There was no Philip, as in Acts 8, to put to him the friendly question whether he understood what he was reading. There was no community or group in which familiarity with Holy Scripture would be prepared for and practised. At the beginning stands the lonely, unschooled, directionless reading of a strange book. And from the book the young man in tribulation encountered quite directly the 'Christ in tribulation', and what came about was a 'fellowship with Jesus, the brother in suffering and the redeemer from guilt', which has never left him since.

In a way which can hardly be conceived of more personally, in this life the *sola scriptura* which gave its stamp to the Reformation proves itself. This orientation on the Bible remains a basic feature of Moltmann's theology. We shall have to discuss later whether and how the central importance of the Bible is reflected on exegetically and hermeneutically. But this much may already be said on these introductory pages: methods of biblical criticism never played a decisive role in the foundations of Moltmann's theology. He did not become a 'Bultmannian', although the influence of the great Marburg scholar was very strong at that time. But on the other hand Joachim Jeremias could not grip him either. Rather, it was exegetes like Gerhard von Rad who helped him to understand the Bible as the great document of God's covenant history with his people Israel and only then, through Christ Jesus, also with his people among the Gentiles, the church. Certainly it was clear to him that the Bible displays a variety of literary 'sources' and 'strata'. But that did not prevent him from reading scripture as the one undivided foundation document of God's unswerving faithfulness. So all his life, as he once said to me, he has remained a 'Bible boy', who allows himself to be addressed by Holy Scripture ever more directly, indeed occasionally in a way which seems all too direct.

5. Friendship in a foreign land

The Dutch students had made it clear that they had really come to the Germans bowed down in shame and scandal only over the bridge which is called Christ. On this bridge an encounter became possible which grew out of a confession of guilt and a request for reconciliation. On this bridge took place the embrace which made enemies friends.

Teachers like Nygren and Soe, leading ecumenists like Mott and Visser't Hooft, came to Norton Camp. Without the ecumenical involvement of the Swede Birger Forell, without the active help of the international Student World Federation and the YMCA and the help of many unknown persons, the theological college behind the fences of Norton Camp would have been quite impossible, indeed inconceivable.

Strangers, indeed former enemies, proved to be friends. That was a surprising, indeed overwhelming, experience for the young prisoner-of-war who had become homeless. The ecumenical movement entered the life of this man who had become alienated from his homeland, indeed had even become a stranger to himself, as a force which offered security and a home. Here was the ecumenical movement, i.e. 'Christ existing as community', to use an expression of Bonhoeffer's, and therefore the communal expression of a grace which does not ask about merit and worth. It went through the walls between hostile peoples, as the Risen Christ went through the closed doors, to give new life with its spirit to the disciples made rigid by fear. Here was the offer of friendship in embittered enmity, the offer of a home in extreme homelessness.

As a child and a young man, Moltmann had known no community which had commended itself to him as a liberating alternative to everyday National Socialism. What he had experienced as an established church presented itself to him as an institution which was all too prone to populism. Thus Moltmann's experiences of the church began abroad; from the start they were ecumenical. So from the beginning this ecumenicity was the hallmark of his theology. The ecumenical horizon is the sphere in which his 'fantasy for the kingdom of God' developed.

Most other theologians develop in the protected 'homes' of their particular traditions and regard ecumenical experiences as something extra, often also as something strange, though quite often also as happy. (Which is why they also have a constant tendency in difficult questions to withdraw into the traditional patterns of thought and models of piety of their familiar tradition.) However, for Moltmann the ecumenical community is his real 'home', in which the confessional 'identities' look like smaller rooms – and sometimes even like constricting cells. That explains why Moltmann never had fears of contact in accepting theological impulses from the representatives of other churches. In the early years the Reformed theologian Otto Weber not only supervised his doctorate but had also become a fatherly mentor, and in the 1980s a deep friendship bound him to the Romanian Orthodox theologian Dimitru Staniloe. Alongside these the Catholic theologian Hans Urs von Balthasar and the black theologian James Cone also played an important role. That also explains why after his return from the prisoner-of-war camp Moltmann did not go back to the Lutheran Church in which he had grown up, but all his life stood apart from the established church groupings in Germany. Anyone who is at home in the ecumene can never again feel at home in confessional domesticity.

6. *After Auschwitz: only the suffering God can help*

Moltmann has always thought that he never had a conversion experience in a narrow pietistic sense. He never 'decided' for Christ. But he does know the moment in which he got the clear impression that this Christ had 'decided' for him and had found him 'in the dark pit' of his soul.[7] This moment is a sentence from the Gospel of Mark, 'My God, why have you forsaken me?' There is no saying in holy scripture which has such a central significance for Moltmann's life and for his theology.

'Christ's Godforsakenness showed me *where* God is, *where* he had been with me in my life, and where he would be in the future,' said Moltmann fifty years later.[8] This now also has particular force in view of the Godforsakenness which is associated with the names of Bergen-Belsen and Auschwitz. That the brotherly acceptance by Christian students from all over the world[9] and the reconciliation with the Dutch students did not become possible through a cautious silence about the Nazi atrocities but through the confession of guilt was the beginning of a 'great hope', the source of a new courage to live. It formed the basis for the decision 'to return to that country of contradictions, between Goethe's Weimar and Buchenwald',[10] and to try again with Germany.

We shall encounter the cry of God's Godforsaken Son more frequently when we are developing Moltmann's remarks about a trinitarian doctrine of God and christology. In this connection it is important to grasp Moltmann's key experience, that God is present precisely also in Godforsakenness. In other words, in the case of God we are not dealing with an unmoved idol of omnipotence who is incapable of suffering, but with a God who loves passionately and therefore has infinite compassion. And only a God who loves so passionately can help us, who have to live in the shadow of Auschwitz.

In this basic experience lies the nucleus of the decision for a

politically conscious theology. Granted, it would be two decades
before Moltmann, together with Johann Baptist Metz, raised the
programmatic demand for a 'political theology', but the political
dimension of Christian faith was already forming in the British
prisoner-of-war camp. The recognition that theology may not
retreat behind Auschwitz, that the churches too must not go
behind this atrocity in conservative zeal, and that being a Christian
has to prove itself in resolute acceptance of the hereditary
historical burdens of the time and in resolute involvement in
the political effects which follow from them – this political
horizon has been planted in Moltmann's theology from the
beginning.

This political horizon also includes the experience of material
poverty and existential misery; it includes the recollection of
a lack of involvement, cynicism and submission in order to
survive. He was reminded of this year of imprisonment, of life in
dirty pits in the earth, when on the occasion of the General
Assembly of the World Council of Churches in Nairobi in 1975
he went into the slum of Mathare Valley. When the Minjung
theologians from South Korea began to speak of the 'people that
walks in darkness', he immediately understood what they meant.
The years of servitude have made him sensitive to poor and
damaged people all over the world. Recollections of the years in
the prisoner-of-war camp turned into the *deep memory of the
suffering and torment* which are not only to be found among
human beings but which burden the whole creation.

What Paul calls the 'anxious waiting of creation' is for
Moltmann reality.

7. *Imprisoned yet free*

To return once more to the encounter with the Dutch students.
Moltmann describes that unforgettable hour in which the guilt of
the people was confessed, the request for reconciliation made,
and the reconciliation sealed with warm embraces, as an 'hour of
liberation'. And he continues: 'I was able to breathe again, felt
like a human being once more, and returned cheerfully to the

camp behind the barbed wire. The question of how long the captivity was going to last no longer bothered me.'[11]

Why could he be happy behind barbed wire? Because although externally a prisoner, really he had already been freed. This is the reason why the word 'liberation' can be regarded as a code word in Moltmann's theology. It characterizes not only liberation from existential meaninglessness but also ecumenical openness from desperate loneliness. It describes the deliverance from national shame and security in a community which transcends all boundaries between individuals and peoples. 'Liberation' thus opens up the political scope of the revelation of what Kurt Marti calls 'God's passion for the world' and does not stop even at the frontier of death. Thus 'liberation' becomes the hallmark and seal of God's history in which human history and the history of our world are hidden.

The kingdom of God breathes freedom.

2

The Community against the Horizon of the Rule of Christ

'In 1959, just after I had arrived at the Kirchliche Hochschule in Wuppertal, I published my first programmatic theological work, *The Community against the Horizon of the Rule of Christ*. It was only thirty-five pages long, and remained quite unknown. Reading it again today, I can discover most of my later ideas in this beginning.'[12] This reference by Moltmann from the year 1997 directs our attention to a writing which stands in the shade of the great 'programmatic writings' which were published after 1964. These were: first, *Theology of Hope* (1964), then *The Crucified God* (1972), and finally *The Church in the Power of the Spirit* (1975). Nevertheless Moltmann himself indicates how important this largely unnoticed work has remained, since it already contains important notions which are developed in the later books. It is therefore interesting to look rather more closely at it. That will also give me an opportunity to examine more closely the first decade of Moltmann's 'theological existence'.

1. *The context: steps towards independence*

In 1948 Moltmann had been discharged. He had returned to Germany and in Göttingen had continued the study of theology that he had begun in Norton Camp. There he met such fascinating teachers as Hans-Joachim Iwand, Ernst Wolf and Otto Weber, who have already been mentioned. Iwand, Wolf and Weber had been active in the Confessing Church, so they represented the 'other' Germany. They had taken part in the resistance against the Hitler dictatorship and were looking for ways to express these experiences in theology and the church. With his interpretation of Luther's doctrine of justification, Iwand was able to deepen Moltmann's experiences of the Godforsaken Jesus. Wolf and Weber were close to the theology of Karl Barth, and with them Moltmann also came under the powerful influence of the great professor from Basel. Barth shone over all. So strongly did he dominate theology that for some years Moltmann thought that there could no longer be any independent theology.

It is nevertheless illuminating that Moltmann never understood himself as a 'disciple' of Karl Barth, just as it is also illuminating that he himself formed no 'school' and did not encourage one. Presumably he instinctively kept his distance because his youthful experiences with the Führer had once and for all satisfied his need for leader figures. Moreover his solitary encounter with Christ had ultimately strengthened him in the knowledge that everyone is alone before the face of God and has to find a personal way into this mystery. If this is 'Protestant', then Moltmann has always remained a 'Protestant', however much he has also been influenced by Catholic, Orthodox and Jewish authors. Precisely because he had no fears about contact, he suspected any 'school'.

Göttingen brought him not only an encounter with impressive professors but also and above all the encounter with his fellow-student Elisabeth Wendel from Potsdam.[13] She had already begun to study theology in Berlin in 1945, having had intensive contact with the Confessing Church through her parents. In contrast to Jürgen, Elisabeth had experienced the Bible studies of the Confessing Church as an 'underground church'. For her the community had provided both a home and freedom at the same time.

In 1951 Elisabeth Wendel gained her doctorate under Weber on Hermann Friedrich Kohlbrügge (1803–1875), the Reformed theologian from Holland who had gained great influence in Wuppertal with his radical theology of justification. A year later Jürgen Moltmann gained his doctorate with a work on Moise Amyraut and the Saumur school.[14] Otto Weber had proposed the topic, but who was Amyraut? Moltmann had no idea. After some research he took up the topic and in this way came into contact with an interesting variant of an early ecumenical theology. Amyraut (1596–1664) was under the influence of Calvin, but had argued for a union between Lutheran and Reformed and also enjoyed great respect among the Catholics.

Elisabeth Wendel and Jürgen Moltmann married in 1952. According to the church regulations then prevailing, as a married woman Elisabeth could not train to be an assistant minister, nor could she look forward to ordination and a pastorate. But her experiences in Potsdam and Berlin will nevertheless have played some role in Jürgen's decision to seek a pastorate in the church of Berlin-Brandenburg. However, after months of waiting this plan had to be given up because the Communist authorities refused them entry. A pastor who had been a prisoner-of-war of the English for three years seemed suspect to them. Might a spy perhaps be being smuggled in in the guise of a pastor? Finally, Jürgen's fatherly friend Otto Weber had an idea which worked. The parish of Bremen-Wasserhorst was vacant, and alongside it work with students could also be developed. So it came about that after an assistant pastorate in Siegerland and the preachers' seminary in Wuppertal, the Moltmanns came to this small Bremen community.

Wasserhorst is a country village in the extreme north-east of Bremen; at that time it was difficult to reach, and even now it is a world apart. For the young couple it was in many respects a laborious time, full of deprivation.

One of the most bitter experiences of these years was that their first child died at birth. It was a help that the community showed great concern for the couple. However, it was only when further children were born that the mourning over this loss came to an end. Over the years Elisabeth brought four daughters into the world; by now they are grown up and standing on their own feet.

If this book were a biography, then it would be important to discuss Jürgen and Elisabeth Moltmann's marriage at length, since it developed into a theological partnership of rare intensity. However, little theological exchange could yet be detected in the first years of their marriage. Whereas Jürgen Moltmann got down to his Habilitation – the countryfolk did not want to be disturbed in the mornings, so there was time for work on the history of theology, which was concentrated on the federal theology of Cocceius -[15] all the energy of the young pastor's wife was taken up by the small children and household chores. Of course the theological partnership suffered under this 'division of labour'. Only many years later, under the impact of the feminist movement in the USA, did Elisabeth Moltmann-Wendel recognize this 'division of labour' which had up till then been taken for granted as the prison which prevents women from 'becoming their own persons'.[16]

It is this liberation-theological dimension which deepened the theological partnership between her and her husband. We shall be discussing this later in the book.[17]

The unforgettable experiences in the prisoner-of-war camp, the proximity to Karl Barth and other representatives of the Confessing Church, and a preoccupation with essential aspects of Reformed theology, led the young Wasserhorst pastor to adopt positions which were politically and ecclesiastically on the left wing. Moltmann chafed against the conservative tendencies which were coming increasingly into the foreground in the young Federal Republic during the 1950s. He distanced himself from the first Federal Chancellor, Konrad Adenauer, since in his whole attitude – stamped by the Catholic Rhineland – Adenauer represented a Germany of the kind that had existed before the Hitler dictatorship. Moltmann's views corresponded more with the position of Gustav Heinemann, who criticized Adenauer's policy of leaning on the Western great powers. Not only did he see it as an expression of a risky taking sides in the 'Cold War' which rapidly became more intense after 1948 and was to govern world politics for four decades. He also felt that the tie to the West and here above all to France took up old models of a Christian Europe which went back to the Middle Ages. For Moltmann, after the experiences of the collapse, all this had the character of 'reactionary' politics.

In parallel to this, the churches also attempted to follow the state church ordinances which had existed before 1933. This resulted in a conservative constellation which again favoured a close partnership between state and church. Granted, this constellation meant that the churches profited considerably from the economic boom in the Federal Republic, the much-discussed 'economic miracle'. But at the same time many people who still clearly remembered the dangerous entanglement of state and church in the Third Reich and the deceptive talk of the 'intact territorial churches' saw this church 'order' as a denial of the Confessing Church. As time went on, the 'new beginning' which had been spoken of in the famous 1945 'Stuttgart Declaration of Guilt' increasingly failed to materialize.

All the same, during the 1950s and even later the protests and reservations about this conservatism continued to remain a clearly recognizable power within the territorial churches. The most important representatives of this protest included Martin Niemöller and Gustav Heinemann. Both were active in the World Council of Churches. Niemöller was one of the first to seek contact with the Orthodox Churches in the then Soviet Union. Thus this kind of ecumenical openness went hand in hand with left-wing politics.

This, in the briefest outline, is the context in which Moltmann spoke with his first programmatic work.

2. *The focus of the programme: the horizon of the rule of Christ*

Moltmann begins with the Jewish theologian Ben Chorin, who had observed that, 'For the Christian church the kingdom of God threatens to disappear behind the figure of the Messiah', and continues: 'This impression in particular touches on our present-day church preaching and our emphatically "ecclesiastical" theology at a sensitive point.'[18] What does he mean by 'ecclesiastical'? This is a reference to the emphatic stress on the central significance of Christ for the teaching and action of the church. Certainly Moltmann also emphasizes that Christian preaching must be 'christological', indeed 'christocentric', but for him this must not lead to the loss of the question of the meaning and goal of this preaching. One can understand the turn away from culture Protestantism which has been unable to hold on to the central significance of Jesus Christ, but along with this there has also been an ominous loss of horizon, and with no horizon Christ cannot be the middle and the centre. 'For there is no middle without a horizon, no centre without a circumference . . . , no Christ without his kingly rule in worldly, bodily life, without the eschatological horizon of the new world, the redemption of the creature in the new heaven and the new earth' (9).

Moltmann takes over from Dietrich Bonhoeffer the insight that the centrality of Jesus Christ can be recognized in its exclusiveness only if at the same time the extent of Jesus Christ and the cosmic breadth of the sphere of his rule is taken into account. For him, this is 'the theme which fascinates us today' because it reflects 'our perplexities in theological and community work': 'How do we say and how do we live out the fact that the kingdom of God is the horizon, that God's world is the infinitely wide circumference which this centre Jesus Christ put around it?' (9).[19]

That is the 'ground bass' of Moltmann's theology. The theme of his life, the kingdom of God, appears briefly and evocatively in the 1959 writing. It is developed in 'four perspectives'. First of all, following Karl Barth, Moltmann speaks of the 'universal foundation of the proclamation of Christ' (10). He refers to Barth's famous first work, the *Commentary on Romans*, because in it the concept of the kingdom of God has been 'subjected to a radical and vehement actualization' (10). He says that Barth has pushed aside all the half-truths which fuse the kingdom of God with human achievements, say in the church, in the state or in culture, and brought out the unique dimension of the kingdom as the revelation of the word of God for all the world. Therefore the one important thing is to proclaim the kingdom of God, as Meister Eckhart could also have said, as God himself and as his infinite being. God in his self-revelation is the 'kingdom in person' (11). That God reveals himself in Christ also makes it plain that God has decided for the world, however much it has also fallen away from him and may itself fall apart. That is the 'objective background . . . the world redeemed in Christ' (12).

From this Moltmann concludes: 'Our church preaching suffers from the fact that this presuppositionless breadth of the rule of Christ which comes first is not expressed with quite a different weight. The expectation with which we go to worship suffers from the limitation that we do not dare to have higher hopes' (13). In our lack of faith we are afraid that the gates will be stuck and the doors will not open. But if we were to believe more boldly in the rule of Christ, we would experience that the gates are already flung wide and the doors are open.

Here, under the heading 'Brothers, remain faithful to the earth', Moltmann turns to concrete developments. Because God has revealed himself in Christ on this earth and in human history, this earth and this history are the horizon against which Christ wills to come to reign. Christoph Blumhardt, Dietrich Bonhoeffer, Richard Rothe and A.A.van Ruler[19] are the authorities which Moltmann follows. The 1949 Dutch Confession of Faith is also important to him.[20]

But how can one as a Christian regard this world as God's world if there is so much blatant injustice and wicked misuse of power in it? This question is raised sharply by the critique of religion made by Feuerbach, Nietzsche, Overbeck or Dostoievsky. And Moltmann concedes that this is *the* problem. 'Doubt in God is an innocence in the face of despair over God's earth and its future' (15). The real boldness of faith consists in maintaining this 'deep yes to this earth' on the basis of the 'passionate love of the cross and the rule of the Crucified One' (15).

At this point the central significance of the Crucified Christ is worth noting. We shall keep coming across it later. It shows that the notion of the rule of Christ does not derive from any utopian belief in progress but is formulated in face of the cross: 'To believe in the lordship of God, i.e. the earth as it is, and to accept and love the cross in the midst of it' (16). And for Moltmann, following Blumhardt, 'love' means God's activity in the world, thus, for example, perceiving 'his mighty acts in the messianic pressure of the workers' movement and in the awakening of the peoples of Asia' (17). It is not a matter of pious feelings, but of concrete political, social and cultural processes. In this context, for Moltmann Richard Rothe is an important authority who has been too little noted hitherto. But more important than Rothe is Bonhoeffer, who maintained in his *Ethics* that the prayer for the kingdom of God compels the church 'for better or worse into the community of the children of the earth and the world' (9). Following God, who remains faithful to his creation, the church too is called and enabled to be faithful. Moltmann quotes the Dutch Catechism, which in Article 18 maintains: 'If we look at the victory which has been won in Jesus Christ, we do not despair in this earth but remain faithful to it' (21). To sum up, then: 'The expectation of the redemptive rule of the crucified and exalted Christ, which puts right all things in our worldly reality, can alone give us the power to take up the "cross of reality" and accept this word in all its reality without reservation, but also without illusions' (21).

This uncompromising acceptance of reality is then developed in a third step under the heading 'New Partnerships of the Church in the World'. Just as Moltmann opposes a 'punctualistic' existential interpretation of the gospel, so too he opposes abstract talk of 'human beings in themselves'. 'We always encounter concrete persons in their social relationships and their social involvement, people with their responsibilities, the father, the mother, the child, the worker, the superior, the subordinate. The church's preaching suffers from the fact that people are still addressed . . . only in relationship to themselves and not to the things on which they work and the power under which they suffer' (23f.). To move forward here, Moltmann refers to Bonhoeffer's doctrine of mandates.[21] In his sketches for an *Ethics* Bonhoeffer had recognized 'divine ordinances in the world' in marriage/family, work, authority and the church (25) and in so doing had continued Luther's reflections on the 'three arch-authorities' or 'states'. It is important for Moltmann that with his mandates Bonhoeffer describes levels and patterns of concrete responsibility which mutually condition one another but do not allow any hierarchy. 'The state, the economy, the family, the church and culture each have their special task in

God's history. They have to carry out these tasks reciprocally in reciprocal limitation and supplementation. Thus the worldly professions are just as related to the service of God in the world . . . as is the apostolate' (27). So it is God who 'serves' his world in these orders. Therefore it is a commandment of faith to enter into this 'service'. Here arguments from natural law are rejected, as is thinking in rigid 'orders of creation'. Moltmann is concerned to integrate Christian life and action into the 'living history of God'[22] and thus to preserve it in a dynamic tension. On the basis of this position he criticized both the doctrine of two kingdoms developed by Lutheranism in the nineteenth century and 'theocratic' tendencies in Reformed Dutch theology. But he immediately adds: 'What seems more important today than drawing such boundaries and making assignations of a theoretical kind is the development of new political virtues in Christianity' (29). Here he takes up some thoughts of his teacher Ernst Wolf, who urges the overcoming of the traditional virtues 'of the authorities' in favour of democratic and participatory values and patterns of behaviour. The important thing is to take seriously the 'material state' (30) of modern democratic and economic conditions so that Christian obedience can be shown appropriately and pertinently in them.

Consequently Moltmann comes to speak on a fourth dimension, which he calls 'the courage for worldly preaching' (30). Church preaching must take on a new form, or more precisely it must attempt to address people in their particular mandates. 'There is no preaching and evangelization in pure culture' (31). Consequently it is a 'dangerous retreat' if the communication of the gospel is predominantly directed towards the family and the private sphere. Here Moltmann recognizes a retreat to the sphere of mandates of the marriage and family. But, he argues, it is important to develop not only 'political preaching' but also 'cultural preaching' and 'economic preaching'.

What such preaching would look like is not discussed in the programmatic writing. But the indication of the need to create 'working groups' (32) to take up social, charitable, cultural and political tasks seems illuminating. The 'call to the kingdom' (32) must be perceived and proved in practical participation in the various tasks of a plural society.

'But in all these things the decisive need is for a new secularization of the gospel and faith' (32), Moltmann writes. Here he understands 'secularization' not as adaptation to the particular fashions of the time but as a force which shapes each particular present. What is called for is not pious internalization but the 'prophetic presence' (32).

In his comprehensive closing thoughts Moltmann once again emphasizes that the worldliness of the Christian life grows out of bold faith in the 'broad horizon of the rule of Christ' (33) and is grounded in it. It is not a question, as in nineteenth-century cultural Protestantism, of deserting pulpit and altar, but of warmly accepting the 'centrifugal power' (34) of the centre, which is Christ. Wherever communities entrust themselves to this centrifugal power which at the same time has a centripetal effect, they will be armed against the temptation of conservatism and a return into the 'horizon of the world of the day before yesterday' (34).

'Bold' is an adjective which occurs with striking frequency in this brief programmatic work. According to Moltmann, a faith must and can be bold which recognizes the rule of Christ not only as the horizon of the world but also of world history, and which consequently regains the 'hope of the last things' (34), so that it knows this earth and its future to be embraced by the 'creation, the reconciliation and the judgment of the world' (34). In this framework of the faithfulness of God which embraces the world and history, Christian faithfulness to the earth and the representative commitment of the community to the world laden with curse and suffering takes on its space, its urgency and also its sense of possibility.

'Today we see Christ and the world (cosmos) in a corresponding, complementary relationship, no longer in diastasis and not in syntheses,' Moltmann finally remarks: 'Just as centre and circumference, discipline and breadth, prayer and openness to the world condition one another, so church and cosmos stand over against each other. We are to gain the freedom to become more churchly

than the church in general and at the same time more worldly
than the world in general and thus break through Christian
mediocrity and illusionary or resigned this-worldliness' (35).

3. A programmatic writing without an echo

Almost forty years later, Moltmann noted that most of his later
ideas are already present in embryo in this beginning. He calls
them 'the messianic dimension, faithfulness to the earth, the
inviting horizon of God's future, the theology of politics and
secular preaching'.[23] If this nearness to the content of the later
works is so striking, the question arises: why did this programmatic writing largely remain unnoticed if the later ones provoked
so lively a discussion?

At a distance of four decades it can perhaps be said that this
work is probably too assertive and too brief. It contains reflections on theology, ethics, homiletics and church politics and thus
basically presents a whole programme for church reform.
Measured by the implications of this programme, however, the
remarks remain too brief and for all their radical nature seem
vague. That can be clarified by a few observations.

What is meant by 'community' in this work remains vague.
We have to note that Moltmann was writing from his experience
as a community pastor, but it would be too narrow to want to
understand his concept of community as being a local community
or parish. This is no mere congregationalism. His reference to
working groups in line with Bonhoeffer's mandates would rather
suggest the model of a city or regional church with differentiated
forms of assembly and action. But it remains unclear how such a
church would have to be organized. The charge of conservatism
is presumably directed not least against forms of church leadership and church movement which became established again after
the war, but there is no indication of what an appropriate form
of government would have to look like. The theological concept
of the community as the fellowship which 'gathers under the
word' needs more concrete treatment in terms of a sociology of
the church to become usable.

Another point which gives rise to questions relates to the

concept of 'preaching'. What are we to understand by 'cultural preaching' and 'economic preaching'? The nearness to the theology of the apostolate which Moltmann had come to know in van Ruler and Hoekendijk suggests that 'preaching' might be meant to be the whole proclamation of the church, i.e. its missionary presence. But that does not clarify the question of the forms and expressions of such preaching.

In connection with this, the relationship between Christ and the cosmos is only imprecisely described by the terms 'corresponding' and 'complementary'. Thinking in 'diastases', i.e. opposite categories, is to be just as firmly rejected as thinking in 'syntheses'. Nevertheless, terms like correspondence and complementarity presuppose reciprocal relationships. But what could the 'cosmos' add to a relationship which was not already there in 'Christ'? What could the 'material' or the character of the reciprocal answer be which is suggested in the word 'correspondence'? How does this definition of relationship relate to the absolute sovereignty of the kingdom of God, which Moltmann had stressed, following Karl Barth?

These questions are not meant to be a belated criticism of this work, but rather to explain why it had so little echo. Basically it represents the foundation for a comprehensive reform of the church. But its mixture of provocation and brevity might have led to the possibility of dismissing the provocation as youthful exuberance and the brevity as a lack of differentiation. Be this as it may, the writing came too late to be able to combat the strong conservative tendencies which had already become established in the state churches of West Germany. And as an invitation to church reform it was ahead of its time, for the great debates on this topic began only ten years later.

A possible reason why Moltmann himself was not concerned to develop his thesis-like suggestions in detail may have been that this would have been a task beyond any individual theologian. It is interesting to imagine what could have been made of this programmatic writing if a whole team had bothered to develop the individual ideas. I shall be returning to this question in my concluding reflections.[24]

For at a distance of four decades it can clearly be recognized that this short work points in a direction which the churches in Germany would have done well to take. For on the whole they have not succeeded in affirming cheerfully and 'boldly' the liberating and challenging horizon of the rule of Christ in the face of politics, above all in the face of the economy and culture. With few exceptions, there has been no intensive contact with the world of culture, say of contemporary literature, music and even more of the graphic arts. Nowhere is the existence of the church in a parochial niche more tormentingly evident than in the helpless speechlessness with which it faces contemporary artists.

Furthermore, this speechlessness also extends to the sphere of the media, especially the electronic media, whose triumphal progress could not be ignored even in the 1950s. The more time has gone on, the less this field of public communication, in which information, education and entertainment are mixed in an ever more tricky way, has been attained by communication in the spirit of the gospel. It is hard to imagine what 'cultural preaching' would have had to look like in this context. Here an alienation has taken place which has further reinforced the reduction of proclamation to its protected areas in the parishes.

The economy has developed no less dramatically. It has established itself as a globalized system of webs of economy and finance and reclaimed its 'autonomy' with a self-confidence bordering on religious certainty. So far the Christian churches have tended to react with fright and timidity to the challenges of economics, although because of their apostolic charge to be 'stewards *(oikonomoi)* of the mysteries of God' (I Cor.4.1) they should have engaged boldly and with commitment for an economic ordering of the earth that reflects something of God's gracious economy, which is in the service of the creation. Faithfulness to the earth – only today, with the incessant bad tidings of ecological crises and socio-political distress in wide areas of the world, does this slogan take on its elementary validity.

With his programmatic writing of 1959 Moltmann shows himself to be a theologian who teaches us to understand the message of the kingdom of God as the broad horizon of

Christian life and the future of God which brings justice as the open sphere of history. Here we can perceive someone who combines passion for the kingdom with prophetic commitment to his time.

Many at that time failed to hear this voice. Five years later it was quite different.

3

Hope, or In the Undertow
of the Kingdom

Bonn 1964

First of all curiosity predominated. For most of us the 'new man' was a clean sheet. 'We' were those studying Protestant theology at the University of Bonn. Some of us lived in the Hans Iwand House; all of us found ourselves in the channel of Barthian theology, which was advocated with indefatigable passion above all by Walter Kreck.

The new Professor of Systematic Theology and Social Ethics was called Jürgen Moltmann. We knew that he had edited the two volumes on the beginnings of dialectical theology in the series Theologische Bücherei[25] and supposed that he would be something like the guardian of the grail of this theological revolution, which 'between the times' of the First and Second World War had thoroughly stirred up the trends in culture Protestantism and liberal thought and had forced them into the background.

So it was curiosity that drove most of us to the new professor's lectures. But after only a few hours this changed into excitement and fascination. For here a tone prevailed which we had not heard before. Here someone was reading the biblical promises as foundation documents of a future hope which was in no way to apply to an invisible beyond, but in concrete terms to our earth and our time. Here someone was discussing eschatology, by no means in the usual sense as the 'doctrine of the last things', i.e. as a doctrine which had to be given obligatory treatment on the last pages of dogmatics, but as the doctrine of hope. This was not about the 'last things', of which in any case one can have no precise knowledge, but about the beginning, the 'earliest day', whose morning glow puts the days of our life in a new life, which gives them a messianic splendour and opens up unsuspected possibilities. The voice was new, but at the same time it corresponded to the *kairos* of our time. Were we not witnesses to unsuspected possibilities? In 1961, at its General Assembly in New Delhi, the World Council of Churches had taken a step which had been thought impossible. The great Orthodox Churches of Eastern Europe and many 'young' churches from the 'developing countries' had joined. This gave the Council a new dimension of ecumenicity. Furthermore the Second Vatican Council dominated our attention. What few had thought possible, the great *aggiornamento* of the Roman Catholic Church, was expanding with revolutionary verve and mobilizing the imagination of Christians far beyond the limits of the Catholic Church. The Civil Rights Movement was increasingly spreading in the United States. The liberation of the oppressed found its compelling expression in the charismatic words and actions of Martin Luther King Jr. Was not the kingdom of God a power which burst open bolts and bars? Was there not reason and occasion everywhere to 'hope on' the kingdom of freedom with impatient solidarity? Even in Bonn, in this 'provisional' capital of the country of the 'economic miracle' in which the old and stubborn Adenauer was attempting to hold back the forces of renewal with the slogan 'No experiments!'?

I still remember vividly how the lectures filled up. Week by week more students came. Even on the last day of lectures, when attention to other teaching activities had already declined considerably, the room in which Moltmann spoke to us was full to bursting.

What we then heard with growing excitement appeared in autumn 1964 as a book and made the 'new man' famous at a stroke: it was, it is, *Theology of Hope*.[26]

2. Theology of Hope: *the most important arguments*

(a) Bloch's *Principle of Hope* baptized?

'To come to the point: is your *Theology of Hope* anything but Mr Bloch's 'Principle' of hope baptized?' This was the question put by Karl Barth in November 1964 in a letter to his young colleague, whom he did not know personally. At the time quite a few echoed this neat judgment by the Basel master. But if one reads *Theology of Hope*, it is striking that Ernst Bloch is quoted relatively seldom. Other authors are allowed much more extensive a say, for example Bultmann or Buber, Ebeling or Hegel, Käsemann or Kant, Luther or Pannenberg, von Rad or Zimmerli, Wittram or Wilckens, and also Karl Barth himself. So what are we to make of this pointed observation?

Moltmann has made various remarks about his encounter with Ernst Bloch and his philosophy. In 1997 he wrote: 'In 1960 I discovered Ernst Bloch's *The Principle of Hope*. I read it in the East German edition during a holiday in Switzerland and was so fascinated that I ceased to see the beauty of the mountains. My spontaneous impression was, "Why has Christian theology let go of its most distinctive theme, hope?" After all, Bloch referred to the "exodus and the messianic parts of the Bible". And what has become of the earliest Christian spirit of hope for the kingdom of God in today's established Christianity? With my 1964 *Theology of Hope* I did not seek to be Bloch's "heir". Nor did I want to "baptize" his *Principle of Hope*, as Barth in Basel suspected. Rather, I wanted to undertake a *parallel action in Christianity on the basis of its own presuppositions.*'[27]

The expression 'parallel action' is, however, ambivalent. It could be understood to mean that Bloch's *Principle of Hope* gives the basic structural features to which Moltmann draws a parallel in his *Theology of Hope*. But would that not have to involve a quite far-reaching similarity in approach and then also in results? And would this not also mean that the young theologian from the Barthian tradition had gone over to the Marxist philosopher from Leipzig?

This suspicion was there, but it missed the nature of the

spiritual affinity between Bloch and Moltmann. Had people taken more precise note of the short 1959 programmatic work *The Community against the Horizon of the Rule of Christ*, it would immediately have been clear that here already was the embryo of what was clarified in the encounter with Bloch. In Bloch Moltmann recognized the overgrown legacy of Jewish messianism, although and whereas Bloch himself thought that he had to play down these roots of his thought and brought his Marxist view of history into the foreground instead. Moltmann did not become a Marxist, but in Bloch reclaimed the misunderstood Jewish teacher of hope. I would like to put it this way: the work of the Leipzig philosopher served as a *catalyst* for Moltmann's theological question. It opened his eyes to a theme which is one of the nuclei of the Christian message, but which lay hidden under a placid and assimilated Christianity, like a glow under a thick layer of ash. Moltmann recognized in the unruly and passionate temperament of the Marxist thinker, who was so unpalatable to his Marxist masters that in 1962 they forced him into exile in Tübingen, his own passionate unrest, his own urgent impatience. *Theology of Hope* is none other than an attempt to free the glow and kindle the fire afresh, faithful to Jesus' messianic cry: 'I have come to kindle fire on the earth; and how I wish that it were already burning!' (Luke 12.49).

This cry can be heard unmistakably in the introductory 'Meditation on Hope'. The impatience already rings out on the first page: 'Owing to the fact that Christian faith banished from its life the future hope by which it is upheld, and relegated the future to a beyond, or to eternity, whereas the biblical testimonies which handed it on are yet full to the brim with future hope of a messianic kingdom for the world, – owing to this, hope emigrated as it were from the church and turned in one distorted form or another against the church' (15f.). Here is reflected what had struck Moltmann in his encounter with Bloch. The atheists had taken up hope: they had reclaimed the future hope for the earth, while the community of the disciples of the Messiah had been unfaithful to the content of his message by transporting the hope from the earth to an abstract beyond or an unassailable eternity. Thus eschatology, as the doctrine of the 'last things', became an ultimately unimportant appendix to theology, although as the doctrine of hope it should really have been 'the medium of Christian faith', the 'key in which . . . everything in it is set, the glow that suffuses everything here in the dawn of an expected new day' (16). Therefore Moltmann draws eschatology from the periphery to the centre, from the end of time to the middle of time, from beyond death to life in this world. In the discipleship of the Messiah eschatology is 'the passionate suffering and passionate longing kindled by the Messiah' (16). And he defines this suffering and this passion as the 'problem of the future' (16). This is basically the only problem that is imposed on theology from its centre and for which it owes an answer to humankind. But of what future can and may Christian eschatology speak? 'Christianity does not speak of the future as such. It sets out from a definite reality in history and announces the future of that reality, its future possibilities and its power over the future. Christian eschatology speaks of Jesus Christ and *his* future. It recognizes the reality of the raising of Jesus and proclaims the future of the risen Lord' (17).

These few references from the 'Meditation' indicate that the development of the relationship between the resurrection of Jesus Christ and the future has to be the central theme. The architecture of the book matches this. It has five long chapters. The middle one is about 'The Resurrection and the Future of Jesus Christ'; in content and in extent it is the core of the book, its turning point and hinge. Chapters I and II serve as it were to prepare the ground, while Chapters IV and V draw some conclusions, above all in respect of hermeneutics and ecclesiology.

So let us make our way through *Theology of Hope*.

(b) Theology of Hope: basic content

The title of Chapter I is 'Eschatology and Hope'. As I have already indicated, its purpose is to make critical demarcations, to open up room in which the problem of the future can be settled and developed. For why does eschatology lead a shadow existence? The reason is that 'the thought forms of the Greek mind, which sees in the *logos* the epiphany of the eternal present of being and finds its truth in that' (40) influence philosophical and theological thought-patterns down to modernity. It is this structure of thought which with an inner logic leads to manifestations of 'transcendental eschatology' as Moltmann finds these with classic eloquence in Immanuel Kant (45ff.) and then also in Karl Barth and Rudolf Bultmann. Moltmann remarks that 'this transcendental eschatology was working with a combination of Ranke's saying that "every epoch has an immediate relation to God" and Kierkegaard's dictum that "where the eternal is concerned there is only one time: the present"' (51). In Barth, he comments, this combination led to an understanding of the self-revelation of God in which the questions about the future and the goal of such a self-revelation could no longer be answered. To put it in another way: Moltmann can no longer recognize in Barth that in the resurrection of Christ an 'eschatological difference' (58) is contained which opens up history. If all times are equally immediate to God and indifferent before eternity, then it is no longer possible to speak of expectation and memory, promise and penitence, certainty and doubt, and then history loses the open character of a process.

Moltmann also recognizes this classical thought-pattern in Bultmann, but here it is not related to the self-revelation of God but to the transcendental subjectivity of human beings. The important thing here is that human beings achieve their authenticity in addressing God. This form of 'fulfilment' consists in the momentary perception of redemption, but as a result it is no longer in a position to state that 'eschatological difference' which can distinguish between what is to hand and the possible, between what is and what is to come. It is significant that in this connection Moltmann combines a 'cosmological eschatology' with the 'eschatological existence of human beings' (69). The first cannot be stated without the second. Where the first is absent, the resurrection hope must become 'the hope of the solitary soul in the prison of a petrified world' and deteriorate into a Gnostic longing for redemption.

The 'clearing-out work' in Chapter I is also part of a concern with the concept of eschatology which appears in the various theologies of salvation history that have been influential from the seventeenth century. They do not begin from the 'eternal movement' of the revelation of God but understand the revelation of God as a process in the self-manifestation of his kingdom. Here the revelation of Christ then becomes the last and decisive 'element in the history of a kingdom' (70). Moltmann points out that these salvation-historical constructions were not in a position to make a critical investigation of their own criteria of historical understanding. Under the conditions of a historical-critical analysis of history and the text, there is therefore something anachronistic about them. The 'disenchanting' of history which has been introduced in modernity by the criticism of the theology of revelation cannot be undone by 'a romantic, meta-historical, believing spell into history again' (73).

Nevertheless, Moltmann maintains that in the idea of salvation 'the question of the eschatological future outlook which the Christian revelation holds for a world involved in history' is still preserved (75). However, the decisive question is whether the concept of a 'salvation history' offers merely the interpretation of an otherwise incomprehensible course of history, or 'whether it itself originates, drives and directs the course of history'. With Barth, Moltmann asks: is revelation a predicate of history? Or can history be understood, experienced and willed in active obedience as a predicate of the eschatological revelation? The answer is clear: if Christ is really risen, then revelation is not a means of giving a meaning to a course of history which is intrinsically meaningless, but in that case it manifests the inner meaning and the promise of history. *Revelation makes history.*

Thus it proves that the concept of revelation and the understanding of eschatology are very closely connected. If Moltmann wants to get beyond the Greek-Western concept of revelation as an epiphany event which he criticizes, he must concentrate on the biblical evidence, and more closely on the message of Christ. 'Christian theology speaks of "revelation", when on the ground of the Easter appearances of the risen Lord it perceives and proclaims the identity of the Risen One with the Crucified One' (84). What does this identity mean? Moltmann formulates it in the two sentences 'Jesus is recognized in the Easter appearances as what he really *was*' and 'Jesus is recognized in the Easter appearances as what he really *will be*' (84–5). There is this same-ness in the cross and resurrection, although there is the greatest conceivable difference between the two, which makes up the qualitative peculiarity of the Christian understanding of revela-tion. What or who forms the ground of the identity of the Crucified One with the Risen One? 'This identity in infinite contradiction is theologically understood as an event of identifica-tion, an act of the faithfulness of God. It is this that forms the ground of the promise of the still outstanding future of Jesus Christ. It is this that is the ground of the hope which carries faith through the trials of the God-forsaken world and of death' (85).

So the leading concepts are 'God's faithfulness' and 'promise'. If revelation is no longer known as an epiphany event but as a promise event and is seized in hope, then history appears as an open sphere full of unsuspected possibilities which are not yet realized. But only then does the work, the praxis of hope, begin, for the important thing is 'to show the world to be history that is open to God and to the future' (93), and that means a battle and a fight with those forces which seek to end history, whether by military or economic means, and also the endurance of suffering which arises from the unresolved contradictions of life and the paralysing, annihilating power of death. Therefore Chapter II (95–138) is about the relationship between promise and history. The theological frame of reference for the understanding of hope is formed by the history of God as this is attested in the biblical texts. Thus Moltmann deliberately dissociates himself from Bloch, who had accepted modern atheism in the tradition of Feuerbach and Marx as the foundation for hope.[28] So here the 'parallelism' between Bloch and Moltmann ends.

Alongside Martin Buber, the main authors quoted in Chapter II are the leading Old Testament scholars of the 1950s and 1960s, i.e. W.Zimmerli and H.W.Wolff, but above all G.von Rad and his great *Old Testament Theology*. In 1957 the first volume (*Theology of the Historical Traditions of Israel*) appeared, and in 1960 von Rad presented the second volume with the *Theology of the Prophetic Traditions of Israel*. This work dominated the discussion, and categories like 'exodus' and 'covenant', 'promise and fulfilment', 'mission and obedience', 'faithfulness and commandment' were on everyone's lips.

What we have already recognized as the motive of Moltmann's theology, namely the question of the relationship between revelation and history, also appears in von Rad when in the Preface to the second volume he declares that he is ultimately concerned 'with the simple question whether history is only an accident of revelation . . . or whether it is to be recognized as the place of the real action of God'.[29] To give another example, the comparable approach is recognized in the critical acceptance of the element of salvation in history, which is indicated in von Rad as follows: 'What I principally see . . . in it (the Old Testament) is the ceaseless saving movement of promise and fulfilment. Then it becomes apparent how the expectations it contains fan out ever wider, then it is no self-contained entity, then it is absolutely open, and the question of its relationship to the New Testament becomes the question *par excellence*.'[30]

To develop the ever broader expectations is the subject-matter of Chapter II of *Theology of Hope*. Here for Moltmann lies the real strength and fascination of the historical and prophetic experiences of Israel with its God. Where the God of Israel is recognized as the God of the covenant, as Ps.146 says, God keeps 'faithfulness for ever', and his identity is not understood as a 'transcendental Super-ego' but in showing 'historical faithfulness to his promises' (104). Then the identity of this God is not recognized in an abstract absoluteness but in the reliability of the relations to his people and his creation in the 'constancy of his electing mercy and faithfulness' (116). The name of God is a 'name of promise' (116).

Those who call on this name refer to the promise, expect its fulfilment and put themselves in the public sphere of the realization of what is promised. This gives rise to something like *an 'undertow' in history*. Faith in the faithfulness of God turns into the expectation of demonstrations of faithfulness and power in the historical process. Such an expectation also chafes against the contradictions between what is and what must come: 'It (the promise) has not yet found its answer, and therefore draws the mind to the future, to obedient and creative expectation, and brings it into opposition to the existing reality which has not the truth in it' (118).

Such a faith hopes with the faithfulness of God also for the sphere where he shows his faithfulness. In other words, where it confesses the Lord, it expects his rule. Where it calls on the judge, it expects his righteousness. Where it longs for the prince of peace, it thirsts for peace. And all this on earth, in the earthly reality and in the course of time.

The obedience which corresponds to such expectation is described in the Torah. The commandments are the 'ethical side of the promise', just as obedience is 'the fruit of hope' (122). But that means that the commandments can no more be understood as rigid norms than the promise is immovable. Rather, they go 'along with the promise, producing history and transforming themselves on the path through the ages to fulfilment' (122). Here, incidentally, another light falls on the debate over 'law and gospel' which has become so sterile. If the Torah is 'faithful to the promise' it is 'gospel'. But where it becomes rigid and threatens to stem the undertow of promise, it presents itself as 'law'.

That the expectations spread ever wider, to repeat von Rad's remark, leads with inner logic beyond Israel into the universality of the world of the peoples. The 'Israelo-centric eschatologies' with intrinsic necessity become 'universal eschatologies of mankind' (130). That is realized with increasing sharpness in the prophetic traditions of Israel. And finally it is characteristic of the apocalyptic traditions of the inter-testamental period that they extend this perspective of mankind to the whole creation and thus first complete the universalizing tendencies. Only with and in this cosmological expansion does eschatology reach its goal. As Moltmann states at the end of this chapter, 'The historifying of the world in the category of the universal eschatological future is of tremendous importance for theology, for indeed it makes eschatology the universal horizon of all theology as such' (137).

Another 'extension' which follows from the event of promise comes at the boundary formed by death. If God keeps faith eternally, then a horizon of expectation opens up which extends beyond the limits of our existence. 'The intensification of the promise finds its approach to the eschatological in the questioning of death,' says Moltmann in respect of the prophetic traditions of Israel (132). If the questioning of death marks the 'threshold' to the eschatological, then with the message of the resurrection of the slain Jesus of Nazareth this threshold is crossed. The 'wide space' in which eschatology achieves its fullness opens up.

That brings us to the central chapter of *Theology of Hope*: 'The Resurrection and Future of Jesus Christ' (139–229). Now it is a matter of developing what is special and new in the Christ event as an expression of God's ongoing history of promise. The God who manifests himself in Jesus is and remains the God who keeps faith with Israel, as surely as Jesus was and remains a Jew. He is the God with 'future as the essence of his being' (a formula taken over from Bloch) and therefore is not to be confused with the God of Parmenides, Plato or Aristotle, which has become one of the essential difficulties of the history of Western theology. Moltmann states as a thesis: who God is 'is not declared by the world as a whole, but is declared by Israel's history of promise' (141). The biblical understanding of revelation is not one of the common variants of the Hellenistic epiphany religions, but the attestation of the God who remains true to himself by being true to his promises (cf. Heb.10.23, etc.).

Moltmann shows that in many ways the writings of the New Testament reflect the character of the gospel as promise. Nor only the letter to the Hebrews and Paul's controversies with the Hellenistic and Gnostic currents in his communities show that. Wherever the resurrection is celebrated in enthusiastic exuberance as the fulfilment and thus the end of the promises, processes are set in motion which transform the Christian faith into a

mystery religion. Therefore, following Paul, Moltmann emphasizes the *eschatologia crucis*: 'Fellowship with Christ is fellowship in suffering with the crucified Christ' (161). As can also be
seen from the sacraments of baptism and the eucharist, discipleship leads to the cross, to suffering and dying. It hands itself over
to the tribulation and the pain of love which cannot be content
with the rebellious world, which is neither redeemed nor re-
conciled, and precisely here it attests the future of the resurrection, which means the triumph of life and the splendour of the
righteousness of God in the midst of the everyday world.

But what kind of a reality is it which is expressed by the resurrection of Jesus from the dead? Moltmann devotes the central
sections of his central Chapter III (i.e. 5 to 9) to this core question. First of all he discusses the historical question of the revelation of Christ and with it also 'the questionableness of the
historical approach to history' (6). After that he takes up the
'form-critical question of the Easter accounts' and discusses in it
'the questionableness of its existentialist interpretation' (7); then
he concentrates on the 'eschatological question as to the future
horizon of the proclamation of the risen Lord' (8). The usual
question is whether and how a resurrection from the dead can be
recognized by those who continue to be mortal, and the conclusion drawn is that something like this is impossible. Against that
Moltmann asserts: 'The resurrection of Christ does not mean a
possibility within the world and its history, but a new possibility
altogether for the world, for existence and for history' (179).
Consequently the resurrection of Christ is not to be explained as
a possible process within world history but as an 'eschatological
process to which world history is subjected' (163). Therefore
there is also no analogy to the reality of the risen Christ in what
is here, but only in what has not yet come and awaits its realization. So the question about the resurrection is not the question
what I can know, but the question what I may expect and what,
in the power of such expectation, I have to do.

It is now all-important to maintain this eschatological dimension as eschatology, i.e. it would be betrayed wherever it was
ordered and dated within world history and apocalyptic. God's

future remains *God's* future; it evades our attempts to determine the passage of time and the course of history, i.e. to give them our meaning. But Christian eschatology is also something different from mere expectation: it is 'the tendency of the resurrection and future of Christ and therefore leads immediately to the practical knowledge of mission' (177). The tendency of the Easter appearances and auditions of Christ therefore leads straight to vocation and discipleship. The theology of hope entails an ethic of hope.[31]

I have already indicated how important the *eschatologia crucis* is to Moltmann. To maintain the identity of the Risen One with the Crucified One is of decisive importance, because otherwise Docetic, Ebionite or Modalistic errors and deviations are inevitable. Even in the New Testament accounts this identity remains an 'enigma' (199), or, better: it remains a mystery which corresponds to the mystery of the faithfulness of God and reflects this. Close as Good Friday and Easter are to each other, in them the contradictions of death and life, God-forsakenness and nearness to God, clash with each other and have to be held together as an expression of the faithfulness of God, a faithfulness which can resolve even the most difficult contradictions of history and make an opening forward. If God becomes all in all, then death too will be no more and all the cries of 'Why?' will fall silent, but only then.

Now how does this God with 'future as the essence of his being' show himself? What are the perspectives of his promises? Moltmann suggests understanding this *promissio* as 'the promise of the righteousness of God, the promise of life as a result of resurrection from the dead, and the promise of the kingdom of God in a new totality of being' (203). Righteousness, life and kingdom are so to speak the 'matter' of which the promise consists, they are the material and the space in which the *missio Dei* unfolds, but they are also to be understood as predicates of God. The God of the promise is known by his righteousness (see Section 11, 203ff.). God's righteousness is therefore an expression of God's faithfulness to fellowship with which he puts right what has separated itself from him, pardons what has rebelliously refused his right and finally also puts himself in the right and thus sets 'in order' what under the torment of an unredeemed world must appear God's arbitrariness or impotence.

Secondly, the God of the promise is known by the 'future of life' (Section 12, 208ff.). God shows himself in the resurrection of Christ from the dead as the powerful one who also overcomes the deadliness of death, since in the biblical sense death essentially means remoteness from God. In that case the overcoming of death means above all the end of remoteness from God and then the gift of life means the making possible of nearness to God and praise of God.

Finally the God of the promise becomes powerful in the 'future of the kingdom of God and the freedom of man' (thus the title of Section 13, 216ff.). The *promissio Dei* develops as the rule of love over all creatures, as the rule of compassion for all those creatures of God who are tormented or deprived of their rights, as liberation for the prisoners, as truth for all who deceive themselves and others. And this rule remains incomplete and unfulfilled as long as the suffering and crying of an unredeemed world lasts. But as it has its foundation in the reality of the Risen Christ, hope and patience of the saints have the greater stamina: just as the *'promissio* of the kingdom is the ground of the *missio* of love to the world' (224), so God's righteousness and the 'hunger for divine right in the godless world' belong together, so the new life of the Risen One seeks the 'true life of the whole imperilled and impaired creation' (205). The gospel of the kingdom develops in the realms of this world as comfort for the fearful, hope for the poor, as a 'homeland of identity' beyond the powers of death. What did Luther sing? 'The kingdom must remain to us.'

Now if the resurrection of Christ is not an event *in* history, but *to* history, then a completely different horizon opens up for any understanding of history. So it is only consistent that Chapter IV should deal with this. It bears the title 'Eschatology and History', but remarkably, after Section 1 an additional title appears: 'The "Solved" Riddle of History' (238). We need not concern ourselves in this context with the discussion of the various modern forms of the understanding of history. The key point of Moltmann's argument lies in the fact that from the leading concepts of promise and mission he arrives at a notion of universal history or world history. 'Only where a knowledge of mission supplies the sense of a future and a purpose' is a 'historical concept of history maintained', and this, too, is there only and as long as this knowledge 'finds its goal in a universal horizon that embraces the whole world'. Therefore 'future is the real category of historic thinking' (263).

But how does that come about? For Moltmann the interest in history is based in a passion for the unresolved unfinished elements in it. We investigate the past by 'seeking traces of vanished hopes' (247). 'The dialectic of past happening and present understanding is always motivated by anticipations of the future and by the question of what makes the future possible' (247). Seen in this perspective, our dealing with history can be understood as eschatological hermeneutics. It is not a matter of studying history like a giant charnel house, but of arousing in the past all that has not yet had any opportunity to live as it was meant to. If this hermeneutical perspective is related to the question how we have to interpret the biblical texts and traditions, then it can only be a matter of becoming aware of what is unfinished and unsettled in this tradition as a reality which is still before us and which comes to us. We must attempt to look in the same direction as the biblical text. From this follows what Moltmann calls 'the hermeneutics of the apostolate' (283). That then has important consequences for the way in which people understand themselves. They discover the mystery of their humanity by recognizing in their history that which is open and not yet settled. Human beings are 'undetermined beings' because and so long as their future still contains prospects and possibilities of which so far they have not yet become aware. Of course this does not mean any abstract existentiality of being human. What people are cannot be separated from what they do and how they deal with the world around them. The hermeneutics of mission and the praxis of mission go hand in hand.

All these considerations lead with an inner logic to the question: what kind of church would it have to be which entrusts itself to this universal process of promise and mission? Which is not in any way determined by its origin but by its future? Which does not know who it is because it comes from a particular history, but which can hope to become the church because God's resurrecting promise comes upon it? Moltmann sums up this 'eschatological understanding of Christianity in modern society' in the term '*exodus community*', and the concluding Chapter V is devoted to it.

Two clarifications which Moltmann makes at the beginning are illuminating. First, like Luther, he is concerned with 'Christianity', i.e. not just the community assembled (for worship), nor even with the church constituted as an institution with social roles. Secondly, he is concerned with 'modern society', a characteristic of which he sees as being that 'the old harmony between *ecclesia* and *societas*' has been destroyed (306). This modern industrial society is shaped on the one hand by a general objectification, reification and functionalization and on the other by the individualizing and privatizing of the person. The pressure towards conformity and levelling down – which is predominantly governed by economics – defines people above all on the basis of their partial utility and their behaviour in multiple roles. Freedom and randomness become almost interchangeable.

For long centuries the church stood for giving an official meaning to society. But modern industry and the society focussed on satisfying needs no longer has need for such a *cultus publicus*. 'Rationalization has "disenchanted" (Max Weber) the world and secularization has stripped it of gods' (287). What room does this society leave for religion?

Moltmann sketches out three functions. First, there is 'religion as the cult of the new subjectivity' (Section 2, 311ff.). Here the solitary absolute I stands at the centre of religious assurance. However, a lack of social consequences goes along with this ongoing existentialistic reflection. Secondly, Moltmann mentions 'religion as the cult of co-humanity' (Section 3, 316ff.): the more anonymous and amorphous modern society becomes, the greater becomes the individual's need for manageable communities. Christian communities can meet this need by offering human warmth and nearness, the intimacy of home and neighbourly responsibility. And thirdly, Moltmann points out that there is 'religion as the cult of the institution' (Section 4, 321ff.). As modern society gets by without 'ideological institutions of meaning' but nevertheless has an inkling of its 'subliminal consciousness of crisis' (323), religion can appear as a more general 'guarantor of life's securities' (298), even if in individual matters it is only voluntary.

These three functions have one thing in common: they function within and at the periphery of modern society, but do not put this in question. But a Christianity which owes itself to the message of the resurrection of Christ from the dead can understand the assignation of such a role only as 'Babylonian exile' (324). Therefore it must venture the Exodus. Because it stands against 'the horizon of the expectation of the kingdom of God' (325), it cannot be assimilated; it remains restless and unadopted. 'It will then be led in this society to a constant unrest which nothing can allay or bring to accommodation and rest' (324). But where the message of the kingdom forms the horizon, proclamation becomes pronouncement (325). It has the truth only in the sense that it confidently awaits it and passionately seeks it.

Wherever Christianity finds itself in the undertow of the future of the kingdom, mission in the power and authority of this kingdom becomes its hallmark. The service which Christ has done to the whole world opens up the broad space of discipleship.

I have already referred repeatedly to the correlation between *promissio* and *missio* in Moltmann. Here it emerges again. The missionary proclamation of the gospel is necessary so 'that no corner of this world should remain without God's promise of new creation through the power of the resurrection' (328). It is immediately added, by way of qualification, that this concept of mission has nothing to do with the extension of the Christian claim to lordship, but everything to do with the task of 'infecting people with hope', as the Dutch theologian of the apostolate, J.C.Hoekendijk, had said (328).

This apostolate of hope has a holistic character. Its concern is 'the eschatological hope of justice, the humanizing of man, the socializing of humanity, peace for all creation' (329). The culmination of this concept of mission in social ethics is manifest. Therefore the concluding section of *Theology of Hope* is explicitly concerned with 'the calling of Christians in society' (329ff.). Following E.Wolf, Moltmann speaks of the 'creative discipleship' which is called for here. Previously Christians had been called on to live out their testimony of faith in the callings and 'states' in which they were, as if these were autonomous 'orders of creation' or 'mandates' of 'fundamental institutions' of God. In contrast to this, Moltmann requires the multiplicity of vocations to be derived from the one call of the kingdom. It is not a matter of how Christians can keep their selfhood under the pressure of the worlds in which they live, but of how they can remain on the track of the kingdom in the mobile and fluctuating conditions of the modern world, how they can preserve the world from going to seed (311) by committing themselves to justice, peace and humanity. Vocations thus have the character of being self-expending. Social institutions, roles and functions are to be understood as 'means' (311) to this, in which conduct must be just, peaceful, human and free.

This understanding of vocation cannot be comprehended without the words 'resistance' and suffering, for the world is not yet finished, but is understood as engaged in a 'history'. Between the 'glory of self-realization' and the 'misery of self-estrangement', both of which arise equally from 'hopelessness in a world of lost horizons' (338), the Christian community holds fast to the call of the risen Christ. It 'raises its eyes, because its redemption is near', and therefore it passionately seeks the ways of the kingdom and looks forward to its many traces.

3. A retrospect

Theology of Hope was, as one would say today, an 'event', a media event. Six impressions within two and a half years is sensational for a book of systematic theology. The reactions and reviews indicated assent, repudiation, objections and questions in great quantities.[32] I want to emphasize only one aspect. Many objections were made to Moltmann's proximity to the philosophy of Ernst Bloch and thus to the one-sided emphasis on futurity in the concept of God. Had not Barth's 'vertical from above' been replaced by just as 'steep' a 'vertical from in front'?

Moltmann goes into this kind of question in his 'Response' by clarifying the concept of the future in a way which is not to be found in his book. Bloch, he said, had spoken of God 'with future as the essence of his being' . For him the *futurum* was the 'actualization of the primal potency'.[33] What he meant was the power of *physis* (from which the word *futurum* is derived). Thus the ambivalence of *physis* or matter – it is *mater* and Moloch at the same time – also appears in the concept of the *futurum*. In contrast to this, Moltmann develops his concept of the future from the concept of *adventus*. In the background is the Greek term *parousia*, which since Paul has been used as a designation for the coming of Christ in glory. The Risen One is the One who is to come. Consequently Moltmann speaks of a 'God with *adventus* as the essence of his being'. We shall keep meeting this 'advent' understanding time and again in Moltmann's work; it plays a determinative role in the 1995 eschatology, as the title *The Coming of God* already indicates.

These two ways of understanding future must be related in practice, for they make possible accesses to reality which are supplementary. Whereas the *futurum* must be *extrapolated* from past experiences, the future is *anticipated. Extrapolation is the medium of the mantics, whereas anticipation arises from the spirit of prophecy.* For the 'praxis of historical action it is necessary to combine the two approaches. Historical action for the future arises out of a combination of what one knows and what one hopes for.'[34]

That also applies to the praxis of Christian life. Where there is no goal there is also no way. Only when one has a *notion* of the goal can one also develop a plan for the road which is to lead to this goal.

Now at this point some critics have objected that Moltmann's *Theology of Hope* is not much more than a kind of 'oracle of the future, nowadays called futurology' when it is concerned with concrete consequences. 'That is evident above all from the fact that its practical part time and again . . . becomes so pale and impractical.'[35] I have already pointed out that the transition from the *docta spes* to the *spes practica* is not as conclusive as that. We shall be discussing this in more detail in Chapter 6. In this connection I would like to quote the critical question of H.E.Tödt. In a letter to Moltmann he writes: 'Reduced to the simplest formula, this is the role which falls to the believer in view of the hope of the kingdom of God. A strong chiliastic component seems to be at work in your writing.' Tödt immediately adds that such a component is important, but he underlines the difference in category between the kingdom of God and all that human beings, even believers, can do. 'The coming of God's kingdom remains exclusively God's act.'[36] There then follows from this the question how hope for God's kingdom relates to hope for the world, in other words 'how hope communicates itself to theological ethics'.[37] Moltmann answers this kind of question in two ways. First he extends the concept of praxis so that it embraces '1. Missionary preaching, 2. The formation of a universal community and 3. Bodily obedience in secular action.'[38] But secondly, he interprets the advent God pneumatologically and says: 'The spirit comes, metaphorically speaking, "from in front" and therefore misery hits all flesh on the front of the present. Through the charisms the spirit comes on the whole front of creaturely misery as the dawn of the new creation.'[39] Thus he wants to overcome the abstract opposition between God's action and human action by a dynamic and kairological theology of the Spirit. That, too, is a fundamental dimension in Moltmann's theology which we shall often be encountering.

I would like to leave this level of critical reflection and express another perspective, that of topicality. More than thirty years ago *Theology of Hope* literally electrified me. And not only me; many people have felt the same. How do we feel today about this book?

First of all, I am struck by how dated it seems. That is not because the authorities to whom Moltmann refers seem antiquated, that the 'fathers' Bloch, Barth, Bultmann, von Rad, Schelsky or Plessner have become 'grandfathers'. What is more important is our distance from the concerns of that generation. How alien to us is the passion of the dispute at that time between 'Barthians' and 'Bultmannians', the 'left' and the 'right'! Those discussions which extended into local church communities centred on the question how God's 'history' occurs in human history, how God's salvation can come to bear in the 'project of history'. From Cologne came the 'Political Night Prayer' and Dorothee Sölle's inimitable commitment. From Berlin came Helmut Gollwitzer's striking talk of the 'crooked wood and the upright walk'. It flourished at the Kirchentage, particularly in the theological themes. What has happened to us during the last three decades of the twentieth century?

It seems to me that in his introduction to the discussion volume W.D.Marsch made a very perceptive remark when he spoke of our 'world history which is infinitely made profane, relativistically and perspectivally destroyed, crumbling and impenetrable'.[40] At that time the term postmodernity did not yet exist, but Marsch mentions some of its characteristic features, namely the impenetrability of circumstances, the unlimited nature of profanation and the removal of taboos, relativism in the canon of values and the loss of perspective for democratic societies. Whereas in the 1960s the dispute was about 'society', now 'I' is there. The individual desire for happiness has taken the place of an interest in social justice. Faith in the possibility of improving conditions seems to have given place to a nameless cynicism. The future is *passé*. The motto now is 'I want everything, and I want it now!' What counts is 'power of now'.

If these points say something about the 'mood' which surrounds us at the moment, then the distance from the advent spirit of *Theology of Hope* becomes clear.

Should we therefore draw the conclusion that Moltmann's book on hope is out of date and therefore obsolete? On the contrary, precisely because it seems to be out of date, because it runs contrary to what seems to be the mood and spirit of our era, the demand and the provocation of this 'programmatic writing' for church and theology, for politics and society, remain in force undiminished. To mention just a few points: what Moltmann has described as 'Babylonian exile' in terms of the churches in Germany, i.e. their social marginalization, their niche existence in the private cult of inwardness or their neutralization in the cult of co-humanity, but also their conceptual and practical helplessness in the face of an ever more heedless disorder in the world economy, all this has increased further by comparison with the 1960s.

We are aware today, in a way which could not yet have been foreseen in the 1960s, of the urgent need to fight for the future of history. That is particularly true of the ecological danger to the planet. Moreover the great hopes of the decades of development have given place to an almost paralysing sobering up. Today the doom of great regions of the earth seems sealed. What once was called the 'Third World' has meanwhile become the 'underworld' of the rich world. The world is dividing into the 'winners', whose number is getting smaller and smaller, and the 'losers', who are becoming ever more numerous.

The pathos of *Theology of Hope* may seem strange to many of us today, but its topicality and urgency consists in the fact that it reminds us that *where the future becomes hopeless, the present becomes merciless.*

4

Everything is Decided by the Cross

1. El Dios Crucificado

In November 1989 a special unit of the El Salvador army forced its way into the Centro Monsenor Romero and shot dead the theology professors of the Central American University of San Salvador who were living there, six men. They also murdered the housekeeper and her fifteen-year-old-daughter.

One of the murdered men was Juan Ramón Moreno. For reasons which cannot be discovered a soldier dragged his body from the inner courtyard into the professors' living quarters and put it in the room of Jon Sobrino (Sobrino was abroad and therefore escaped this massacre.) Was the dead brother in his room an indication that he too had been an intended victim? In the process a book was knocked off the shelf; it lay there in Juan Ramón's blood.

This blood-soaked book can now be seen in a little exhibition devoted to the memory of the murdered Salvadorean Jesuits. It bears the title *El Dios Crucificado* and is the Spanish translation of Jürgen Moltmann's book *The Crucified God*.[41] This remarkable event is not just an evocative symbol for Jürgen Moltmann. The 'crucified' God finds himself again in the blood of his many murdered martyrs. The cross of our God is recognized in the death of his witnesses. The loving God suffers in the suffering of the poor and persecuted. This is the central statement of the book. It is made present at a stroke in the death of Juan Ramón.

2. The Crucified God

In retrospect, Moltmann says that this is the work that moved him most. In fact, with this book he keeps taking up the question with which his theological thought had begun. At that time, in 1943, in the midst of the firestorm which engulfed his home city of Hamburg, in 'Operation Gomorrah', when a grenade tore his best friend to pieces by his side, for the first time he had cried to God. Then later, in the British prisoner-of-war camp, Jesus' dying cry reached him, 'My God, why have you forsaken me?' And in this cry he had recognized his own cry; in this man forsaken by God he discovered his brother, and with him the basis of a hope which knows that death is behind it.

The cross is the point at which and in which everything stands and falls. 'The churches, believers, and theologians must be taken at their word. And this word is "the word of the cross". It is the criterion of their truth, and therefore the criticism of their untruth. The crisis of the church in present-day society is not merely the critical choice between assimilation or retreat into the ghetto, but the crisis of its own existence as the church of the crucified Christ' (2).

These theses from the introduction indicate why this book, too, is a 'programmatic work'. If the word of the cross decides on the truth and untruth of faith, church and theology, then the theology of the cross as an inner critical criterion comes into the centre and puts all criticism which comes from outside in second place.

Does this take back the programmatic impulse of *Theology of Hope*? It has occasionally been seen in this light. But Moltmann emphatically emphasizes that his theology of the cross represents the other side of his theology of hope. Just as he has always conceived his eschatology as *eschatologia crucis*, so too his theology of the cross centres on the 'cross of the risen Christ' (5). Whereas hope lives by the memory of the future of Christ, so here hope draws on the memory of Christ's death. The gravity and bodily nature of the hope in God's faithfulness to his promise is decided by the incarnation of this hope in the history of the suffering of Christ.

Nevertheless, we should not overlook the fact that during the eight years which lie between the appearance of the two works, Moltmann's sense of time had changed. Between 1964 and 1974 the key in which music was made in the church and in politics became shriller and more dissonant. Moltmann himself describes the year 1968 as the 'climax and turning-point in the mood of a new awakening'.[42] In Rome the first attempts were being made to put a brake on the verve of Vatican II; Martin Luther King Jr was murdered; the 'Prague Spring' was stifled. Many ghettos of the black population of the USA went up in flames. The student revolt and the often disproportionate reaction of state organs exacerbated the bitterness and the readiness for violence. The revolutionary verve seemed to shatter on the immobility of a world which was appreciably more orientated on success and profit.

(a) Who is God on the cross of the Godforsaken One?

If *Theology of Hope* had been understood as a parallel action to Bloch's *Principle of Hope*, yet other conversation-partners appear in *The Crucified God*. These are above all Adorno's *Negative Dialectics*, Horkheimer's *Critical Theory* and Abraham Heschel's understanding of 'pathetic theology'.

'Only the suffering God can help,' Dietrich Bonhoeffer had written in prison in 1944. Only the 'dangerous memory' of the cross and the 'presence of God in the crucified Christ'[43] could remind churches and theologies of their deepest foundation and at the same time make them ask critically whether they were ready to take their place beside those who sit in the shadow worlds of death that are continually deepening. Hence the subtitle 'Foundation and Criticism of Christian Theology'.

Here, in the link with the '*pathos*' and '*sympatheia*' of the cross, the *pathos* of the theology of hope, which had seemed to some readers to be 'utopian', takes its place. This point by which Christian faith stands and falls is anchored in the concept of God, thus at the centre of theo-logy, and thus manifests the 'hard core' of the Christian understanding of the self and the world.

So the question is one of both the identity and the relevance of the Christian faith. It is thus at the same time also a question of the crises of the relevance and identity of Christianity in the modern world. The two are very closely connected, since how one determines one's identity is shown by those with whom one shows solidarity and those with whom one does not. The 'word of the cross' now denotes the event with which Christian faith must identify itself time and again and which at the same time provides the criterion for all forms of self-emptying and solidarity: 'Christian existence finds its Christian *identity* in that twofold process of identification with the Crucified Christ. His cross distinguishes belief from unbelief and even more from superstition. Identification with the crucified Christ alienates the believer from the religions and ideologies of alienation, from the "religion of fear" and the ideologies of revenge. Christian theology finds its *relevance* in the well-thought-out and practised hope of the kingdom of the crucified Christ, by suffering in the sufferings of this time and making the cry of tormented creation its own cry for God and freedom' (24, author's italics).

Here Moltmann brings something into the centre of Christian faith which is difficult not only for him 'by nature', namely to identify himself in others, in strangers and those of opposite views. How does one avoid mere assimilation on the one hand and sectarian encapsulation on the other? How does one become strong enough to endure the challenge by the stranger and the alien and to give up the temptation to seek hasty parallels?

Underlying this is an important basic epistemological decision. On the one hand we are shaped by the principle that like can only be recognized by like. But this does not get us anywhere with the question of the knowledge of God. Here the 'dialectical principle of knowledge' (27) must come into play, according to which something can be recognized only by its opposite. 'Applied to Christian theology, this means that God is only revealed as "God" in his opposite: godlessness and abandonment by God. In concrete terms, God is revealed in the cross of Christ who was abandoned by God' (27). Applied to church life and church praxis this approach means that the principle 'like seeks after like' cannot be used. 'But for the crucified Christ, the principle of fellowship is fellowship with those who are different, and solidarity with those who have become alien' (28). This brings the cross, 'in all its harshness and godlessness', as Moltmann says, following Hegel, into the centre. It must therefore first be rescued from the manifold falsifications, banalities and trivializations in which it has become involved through Christian piety and art, through custom and adaptation. The second section of the chapter ('The Resistance of the Cross against its Interpretations', 31ff.) is concerned with this. The manifold decorations which have overgrown the cross must be torn away to know it in its repulsive nakedness. The 'cult of the cross', the 'unbloody repetition of the event that took place on Golgotha on the altar of the church' (41), must be criticized, because and in so far as it puts the profane strangeness of the crucifixion in a religious context and makes it 'manipulable' by church and cult.

After this Moltmann turns to the 'mysticism of the cross'. In particular in its diverse forms he recognizes 'the devotion of the poor and the sick, the oppressed and the crushed. The "God" of the poor, the peasant and the slave has always been the poor, suffering, unprotected Christ, whereas the God of empires and rulers has usually been the Pantocrator, Christ enthroned in heaven' (45f.). This line can be traced from the Middle Ages to our time. Just as it characterizes the longing of the wretched in the plague houses of the Middle Ages, so it stamps the piety of the poor of Latin America and the faith of the slaves taken from Africa to America. However, a mysticism which humbly accepts its own cross as merely corresponding to the cross of Christ comes near to a piety of fate. But where it recognizes that the cross of Christ is also in contradiction to its own suffering, the potential of this messianic difference becomes visible: 'The church of the crucified was at first, and basically remains, the church of the oppressed and the insulted, the poor and wretched, the church of the people . . . As the people of the crucified Messiah it is the church of liberation for all . . . but not for everyone in the same way' (52).

This generally affirmative acceptance of the mystical traditions is then followed quite consistently with reflection on the 'following the cross' (53ff.). Anyone who wants to live in the light of the Risen One bears the dying of Christ in his body, as Paul writes (II Cor.4.10). There are different forms of following the cross. Moltmann distinguishes the cross which arises with the apostolic preaching of the obedience of faith from the cross of the martyrs who bear witness before the authorities to the rule of the Crucified One and also from the suffering of love which seeks to reach people who have been made contemptible, and finally from apocalyptic suffering with enslaved creation over a godless world. These clarifications then bring Moltmann to the question of a 'theology of the cross' (65ff.). He understands it as a 'critical theory of God' (69), in the sense that criticism in the light of the cross is directed towards human beings who know and destroys their heuristic interests, thus above all their tendency towards self-justification, their striving for power and their desire for self-divination. Moltmann thinks that – alongside Paul – Martin Luther is the most important witness to this approach, Luther who in 1518 set the concept of a 'theology of the cross' as a programmatic concept of the Reformation over against the mediaeval *theologia gloriae*.

This 'critical theory' is developed in respect of two tasks. First of all it is necessary to clarify whether it corresponds to the biblical witness of Jesus Christ, i.e. it must be developed in material terms as christology. This is done in Chapters 3 to 5 (82–199). Secondly there is a need to elucidate what consequences follow from this for the doctrine of God, anthropology and political ethics. That is the material for Chapters 6–8 (200–340). With questions in these two directions Moltmann continues the key words 'identity' and 'relevance'.

(b) Who is this man?

We cannot consider the cross of Christ without coming up against the historical Jesus. Who was this man? What was and is the truth of his life and his death? What and who is God in this life and in this death? Is this Galilean the one who is to come, the messianic emissary, and to what degree is he this person? These are questions which Moltmann investigates in the course of christological approaches, finally turning all the questions round with reference to the question which Jesus puts to his disciples: 'Who do you say that I am?'

So the central problem consists in linking historical-exegetical and theological perspectives. Therefore here, too, a dialectical figure of thought emerges in order to avoid the mistake, commonly made, that preoccupation with the life and death of (the historical) Jesus degenerates into a kind of 'Jesuology', or that preoccupation with the death of Jesus Christ in the light of the resurrection ends up in a(n unhistorical) Christ myth and thus a mystery religion. 'We shall then attempt to treat the *historical task* of describing the death of Jesus within the framework of his life as a *theological task*; for his life, preaching and ministry, and his death too, were in his own mind theologically determined. We shall then approach the *theological task* of setting forth and interpreting the Easter faith as a *historical task*, in so far as all statements of faith concerning his resurrection and exaltation by God and his functions as Christ, Kyrios and Son of God are related to his life and his death' (113). It is as part of this dialectical reciprocal relationship that Moltmann discusses the 'trial' of Jesus as a 'historical trial' (and not just as a legal trial) which is about the truth of God.

How did the preaching Jesus become the preached Jesus Christ? What in this is the 'truth of God'? The decisive point which is critical in this sense is the cross, or more precisely Jesus' cry on the cross, 'My God, why have you forsaken me?' Here it becomes evident that Jesus died not only as a blasphemer (as his Jewish accusers thought) or as a political rebel (as the Roman occupying forces thought); he also died as God's witness and thus for the sake of God. In other words, the theological process takes place in and behind the historical process. And whereas the issue in the historical process is who this Jesus was, the theological process decides who is the God whom this Jesus proclaims as his 'Father', i.e. as his dear Father. 'The history of Jesus which led to his crucifixion was . . . a theological history and was dominated by the conflict between God and the gods; that is, between the God whom Jesus preached as his Father and the God of the law as he was understood by the guardians of the law, together with the political gods of the Roman occupying power' (127).

The all-important question is how to understand this theological depth dimension. And it is recognized in all its harshness only in the cry of the godforsaken Jesus. 'Why did Jesus die? He died not only because of the understanding of the law by his contemporaries or because of Roman power politics, but ultimately because of his God and Father' (149). The cry of the forsaken one to God also tears open the fearful possibility that this is not at all the God on whom Jesus relied body and soul and is not at all the Father whom Jesus confessed him to be. 'Thus ultimately, in his rejection, the deity of his God and the fatherhood of his Father . . . are at stake' (151).

By and in this cry a decision is made: either theology is utterly impossible or it is now possible only as specifically *Christian* theology.

We recall that the apodeictic passion of this approach is connected with the fact that for the young Moltmann in a prisoner-of-war camp this cry of godforsakenness opened up an encounter with God. It was vitally important in the truest sense of the word, and decided the direction which his life was to take.

So if the cross of Jesus Christ is about the deity of God, then this 'process' takes on an eschatological tension which must be immediately connected with the Easter event. For what does it mean for God that the godforsaken Jesus is recognized and confessed as the Risen One? The primitive Christian communities had no doubt that the resurrection was a reality, and they also took it for granted that this had been the work of the Father. Thus it was also necessary to think that in this man God had gone to the uttermost limit, into the hell of the death of God, so that the breadth of his love might become manifest. That was – and remains – a mystery which it is impossible really to understand. Nevertheless, if one puts one's trust in it, it proves to be the transforming power of a new life which hitherto had to be thought impossible.

For if the Crucified One has been raised, then the resurrection of all the dead is possible. The impenetrable curtain which death has drawn over the world has been torn 'from the top down'. Now the creation stands there in a new light. The breadth of God's love and righteousness can be expressed only in apocalyptic categories. Death is swallowed up in victory. The expectation of the Christian communities extends into cosmic dimensions: these communities expect a new heaven and a new earth in which righteousness – the righteousness of the one who raises the dead-can dwell.

But what does it mean that this Risen One is the Crucified One? Does the cross become the passageway towards a heavenly mystery play? The communities of the New Testament understood the cross as a sign of the salvation which embraced them. The cross is 'for us', because in it God opposes our unbelief and superstition, our religious and political 'gods', and it is 'for us' because in our godlessness and blindness to God we are 'dead' and therefore can be brought to a new life only from outside. 'The resurrection from the dead qualifies the person of the crucified Christ and with it the saving significance of his death on the cross for us, "the dead". Thus the saving significance of his cross manifests his resurrection. It is not his resurrection which shows that his death on the cross took place "for us" that makes relevant his resurrection "before us". This must be stressed, because the early Jewish-Christian idea of the dying Christ as an expiatory offering for our sins, which has constantly been repeated throughout the tradition in various forms, cannot display any intrinsic theological connection with the kerygma of the resurrection' (182f.). Everything depends on this tension between the 'for us' and the 'before us'; the usual theories of atoning sacrifice may support the 'for us', but they cannot provide the eschatological orientation and scope of the 'before us'.

Unfortunately I cannot discuss here the manifold christological reflections in Chapters 3 to 5. It seems to me more important to concentrate on the question what this christology says about our understanding of God. What does it mean to speak of the 'crucified God'? So we turn to Chapter 6 (200ff.).

(c) The cross – the suffering God

This chapter, of more than seventy pages, is the most comprehensive part of the book, not only externally but also in terms of content, for here the issue is the 'truth' of theology and the truth of a truly Christian doctrine of God. When Moltmann says with Luther that everything is decided by the cross (*crux probat omnia*), here the problem of the Christian understanding of God is decided. Where was God when Jesus died on the cross? Did the agony of this Son of man leave God untouched? Or did God suffer with him? But how can one suffer with a death without also dying? So did God die on the cross of Jesus? We may recall that the question of the 'death' of God took up a good deal of the theological debates of Europe and America in the 1960s. It reflected among other things the dispute over theism and atheism which has constantly been a marked preoccupation of the modern era.

Moltmann involves himself in this debate by taking up the challenge of understanding the being of God from the death of Jesus. Here he knows that he is close to approaches which have been developed both by Catholic theologians (K.Rahner, H.Mühlen, H.Küng and H.U.von Balthasar) and by Protestant theologians (K.Barth, E.Jüngel, H.G.Geyer). All, if with different accents, have relied on the Christ hymn in Philippians 2 to describe God's self-emptying in Jesus Christ. Here they run into problems connected with the doctrine of the two natures. This theory had been developed in the church fathers to make it possible to distinguish the divine nature of Jesus from his human nature. Why was this so important? This doctrine of two natures on the one hand sought to maintain the classical doctrine of the impassibility of God, but on the other it had to link up with the history of the suffering of Jesus. However, if one takes the approach of kenosis seriously, this theory is difficult to maintain.

Moltmann adopts Luther's theology of the cross to overcome this dilemma. Luther fights against inferring God's invisible and inaccessible being in an indirect and analogical way from his works which are visible to us. That had been the classical approach of philosophical theism. It had been this particular approach which was radically disputed in atheism in modernity (here Moltmann also speaks of a 'protest atheism'). Now Luther says that God's nature is visible and accessible only from its opposite, i.e. in the suffering and death of Christ. But that means renouncing both theism (and its 'proofs of God') and atheism (and its challenges to the existence of God). At the same time it means leaving behind childish projections on to God's omnipotence as a compensation for human impotence and loss of power and also metaphysical revolts against such an image of God in the name of human suffering (a perspective which Moltmann notes above all in Dostoievsky and Camus). If the statement 'there is a God' must be bought at the price of the torments of creatures which do not touch the Creator, then one can understand the atheism which in the face of the torments of the world comes to say that there cannot be a God, and if there was, then such God would be a monster.

Now if one allows the notion that the cross of Jesus took place in God, and that thus the death of the crucified Jesus becomes the death of God, then theology can deliver itself from the straits of both theism and atheism. It liberates itself from the notion that there must be a contradiction between God and suffering, and begins to understand that 'God's being is in suffering and suffering in God's being itself'. Why? Because 'God is love' (230). How can this principle that God is love be stated theologically? Here Moltmann refers back to the doctrine of the Trinity in the Cappadocian church fathers.[44] For him, its strength consists in the fact that it does not presuppose an abstract doctrine of God on the basis of which the trinitarian definitions of relationship would then have to appear as later speculation. If, rather, 'the theology of the cross must be the doctrine of the Trinity and the doctrine of the Trinity must be the theology of the cross, because otherwise the human, crucified God cannot be fully perceived' (241), then God's being and essence are *a priori* developed as trinitarian. 'The material principle of the doctrine of the Trinity is the cross of Christ. The formal principle of knowledge of the cross is the doctrine of the Trinity' (241). Here Moltmann follows the long-forgotten theologian B.Steffen, who as early as

1920 had stated that if one wants to seek traces of the doctrine of the Trinity in the New Testament, then one must seek out the message of the cross, for this is the real basis and the inner necessity of a trinitarian theology. 'In that case the doctrine of the Trinity is no longer an exorbitant and impractical speculation about God, but is nothing other than a *shorter version of the passion narrative* of Christ in its significance of the eschatological freedom of faith and the life of oppressed nature' (246, my italics).

When we remember that Moltmann wanted to understand the trial of Jesus as God's 'trial', we can also now also understand that the history of Jesus' passion manifests the history of the 'passionate' God. The emphasis here lies on 'history'. 'To think of God means to think oneself into God's history and know that one's own history, with all the happiness and pain that belong to it, is taken up into this history.' 'All human history, however much it may be determined by guilt and death, is taken up into this "history of God", i.e. into the Trinity, and integrated into the future of the "history of God"' (246).

It is clear that thus aspects of a 'process' are introduced into the understanding of God and break up the fixation on personalistic terms. We shall be concerned in another context with what this means for classical terms like 'Father' and 'Son'.[45] Taking prayer as an example, Moltmann shows that it can be quite meaningful to understand prayer as a movement in an 'inner trinitarian event'. If we pray, we turn 'in' the Spirit 'through' the Son 'to' the Father; in other words, we open ourselves to the love which grounds, sustains and drives on this event of the Trinity. In our complaint we also claim this love for us; we celebrate in our praise this love as a liberating power in our life.

If the essence of the Trinity is love, we can see that the classical attribute of impassibility is inappropriate. Rather, we are led to see the 'omnipotence' of love precisely in God's capacity to suffer. Only if death is 'in God' are we, too, saved 'in God' in our deaths. And because death is swallowed up 'in God', a life of liberation from all the ties of death also opens up to the creatures of 'God'.

(d) Following the Crucified One – the compassionate

Thus to the 'pathos' of God there corresponds the '*homo sympatheticus*'; the compassionate person responds to the suffering God. That is a conclusion which associates Moltmann with the Jewish theologian Abraham Heschel, who on the basis of his studies on the prophets of Israel arrived at a 'pathetic theology' (270ff.). It is an approach which also brings Moltmann near to Elie Wiesel, who speaks of God as suffering with those in Auschwitz (273f.). These brief references attest that the understanding of a suffering God not only sets off a 'revolution' in our current notions of God but also must have far-reaching consequences for our picture of human beings and, starting from that, for our political and social ethics. The 'revolution' lies in the fact that the real criterion of power consists in the force of a passion which is capable of suffering or a capacity for suffering which is capable of passion. The perspective for human behaviour and action changes radically. If it comes into the horizon of the 'passion of the crucified God' (291), it also enters into a new horizon of freedom.

What can be said specifically about this horizon of freedom? It is not enough to persist within theological reflection. Rather, an attempt must be made to develop the 'psychological hermeneutics of the word of the cross' as well as its 'political hermeneutics' (292). Here 'hermeneutics' is understood as the 'translation of the theological language of liberation for a particular sphere and into a particular dimension of life' (292). Because of the complexity of human life, a variety of such hermeneutical processes are necessary.

In Chapter 7, under the title 'Ways towards the Psychological Liberation of Man' (268ff.), Moltmann develops his psychological hermeneutics in an exemplary way in a critical discussion of the psychoanalysis of Sigmund Freud. The point of contact is immediately obvious. A theological anthropology which speaks of a suffering God must prove its relevance in particular in the encounter with images of human beings which grows out of a concern with human suffering. In other words, the hermeneutical and therapeutic interests coincide. As a rule theology works with the dialectic of law and freedom. But in psychological interpretation 'law' appears as a compulsion. Psychologically sick people suffer from obsessions and compulsive actions, and their liberation consists in living in an unforced way. Whereas Paul speaks of sin, law and death as vicious circles (cf. Rom.7.7ff.), we speak of 'fatal legalistic patterns' or 'processes of negative feedback in which orientation on life shifts over to become orientation on death' (293). This structural analogy is easily recognized. Consequently practical hermeneutical work consists in showing freedom from the vicious circles which faith asserts, as present liberation which can actually be experienced from the destructive processes of negative feedback, whether psychological or political.

It is evident from Freud's criticism of religion that such an encounter between theology and psychoanalysis also has a feedback on theology. In his therapeutic work he saw himself confronted with pathological forms of private religion (that of his time) which essentially had arisen out of the historical effect of Christianity and Judaism. Thus in a preoccupation with Freud's criticism of religion a question recurs which has also occupied many theologians, namely the distinction between faith and religion.

I cannot describe here the ramifications of Moltmann's dialogue with Freud, but do want to take an example to show how the argument goes. Neurotically sick people develop forms of behaviour which come close to the 'religion of anxiety', in which the religious can, for example, be recognized in ritualized patterns of suppression and crazy practices. These 'pattern formations for repression and the idols and laws of the religion of anxiety may not either suffer or die, since they have been erected against suffering and dying. They must be omnipotent and eternal, because they are meant to help impotent and mortal man and to relieve his anxiety . . . But the crucified God renounces these privileges of an idol. He breaks the spell of the super-ego which men lay upon him . . . In becoming weak, impotent, vulnerable and mortal, he frees man from the quest for powerful idols and protective compulsions' (303). So it becomes evident that it is precisely infection by suffering which can break up the deadly rigidity in suffering. In the discipleship of the suffering God a capacity to suffer becomes a sensitivity which serves life.

However, it very quickly becomes evident in psychological hermeneutics that psychological suffering passes over into social suffering or is stamped by this. Therefore it must be supplemented by a political hermeneutics. This brings us to the goal of the last chapter ('Ways towards the Political Liberation of Man', 317ff.). Here Moltmann bases himself on the discussion over 'political theology' which he and J.B.Metz had proposed at the end of the 1960s and the 'theology of liberation' which began with Latin American theologians like Gutiérrez. Here too the important thing is to define the vicious circles in which human life is wasted or destroyed under oppression, servitude and exploitation. 'The freedom of faith is lived out in political freedom' (317), Moltmann states categorically. Those who enter the sphere of influence of the crucified God can break through the vicious circles of a lack of freedom and misuse of power; they therefore seek collaboration with other freedom movements, and these will have above all a socialist, democratic, humanist and anti-racist orientation. Here too a reciprocal criticism arises, for here too we have a (self-)critical working out of the ideological functions of Christianity as political religion. 'Unless Christian theology frees itself from the needs and demands of the prevalent political religions, there can be no liberating theology' (322). The point of reference of this 'self-liberation' is the fact that Jesus was crucified by the political occupation forces as a rebel and that the early Christian communities were also persecuted by the Roman state and by pagan philosophers as 'godless'. Faith in the Crucified One was a striking and provocative counter-symbol to the emperor cult. Faith in the resurrection of this Crucified One created an eschatological tension which opposed all the chiliastic and salvation-historical restrictions of history. The trinitarian understanding of God, which explicitly included the cross, was not suited to the ideological over-exaltation of hierarchical conditions of rule. 'The consequence for Christian theology is that it must adopt a critical attitude towards political religions in society and in the churches. The political theology of the cross must liberate the state from the political service of idols and must liberate men from political alienation and loss of rights' (304).

This work of liberation must take place in five 'vicious circles' which Moltmann designates with the key words 'poverty', 'violence', 'racial and cultural alienation', 'the industrial pollution of nature' and 'senselessness and godforsakeness' (330ff.). Against poverty Moltmann sets liberation as 'the satisfaction of the material human needs for health, nourishment, clothing and somewhere to live', and for this the key word 'socialism' serves him as a symbol (332). On the political level liberation from violence means democracy; here the Universal Declaration of Human Rights offers a framework of orientation, even if it needs to be supplemented. At the cultural level the key word 'emancipation' (333) is the leading term, and at the ecological level 'peace with nature' (334), while at the existential level Moltmann speaks of the 'courage to be' (335).

As these 'vicious circles' constantly work together and thus intensify their destructiveness, liberating praxis must similarly attempt to intensify its constructive forces by community and networking.

This already brings us to ecclesiological and ecumenical questions, which Moltmann has developed in his book *The Church in the Power of the Spirit*. We shall be dealing with them in the next chapter.

3. *Summary: the programmatic element in* The Crucified God

What makes this book *The Crucified God* a 'programmatic writing'? In other words, what statements have been understood as 'programmatic'? The German discussion volume on *The Crucified God*[46] offers an illuminating survey. I want to emphasize the following perspectives.

1. The central programmatic focal point, namely the emphasis on the suffering God, has clearly provoked the most criticism. It was above all Reformed theologians like Lochman or Miskotte who expressed the suspicion that God's freedom was being damaged if God's capacity to suffer was brought too strongly into the centre. Moltmann counters that it is not enough 'to regard God's freedom as self-determination and to characterize this freedom as freedom of choice'.[47] By contrast he brings the

concept of freedom near to friendship, because he thinks that such a 'domination-free' concept of freedom would correspond better with a God whom we seek to understand as love.

If the critical objections of Lochman or Miskotte seem to be stamped more by preserving a certain 'balance' in classical (Reformed) theology, Dorothee Sölle's criticism comes from quite a different side. It is prompted by Moltmann's reflection that the real sharpness in the suffering of Jesus on the cross is achieved only where he believes himself to be betrayed and destroyed by God. 'The decisive point which I do not understand is a thought about suffering which remarkably blurs the difference between victims and executioners . . . The Father is . . . one who . . . makes the Son sacrifice himself.'[48] Sölle regards the belief that Jesus 'came to grief over God, that God, at any rate in one person, is an executioner' as a projection of sado-masochistic needs which are incompatible with the real motif of Moltmann's book as she sees it. For she emphatically supports what colleagues like Lochman have criticized as 'one-sidedness', namely the overcoming of impassability and immobility in the traditional concept of God. Sölle sees it as the real strength of Moltmann's book that God does not look on helplessly or even unmoved where human beings suffer, but suffers and dies with them. And she sees this revolutionary criticism of traditional images of God watered down where Moltmann again puts them in a traditional trinitarian pattern of thought.

Moltmann has been considerably occupied with Sölle's criticism, especially as it is repeated so often, particularly from the feminist side, that finally, as Moltmann says, a 'legend of my "sado-masochistic God" who "kills" his own son' has come into being.[49] In this connection he recalls the blood-soaked book *El Dios Crucificado* in Jon Sobrino's room. He sees the martyrdom of the El Salvador Jesuits and the two women as a concrete expression of a passionate theology which is capable of suffering, which has nothing to do with sado-masochistic projections, but does as much justice to the actual harshness of the darkness of God in which we human beings find ourselves as to the boundless love with which God also endures this darkness.

In my view this is the real programmatic renewal which has been achieved with this 'programmatic writing'. It is still far from having found a home in the everyday piety of most Christian communities. There the impassible 'Almighty' still 'rules' and therefore the question 'How can God allow it (if he is really almighty')?' is still time and again the most laborious problem with which people fight. In addition, the message of the suffering God asks far too much of many people, since it does not fit with the images of success, competitiveness and unassailability which are glorified today.

2. A series of objections are made to the programmatic point that Moltmann combines his theology of the cross with the theology of the Trinity. Is this approach appropriate for transcending the centuries-old dispute over theism and atheism? Precisely because the theology of the Trinity largely leads a shadow existence, its central significance for Moltmann is in a way surprising. But he insists that the doctrine of the Trinity is no way a Greek speculation developed subsequently, but the valid expression of the New Testament theology of self-surrender. At the centre of the message of Jesus now stands the cross, and the whole harshness of the godforsakenness must be endured theologically. That is conceivable only with a doctrine of the Trinity. When Moltmann wrote this counter to his critics he was already occupied in composing his doctrine of the Trinity. (His work *The Trinity and the Kingdom of God* appeared in 1980, a year later.) I shall return to this theme in Chapter 8.

3. In her criticism Sölle found fault with Moltmann for aiming at a trinitarian involvement of his theology of the cross, and said that 'nothing new' had come out 'about the Holy Spirit and his functions'.[50] If there was already a theology of the Trinity, then also and with equal weight there should be pneumatology. Sölle was not alone in making this objection. In his retort Moltmann conceded this lack and pointed out that he was attempting to fill this gap in his book *The Church in the Power of the Spirit*. That brings us to the last 'programmatic writing', to which we must now turn.

5

In the Fellowship of the Spirit of God

1. Convergences

The Church in the Power of the Spirit appeared in 1975,[51] three years after *The Crucified God*. But it would be wrong to assume that Moltmann wrote this book only after the other was completed. Things don't turn out like that in a professor's work. He had been offering lectures on ecclesiology since 1966; the themes 'Spirit of God' and 'Church' formed a significant focal point alongside the fields around the motifs of 'Hope' and 'Cross'. ('Ethics' represents a further focal point, and we shall be concerned with that in the next chapter.)

(a) The trinitarian dynamic

Theology of Hope has been associated with Easter and *The Crucified God* with Good Friday. So should *The Church in the Power of the Spirit* be associated with Pentecost? These allusions to the church's liturgical year are not without interest, but are unsuited to constructing a chronological sequence between the three writings or even a sequence in content. As I have already indicated, the specific conditions of academic work meant that the topics of these three books constantly overlapped and were worked out in such a way that they complemented one another.

Nevertheless the allusion to Good Friday, Easter and Pentecost is illuminating because it demonstrates the inner dynamic in these three books and refers them to one another. Whether we begin with the promise of the resurrection hope or the passionate surrender in the event of the cross, or the messianic power of the Spirit of God, each time new aspects of the one history of God appear, as if in a magnifying glass. Each time God, Christ and the Spirit are talked of in different ways. The three books are always about christology, the doctrine of God and pneumatology, i.e. the whole of theology, at the same time. In other words, *they are about the trinitarian history of God with the world*. It is therefore not at all surprising that the theology of the Trinity depicts the intrinsic connection between these three programmatic writings and then also, from 1980, becomes the starting point of the second great cycle of theological 'contributions'.

(b) The 'oppressed Christians throughout the world'

But at the same time the aspect of Moltmann's theology which was directed towards the world intensified. The basic ecumenical trait that we could already make out in his first theological writings becomes increasingly clear in the years between Wuppertal and Tübingen. *The Church in the Power of the Spirit* is dedicated to the World Council of Churches, its (then) General Secretary Philip Potter, and 'the oppressed Christians throughout the word'. This dedication indicates what 'church' the Tübingen theologian has in view. By now the pastor of the small congregation of Wasserhorst had 'got around' the whole world. For example, in 1968 he spent a visiting semester with his family in Duke University, North Carolina. The murder of Martin Luther King Jr happened at this time, an experience which shook him. There were also lecture trips to different areas of the world, and participation in ecumenical conferences put him in intensive contact with churches in very different situations. Korea, Kenya, Ghana, the Philippines, Latin America are stages in the discovery of the ecumenical church which at the same time represents an introduction to the suffering, persecutions and tribulations of large parts of Christianity all over the world.

His friendship with Philip Potter, the charismatic church leader from the Caribbean, comprises so to speak in embryo what tribulation and liberation can mean. Potter's grandfather

had been a slave and he himself constantly suffered under forms
of racism, open and concealed. Potter's home, the West Indies, is
'Third World', in direct proximity and in ecumenical dependence
on the 'First World', above all the USA, and with the cultural
stamp of European colonial powers, especially Great Britain.
Philip Potter embodies what the solidarity of young Christians,
for example in the World Student Christian Federation, could
mean for oppressed and suppressed young people; what the
ecumenical movement could bring in the form of militant renewal,
a critical spirit of resistance, and messianic impatience. In dedi-
cating his book to such a representative of oppressed Christianity
fighting for its liberation, Moltmann makes it clear that he wants
to set his reflections in the context of the great schemes of liberation theology.

What does it mean in this perspective and against this background to repeat the words of the old creed of 381, that we
believe in the one, holy, catholic and apostolic church? In a
concluding meditation (337–61), Moltmann offers an interpretation which I shall refer to briefly here, since it makes clear the
approach which governs the whole book. The unity of the
church is associated with freedom, its catholicity with partisanship, its holiness with poverty and its apostolicity with suffering.
At first sight these associations seem surprising, but their logic
becomes evident when they are understood as signs of the history
of God with his oppressed creation, craving the freedom of the
children of God: 'What form is to be taken by the *one* church in
Christ in a world of hostility? By the church made *holy* in the
Spirit in a world of poverty? By the *catholic* church as it testifies
to the kingdom in a world of violence? By the *apostolic* church in
the world of the cross?' (341f., my italics).

So if we bring these messianic perspectives into the centre, we
cannot strive for a unity which does not at the same time leave
room for freedom, just as we cannot also desire a freedom which
is ready lightly to sacrifice unity. A consistent 'fellowship of
Christ' (347) is then the criterion for both unity and separation,
for the relative right of conflicts and the need for reconciliation,
for confrontation and for collaboration.

The same is true of the clause about catholicity. As an expression of the universal presence of the Spirit of God this is essentially related to the whole of humankind. But precisely for that reason the church cannot be content for particular parts of humankind always to be excluded and dehumanized, for whatever reason. Partisan support for the poor and needy thus becomes the hallmark of resolute universality.

The same is true of the confession of the holiness of the church. A church does not become holy by separating itself from guilt and suffering, but conversely by recognizing that with its guilt and its suffering it is justified by the suffering of Christ. Surrender, emptying and poverty are characteristic of the Son of man, and precisely in this he is the Exalted One. Thus the holiness of the church is first disclosed in fellowship with the poor and in protest against the impoverishment of the world.

Consequently the apostolate, too, is a category of mission which can lead to martyrdom. As can be demonstrated by many examples from the history of the martyrs, which indeed has come to a sorry climax in the twentieth century, the proclamation of the Crucified and Risen One leads to protest against the 'principalities and powers' of this world and therefore provokes its furious resistance. Therefore in fellowship with the apostles it is true for the church of all times that it comes very near to the cross wherever it clearly and unmistakably bears witness to the kingdom of God.

(c) The messianic Spirit of God in a time of uncertainty

Finally, a third point which can contribute towards understanding this book needs to be addressed in this introduction. If we compare *The Church in the Power of the Spirit* with *Theology of Hope*, published eleven years earlier, then the changed feeling for the heightened crisis of the world situation is evident. 'The word "crisis" is on every lip,' Moltmann says in the Preface. 'Instability, both inward and outward, is growing. Our political, economic, ethical and religious systems are more vulnerable than many people thought. Consequently the longing for security in all spheres of life is growing as well' (xii). This gives the key phrase 'oppressed Christians throughout the world' its depth. It is evidently not just about the economically and socially impoverished people in the 'Third' World, but about a more radical understanding of oppression, and the bringing of fear and uncertainty to all parts of the world, including the rich and prosperous societies of Europe and the USA. In this connection the first report of the Club of Rome, which appeared in 1972 under the title *The Limits to Growth*, should be mentioned.[52] For the first time the threatening situation of humankind as a whole is presented in a scenario. That the ecological devastation caused by over-exploitation and mismanagement is as dangerous as the military arms race, the atomic overkill between the two superpowers and the increasing economic imbalances in world society heightens the sense of doom which seized many people in the 1970s and in some religious groups deepened into a sense of the end of the world.

Moltmann's book must now be read as the work of someone who in the tribulations of these years understands himself to be both a contemporary and also a 'comrade of the kingdom', who combines his pastoral with his prophetic interest. Moltmann wants to understand the crisis as an opportunity, the uncertainty as an invitation once again to root himself firmly in what lasts. Thus the messianic in the history of the Spirit of God comes on the scene as a constructive counter-force to the fatalistic and destructive phenomena of the paralysis of the 'spirit of the time'.

2. The Church in the Power of the Spirit – *a sketch of the content*

Three key words give the book its structure: 'foundation', 'future' and 'commission'. 'Foundation' means the foundation of the church in the Gospel of Jesus Christ (Chapter III); 'future' implies the 'church of the kingdom of Christ' (Chapter IV), and 'commission' refers to the questions about the tasks and structure of the church in the 'present' (Chapter V) and the 'power of the Holy Spirit' (Chapter VI).[53]

(a) 'The church of Jesus Christ'

Without Christ no church. That is the foundation. There cannot and may not be another. But how is this relationship to be understood? Is Jesus Christ the founder of the Christian religion, the one who gave it its original impulse, who continues to have an impact in the 'kerygma'? Or is the church the *Christus prolongatus*, the extension of Christ? Moltmann rejects all these descriptions of the relationship between Jesus Christ and the church. He understands Christ as 'eschatological person' (73), i.e. in the light of Easter. 'Through his resurrection from the dead Jesus was enthroned as Kyrios, the Christ of God. The resurrection establishes Jesus' "eschatological position". In him the God who is to come, with his lordship and glory, is already present. The risen Christ represents in this transitory era of the world the God who is to come. He therefore represents the coming freedom and salvation of creation at the same time' (74).

Where this Christ makes himself present, the church comes into being and also exists. But this sentence cannot be turned the other way round. Christ need not be where the church is. It must pass away where he withdraws his power. Therefore it must pray steadfastly and urgently to remain in the field of the activity of the Spirit and to correspond in its being and activity to the ways in which Christ works.

In order to be able to describe such relationships of correspondence Moltmann starts from the titles of Christ in the New Testament and develops functions of the church from them. At the same time he leans on the traditional doctrine of the 'threefold office' of Christ which had spoken of a prophetic, priestly and royal dimension in the saving work of Christ, but goes beyond it in an illuminating way.

Moltmann begins with the messianic mission of Jesus and relates the church to this as an 'exodus community' (Section 2, 76ff.). The messianic mission consists in the fact that as the eschatological 'evangelist' Jesus opens up the good news of the imminent kingdom of God to the poor. He is the 'herald of joy' (76), and his prophetic preaching is addressed to those who in body and soul must spend their lives in the shadow of death. 'In a divided, unjust and violent world, the *partisan* gospel reveals the true universality of the coming rule of God and the indivisible liberty' (80).

Where the church is prepared to follow this gospel, it finds itself in an 'eschatological exodus' (38), since it finds itself opposed to all the powers which divide this world among themselves, and cover it with injustice and violence. As the 'community of Christ' it is therefore at the same time 'the people of the kingdom'. The universal world mission of the Messiah in no way means that as an exodus community his community takes leave of the world, but that it understands itself as an advance guard of the new world that is dawning in the midst of a world age which is passing away.

At the same time, however, the church has to remember that its herald of joy is the crucified Christ and that consequently as an exodus community it is also the community of the cross (Section 3, The passion of Jesus and the 'community of the cross', 85ff.). Although it sounds paradoxical, the glory (*doxa*) of Christ consists in his death on the cross and his dignity rests in his self-surrender. This is the place at which the church sees the light of day. It is born 'out of the cross', and 'under the cross' it pursues its calling (89).

As Jesus was brought to the cross by the Roman forces of occupation because they regarded him as a politically dangerous rebel, the political dimension of the criticism of power also remains established in the community of the cross. Here there is an either-or, either Christ or Caesar: 'The idolization of political power and the religious legitimation of economic, social and political conditions of rule are compulsions which no people and no society and hardly any political movement escapes' (90). For as Moltmann says with Calvin, the heart of man is a 'manufactory for idols'; therefore the disempowering of the enslaving idols and the desacralizing of political and economic conditions become the core of a message which appeals to the crucified Christ.

But the cross does not just stand for the political rebel; it is also the sign of the utmost godforsakenness. 'In his godforsakenness the Son of God takes upon himself the fate of the man who has been handed over' (94), and precisely in so doing brings God to all those who believe that they have been abandoned by God. In the previous chapter I spoke at more length about this extreme tension in the concept of God which leads Moltmann to the theology of the Trinity. Here it is taken up to express the priestly dimension of Christ. In the language of the letter to the Hebrews he is the spotless sacrificial lamb and at the same time the 'true high priest', so that in his death the sins of the people are blotted out once and for all. Consequently the priesthood of all believers will prove itself in a life which fundamentally dispenses with scapegoats and sacrificial mechanisms. 'Fellowship with the crucified Jesus is practised where Christians in solidarity enter the brotherhood of those who, in their society, are visibly living in the shadow of the cross: the poor, the handicapped, the people society has rejected, the prisoners and the persecuted' (97).

The Easter reports speak of the crucified Jesus as the Lord over life and death. His rule is the 'radical alternative to human forms of sovereignty' (98), because it promises deliverance from human systems of sovereignty. When it is said that Christ has power in heaven and on earth, this is not a triumphalistic arrogance but the devaluation of unjust conditions in which the rich remain rich but the poor poor, the masters remain the masters and the slaves slaves. *If the crucified Christ is the Lord of the world, then notions of sovereignty are turned upside down* and 'dominion-free brotherhood is the last goal of the history of Jesus' (104).

If this is the kingly office of Christ, then for the form of the church it means that all believers, regardless of status, sex, possessions or race, are 'comrades of the kingdom', equal comrades on the same footing who approach their tasks and conflicts in a comradely and conciliar way. Consequently the universal kingship of all believers is expressed in a radical democratization of conditions in the church and calls for a radical democratization of all political conditions.

Now it is interesting and illuminating that Moltmann extends this Easter notion of rule beyond the political dimension and expands it by the categories of play and festival. Where we have to do with the 'Lord of glory', it is not just a matter of obedience, of conversion and work on changing the world, but equally the 'feast of freedom', 'joy in existence' and the 'ecstasy of happiness' (109). Without this aesthetic dimension, discipleship of Christ would inevitably degenerate into joyless and legalistic efforts.[54] But the kingdom of glory is meant to be celebrated in joyful anticipation. 'For the feast of freedom does not play with unreal possibilities but with the actual potentialities of the future of Christ in the creative Spirit' (111).

Where the 'comrades of the kingdom' experience and recognize themselves as children of freedom, the space of friendship opens up. Section 6, under the heading 'In the friendship of Jesus' (114ff.), is about this. Even if the New Testament evidence which describes the relationship of Jesus to his disciples with the term friendship is relatively scarce, Moltmann sees here a pioneering category for describing the spirit of fellowship which is filled with God's friendliness towards human beings: 'Thus, theologically, the many-faceted work of Christ, which in the doctrine of Christ's threefold office was presented in terms of sovereignty and function, can be taken to its highest point in his friendship' (119). The way in which here Moltmann takes the prophethood, priesthood and kingship of all believers out of its narrow official setting and combines it with the respect, mutual well-pleasing and open-hearted appreciation which is possible only among friends, invites reflection. Therefore the church of Christ is above all the place of friendship and friendliness, which is not to be confused with the cliquish 'circles of friends' as they are to be found in all 'lifestyle enclaves' (to use R.Bellah's phrase).

Moltmann concludes this Chapter III with a reflection on 'the place of the church in the presence of Christ' (121ff.). If initially the slogan had been 'without Christ no church', so here the thesis is *'Ubi Christus – ibi Ecclesia'* (Where Christ is, there is the church). But where is Christ to be found? It is obvious that he is not simply to be found where there are churches. Therefore Moltmann states that the presence of the crucified and risen Christ is to be believed where it is promised, which means in the apostolate and in the poor. By 'apostolate' he understands 'the medium of the proclamation through word and sacrament, as well as the persons and community of the proclaimers' (123). Again this is not to be misunderstood to mean that the presence of Christ can be assumed as it were automatically under word and sacrament or in the community of preachers. There is no identity here which would make such inferences possible, but only an 'identification' of Christ with his own which is irreversible.

This identification is also to be found in the presence of Christ in the poor. 'According to this story (the reference is to the parable of the judgment of the world in Matt.25) the coming judge is already hidden in the world – now, in the present, in the least of his brethren – the hungry, the thirsty, the strangers, the naked, the sick and the imprisoned. Whatever we are doing to them we are doing to him' (126). Moltmann thinks it important that the hidden presence of the Coming One in the poor must not be understood as an ethical programme but first of all as a dimension of ecclesiology. Why is this necessary?

If Christ has promised to be present in word and sacrament, this cannot mean the performance of a ritual which takes no account of existing circumstances. Rather, the fellowship under the word and the sacraments is focussed on filling and satisfying, on friendship and friendliness, on joy in life and affection. In short, the power of Christ to change society is anticipated and tested each time his disciples gather under word and sacrament.

Precisely that ought also to happen where the presence of Christ in the poor is believed in. For his presence in the poor implies anything but the sanctioning of distress. The hungry are to get food, the naked clothing, and prisoners are not to remain isolated and alone. *If the coming Christ awaits us in the poor, then he awaits us at the sore point of history,* so that there the power of the kingdom which elevates and sets upright can be anticipated and tested. This force which sets upright and puts right is the prevenient judgment of the eschatological Pantocrator.

(b) 'The church of the kingdom of God'

This has already brought us to the second focal point of Moltmann's ecclesiology, namely the future or, as the title to Chapter IV states, 'The Church of the Kingdom of God' (133). Moltmann states as a thesis, 'In this chapter we must now assess the breadth of the *horizon of hope* opened up through Christ for Christianity as it lives and suffers in history', and then explains that he is concerned with 'the concrete doctrine of hope for Christianity's relationships in the world'; for 'eschatology is always specific only as relational eschatology' (134). Four relationships are identified: the 'hope of Israel', the 'hope of the religions', the 'hope of human society' and the 'hope of nature' (135). Whereas Israel and the nations are discussed in separate sections, Moltmann takes the key words 'society' and 'nature' together in a single section under the title 'Christianity in the processes of the world's life'.

'Israel is Christianity's original, enduring and final partner in history' (135). This approach determines what is said in Section 2 about 'The church and Israel' (136ff.). It emphasizes the deep connection between the two but of course also prompts the question what distinguishes them and in what the special calling of Christianity is to be seen. Moltmann maintains that 'the church is not the organization that succeeds Israel in salvation history', nor is it 'a revival movement within Israel'. The independent calling of the church consists 'in precisely this service of reconciliation between the Gentiles and God which heralds the redemption of the world' (148). And 'the redemption of Israel coincides with the redemption of all creation' (149).

Thus here there is the assumption of a kind of economy of redemption which puts Israel and the church side by side and nevertheless gives the two different tasks, in the expectation that they will fuse together in the consummation of the kingdom.

Now this special relationship determines the question of the relationship between Christianity and the religions (Section 3, 150ff.). Here first of all it is said that the situation in world history must be taken seriously: among other things this consists in the fact that the one humankind represents the future of all peoples. Some clarifications for dialogue with the religions emerges from this. Not only has traditional Eurocentrism become obsolete, but church absolutism, as a consequence of which there is said to be no salvation outside the church, must be overcome along with the absolutism of faith which postulates an *a priori* difference between Christian faith and the forms of faith of other religions. But on the other hand an Enlightenment relativism is also finished. What remains? If Christianity renounces all claims in the direction of exclusiveness or inclusiveness, it can still understand itself as a 'critical catalyst' which can exercise an indirect transforming function with its message. Moltmann thinks that 'this can be called the indirect infection of other religions with Christian ideas, values and principles' (180). However, this would also mean Christianity allowing itself to be 'infected' by the notions, values and principles of other religions.

If we take the development towards an interdependent humankind seriously, then the process of indigenization in various worlds becomes very important. Here the suspicion of syncretism immediately presents itself. But Moltmann thinks that this danger can be avoided where religious and cultural forces are activated charismatically for the messianic future. If Christians can open themselves to the notion that the 'future of the liberating and redeeming kingdom' is to be expected '*in* the potentialities and powers of the world religions' (185), then a new 'dialogistic profile', which is there only in embryo, comes into existence.

The term 'catalyst' is appropriate for defining the significance of 'Christianity in the processes of the world's life' – thus the title of Section 4 (163ff.). What concrete doctrine of hope comes into play here? Moltmann distinguishes three dimensions and speaks of: 1. the '*economic* process which is acted out in economic struggles and the exploitation of nature'; 2. the '*political* process which is acted out in the struggle for power and the control of power'; and 3. the '*cultural* process, which is acted out in the struggle for educational, racial and sexual privileges' (165). These processes are at the same time crises in which the human 'will for life' is shaken. Therefore Christian preaching must first prove itself by living out for people and bringing to people 'courage to be', an 'affirmation of life' and 'loyalty to the earth'. The passion for life can overcome the addiction of disheartened people to death only if it combines the 'power of hope' and the 'capacity for suffering'. These three belong together; they are 'directed towards the future of creation in the kingdom of God and are actualized in the powers of the Spirit and the potentialities of history' (168).

Moltmann now applies this spiritual-pastoral triad to the three processes of life which have been mentioned. In the case of the economic process he comes to speak of the ecological scenario of dangers which at that time had been presented in their urgency by the Club of Rome. He criticizes the notion of growth driven by the economy: 'The limitless growth of claims for more life, greater power and expanded rule has up to now been the inner fuel of "progress". We can now look ahead to the time when it will be the fuel of catastrophe as well' (195). Therefore Christians can no longer accept the claim of the economy to its own 'laws' and 'pressures'; over against the paradigm of limitless growth it must set the model of 'symbiosis' (174). Symbiotic life prefers the satisfaction of the needs of the community to the heedless forcing through of private claims; it opens up the way from the exploitation of nature to peace with nature, from the struggle of existence to 'peace in existence' (174). The driving categories here are 'social justice' and an 'ethic of solidarity' (175).

Where Christianity preserves its function of being a catalyst in the political programme, it will take the side of human rights. Moltmann emphasizes that human rights may not be related only to individuals, but must be understood in their collective and economic extensions as 'rights of humankind', i.e. as a collection of rights and obligations which have in view humankind as a common subject in law.[55] Human solidarity has priority over popular, ethnic or national loyalty. Therefore here ecumenical Christianity is called for. It must perceive its universal political responsibility.

When we turn finally to the third, the 'cultural process', we note that Moltmann limits himself to a few 'typical cultural conflicts'.

He mentions racism (183), which he describes as a spiritual mechanism of self-justification and as an ideological mechanism of subjection.[56] He goes on to speak of 'sexism' (184), at that time a brand-new word – which is similarly about male self-justification and the safeguarding of predominance. Then he refers to the conflict between the healthy and the handicapped, this too a theme which at that time was only slowly attracting attention. 'It is only when the healthy cease to present a problem for the handicapped that the practical problems of the handicapped can really be solved' (186), Moltmann remarks laconically.[57]

Obviously these cultural conflicts are intensively bound up with the problem of self-justification and therefore call forth the Christian message of justification by faith. The social nature of justification shows itself in the fact that people can renounce confirming their identity with privileges and claims to power and thus at the same time live out their respect for the rights and dignity of others. 'The Church of the Kingdom of God' is the title of this part of Moltmann's messianic ecclesiology. But what about the future and present of this kingdom, and what does the power which develops in this kingdom look like?

'The eschatological fulfilment of the liberating lordship of God in history is termed *the rule of God*.' However, in the sphere of our history this rule is hidden and disputed. But that does not mean that its immanent power can be given up in favour of a total other-worldliness. It is important to understand God's rule as 'change within the system' and at the same time as a 'future which transcends the system' (215), just as the obedience to the will of God that changes the world and prayer for the kingdom of God indissolubly belong together. Moltmann sees the dynamic interlocking of these two perspectives of history safeguarded in the concept of the messianic. Consequently, 'the messianic life is . . . not life in constant deferment, but life in anticipation . . . Its freedom lies in its transcending of the present through the power of hope for what is to come, and the actual in the light of the potential. But this is also its pain: it has to seize the new against the resistance of the old, so that a new beginning cannot be made without an ending, and freedom cannot be realized without a struggle' (217). Now if the church is the place of this messianic life, it has a share in this freedom and in this pain. It has to prove its role as messianic forerunner by being taken out and driven beyond its social and historical limits. That it has a share in God's 'project' gives it the certainty and joy to sustain the pain of its recalcitrant everyday life. 'In this sense the church of Jesus Christ is the *people of the kingdom of God*' (196).

(c) 'The church as a community of messianic service to the kingdom of God'

After the discussion of the 'foundation' and the 'future' of the church, Chapters V and VI are about its task. Here the questions of specific expressions of the life of the church and its form are discussed. In terms of tradition Moltmann distinguishes between the 'means of salvation' (Chapter V) and the 'offices' (Chapter VI). However, in order to avoid the intractable discussion about the number and value of the church's sacraments and offices he inserts in the section 'The sending of the Spirit as the sacrament of the kingdom' (199ff.) a reflection in which he takes up approaches of Rahner and Barth. Rahner had designated the church the 'fundamental sacrament' and had derived this in turn from God's self-expression in Christ as the 'primal sacrament'. Barth had started from this 'primal sacrament' and wanted to reclaim the use of the term 'sacrament' exclusively for God's revelation in Christ. Moltmann proposes opening up this christological concentration in a trinitarian direction and speaking of the 'eschatological gift of the Holy Spirit as the sacrament' (202). 'This *trinitarian concept of the sacrament* includes the eschatological history of God's dealings with the world in the "signs and wonders" of the Holy Spirit and the "signs of the end". In the eschatological gift of the Holy Spirit "word and sacrament", "ministries and charismata" become comprehensible as the revelations and powers of Christ and his future' (205). Thus all expressions of the life of the church are as it were 'loaded' with God's power and orientated messianically on the kingdom. That explains why Moltmann designates the church the 'messianic fellowship of service for the kingdom of God' (198).

What does this 'fellowship of service' need for its life and witness in the world? It must gather around the gospel (Section 2, 206ff.), i.e. it must continually assure itself of its foundation in order as a 'fellowship of hope', to find 'freedom from the perspectives of its society' (225). There follows (in Section 3, 226ff.) an account of baptism. Its messianic quality singles it out as an 'event of liberation' (239), which takes those baptized out of their natural identifications (by family, people and society) and sets them free for their calling into the kingdom of God. It is only consistent for Moltmann to prefer the baptism of adults who have consciously decided for Christ to the traditional infant baptism.

The next section (242ff.) logically deals with the 'Lord's supper'. This too is qualified in messianic terms as a fellowship meal, and here in principle an 'open invitation' to those who have committed themselves to their community applies. No kind of 'office' and no 'discipline' can force themselves between the Lord of the supper and his guests as an admission authority. 'His invitation involves no condition about the acknowledgment of ministries in the church. It is gracious, unconditional and prevenient like the love of God itself' (272). Therefore as the people of the kingdom the church experiences itself in undivided fellowship with its Lord, and the more it becomes the 'fellowship church of the people', the more important will this 'fellowship in the meal' become for it (258).

In a separate section (261ff.), Moltmann then discusses 'worship' as the 'messianic feast' which 'sets the assembled community, with its daily pains and joys, in the broad context of the trinitarian history of God with the world' (260). That today these services have also to provide for such religious functions as a suspension of workaday activities, a safety valve, relaxation and compensation must be deliberately noted, so that they can be taken up into the messianic freedom.

Worship understood as a 'feast' and a 'messianic intermezzo' (to use van Ruler's term) presupposes that the community is an active subject which forms spontaneously, whereas the liturgically regulated 'celebrations' of the churches that 'look after people'[58] are inclined to tone down the ferment of the spontaneous in favour of routines that can be repeated as a ritual.

In a separate section headed 'The messianic way of life' (6, 275ff., Moltmann grapples with the problem which again had become a marked concern in the 1970s, namely the question of an appropriate 'spirituality'. What does a Christian life look which has been 'infected' by the messianic? Moltmann resorts to the concept of 'rebirth'. He thinks that *regeneratio, renovatio* seem to capture the sense of what is meant better than sanctification, with its many levels of meaning' (278).[59] This is not of course a spiritual matter but a life which gives itself over to the messianic *vivificatio* body and soul. The living hope sparks off 'creative tensions' (282) in each reborn life. Reference is made to 'the tensions between *prayer and faithfulness to the earth*, between *contemplation and political struggle*, between *transcendental religion* and *the religion of solidarity*' (282). In this connection Moltmann recalls the Blumhardts and Dietrich Bonhoeffer, the lifestyle of Taizé and Martin Luther King Jr. Their common feature is the quest for a political spirituality in solidarity: 'No one who . . . in Christ's name cries out for redemption can put up with oppression. No one who fights against injustice can dispense with prayer for redemption' (314). To preserve this reciprocity is indispensable for a messianic lifestyle.

Now, of course, the dimension of the messianic also determines the 'offices' of the church. To begin from fellowship implies that first the community' comes into focus (Section 1, 'The community in the process of the Holy Spirit', 291ff.). It is the 'fellowship of the free', and their ordinances must therefore be 'ordinances of freedom' (292). For as the rule of Christ essentially consists in liberating people from the pressure and compulsion of the 'powers and authorities', every community order and every church government must judge itself by this criterion.

But where the messianic power of the Spirit of God gains

ground, all powers are 'loaded' with grace, i.e. they are determined charismatically. 'In principle every human potentiality
and capacity can become charismatic through a person's call, if
only they are used in Christ' (297). Now charismatic gifts are
very often understood in enthusiastic terms and misused.
Therefore Moltmann emphasizes that 'the crucified Jesus is the
measure of the fervency of the charismata' (299). He also makes
it clear that charismatic 'reversals of polarity' of natural possibilities and capacities do not create a special, as it were 'ontological',
state but are always effected in relation to the presence of the
Spirit, i.e. modally. So one can gain charismatic powers, but one
can also lose them!

This perspective now shapes the reflections in Section 2, which
is about the 'charge to the community and the assignments
within the community' (327ff.). The individual callings in the
community have to start from the call of the community. All
offices in the community result from the threefold office of the
community and must be qualified in the light of this. Now that
does not just mean that the community defines its office. The
messianic dimension implies that all offices live and are active by
the charismatic power of Christ. 'Any member of the community
who stands up in front of it is therefore commissioned by it to act
in Christ's name . . . It has not the right to stop assigning the commissions themselves' (304). Questions of status are secondary:
'According to the powers and possibilities available, the charges
we have named (here Moltmann is thinking e.g. of preachers,
teachers, pastors, sick visitors, missionaries) can be full-time or
part time. They can be carried out by *men* and *women*, by the
married and the *unmarried*, by the *theologically trained* and by
people without any theological training. They can be exercised
by *individuals* and *groups*' (335).

It is in keeping with these principles that the form of leadership
of the community must be presbyteral and democratic and that
the structures of decision between individual communities must
be organized in a conciliar way. What does this mean for the
notion of the apostolic succession? This is strictly related to the
community as the apostolic people, but not to offices of leader-

ship that are specially singled out: 'Even a succession of bishops is no guarantee of the permanent identity of faith, nor of faithfulness to the apostolic gospel' (313).

From this, finally, it follows for the 'form of the church as fellowship' (thus the title of Section 3, 314ff.) that the 'fellowship of friends' (314) should be the leading idea. In this sense the famous formula of the 'community of brothers' from Thesis 3 of the Barmen Theological Declaration is determined. It is no surprise that the historical transformation of communities of discipleship open to the world into the imperial church in the Roman empire implies a grave questioning of the charismatic openness of the church. As Moltmann says, 'This transition from the church open to the world to the imperial church still determines the church's structure and organization today in what were for long "Christian" countries' (318f.). Certainly the Reformation attempted to replace this kind of 'church' with the 'principle of community', but did not carry it through, so that even in the Reformation churches a 'territorially and socially closed church' (319) has come into being.

Moltmann explains the fact that over the course of church history, time and again there has been a conflict with sects as a result of the unresolved and unresolvable conflict between charismatic calling and assimilation to the imperial church. 'Because Christianity, by virtue of its messianic hope, points beyond itself and the church, prophetic and messianic sects always come to the fore whenever the church surrenders its hope for the coming kingdom' (320).

Manifestly these radical church groups in times of radical upheavals represent the necessary agencies in which the messianic alternative to the closed institution of the mainstream church is expressed. Therefore it makes sense always also to read church history as the history of sects, 'in order to understand the whole of Christianity' (320).

Another alternative movement which has accompanied the imperial church critically from its beginning was the eremetical and ascetic movement from which the monastic communities arose. Radical discipleship groups remain the charismatic counter-force to mainstream church organizations; in them the memory of the energy of the kingdom of God that brings radical renewal is more alive than in the assimilated apparatuses of established churches.

Nevertheless, even Moltmann, despite all his sympathy for the communities of radical discipleship, does not go so far as to reject the justification for mainstream church institutions as anti-Christian: 'The mainstream churches and the discipleship groups remain dependent on one another in a kind of double strategy until the *community principle* can be realized' (326).

But how is that to happen? Moltmann thinks that while the old established churches still have an important 'organization for the care of the people' (326), they less and less have a people. Most of the proposals for church reform have come from above. However, he sees that the counter-movements in which a 'reform of the community from below' (328) announces itself have arisen primarily in the base communities and above all in Latin America, and from there have spread all over the world. 'In these communities people are the subject of their own Christian fellowship. In place of the "church for the people" we have the beginnings of the "church of the people", which lives, suffers and acts among the people themselves and with them' (329f.).

Moltmann recognizes another alternative movement in the community work which was first developed in slums as 'community organization' and which in a very great variety of ways has been expressed in civil initiatives.

Moltmann observes that these alternatives are bound into the traditional structure of the established churches in a 'double strategy'. People then like to speak of the 'church as institution' and the 'church as event'. But the combination of these two approaches creates an indecision that leads to compromises on both sides. Moltmann sees the way out in concentration on the 'gathered community'. 'Where the community gathers round the gospel and the Lord's table, it becomes recognizable in the world and unmistakably the people of Christ, the messianic community of the coming kingdom' (334). Messianic calling, the charismatic differentiation of its ministries, and openness to the world can be depicted in these gathered communities. Consequently a church reform worthy of the name would have to 'make the build-up of the living congregational church its priority, not the extension of supra-regional offices' (335f.). 'The goal of all strategies is the building up of mature responsible communities' (336). With this consistent congregationalist focus, Moltmann concludes his remarks on the 'commission' of the church in the power of the Spirit of God.

3. *Unclear signals? Notes on a programmatic writing which is not one*

After the two programmatic writings, *Theology of Hope* and *The Crucified God*, the publishers brought out discussion volumes – an indication that both books had had so broad a response that this was worth separate documentation. No such discussion volume came out after *The Church in the Power of the Spirit*. This is an indication that this book did not find a comparable echo. Why was that? I do not propose to go into the question of the reception of *The Church in the Power of the Spirit* in detail. Rather, on the basis of my own impressions after reading it I want to point to a few features which are open to misunderstanding.

(a) *Comparisons with 'The Community against the Horizon of the Rule of Christ'*

It is striking that there is no reference to the 'first programmatic writing' – perhaps it would be better to speak of a 'zero number'. The short work 'The Community against the Horizon of the Rule of Christ' does not appear, although the overlaps of topics in ecclesiology might have led us to expect references back to it or even critical correction. The fact that these nevertheless do not appear suggests that the author must have felt that he had moved a very long way from his early approach.

And in fact the distance is tremendous. Granted, only sixteen years lie between these two publications, but the scope of the experience and impressions have expanded to a degree which is amazing, given this short period of time. As I said in the introduction to this chapter, the pastor of Wasserhorst has become an international and much sought-after theologian. Thus the 'horizon' of the problems and methods of argumentation have emphatically changed.

However, if we take a look at the theological outlines the common features emerge. What in 1959 was called the 'rule of Christ' is developed in *The Church in the Power of the Spirit* under the key words 'foundation' and 'future'. The christological anchoring is at the same time the motive for the universal claim expressed in the term 'kingdom of God'. However, the trinitarian lay-out of this kingdom-of-God theology is new.

Also familiar is the concentration on 'community' and with it the impulse towards church reform. However, in the 1975 book the theological and above sociological inconsistencies in the concept of community which already struck us in the first writing are repeated. We shall have to go on to talk about them.

It is striking that the reflections on preaching – in 1959 Moltmann had spoken of 'economic' and 'cultural' preaching – do not appear again, although the extended sections on 'Gospel' and 'Worship' (206ff., 261ff.) lend themselves admirably to a development of these approaches. Here among other things, a dialogue with the theorists and – above all – with the practitioners of the sciences of communication should have been carried on, though systematic theologians are fond of shifting this into the sphere of practical theology. I do not want to dispute that it belongs there. Nevertheless, a somewhat more detailed account would have been desirable, even in the framework of a systematic theological treatise.

However, one should not ask of a book what it explicitly does not promise. And in his 'messianic ecclesiology' Moltmann wanted to concentrate on the questions of systematic theology. He deliberately neglected the ecclesiological, sociological and historical questions relating to the church in order to devote himself to the theological foundation of the church. The church becomes and remains the church only where and in so far as it

remains and becomes the church of *Jesus Christ*. The church is
and remains only where and in so far as it remains the church
against the horizon of the coming kingdom of God. The church
becomes and remains the church only where it understands itself
as *the people of God changed charismatically by the urging of the
Spirit of God*. These are the principles which give the whole book
its liberation-theological stamp.

(b) Universalism and the church

It is this liberation-theological universalism which gives
Moltmann's ecclesiology its distinctive verve. That is evident in a
particularly impressive way in Chapter III, for there with the key
words 'exodus community', 'community of the cross', 'comrades
of the kingdom' and 'fellowship of the friends of Jesus', guiding
images are presented with which further creative ecclesiological
work can be done.

However, it is precisely this liberation-theological universalism
which creates the ecclesiological problems. If the kingdom of
God embraces and comprehends the whole world, either the
consequences for the understanding for the church are gigantic,
with the result that triumphalistic claims are inevitably made, or
the fatal inappropriateness of this relationship painfully emerges.
What image of ecumenicity can do justice to trinitarian universalism? This book may be dedicated to the World Council of
Churches, as I have already mentioned, but Moltmann pays no
attention to the ecclesiological difficulties of this ecumenical
construction.[60]

That becomes clear in what in my view is a particularly striking way in the question of the relationship of the church to the
world religions. Why should not the dynamic of messianic
universalism also find expression in the other religions of the
world? To put the question another way, if God's Spirit really
fills all the world, how can it not also manifest itself in the other
religions of humankind? So what is the specific mission of the
Christian church? What conclusions follow from messianic
universalism for the understanding of dialogue and world

mission? Cannot far more incisive conclusions be drawn than seem possible from our perspective, which is still all too strongly stamped by the heritage of the 'Christian West'? Here Moltmann's remarks remain comparatively hesitant and half-hearted.

(c) Church and community

I have already pointed out that Moltmann does not go into sociological and confessional differences in the church. However, this strictly theological approach does produce conceptual blurring which becomes increasingly difficult as time goes on. First, Moltmann uses the terms 'church', 'Christianity' and 'Christendom' without differentiating them precisely. Only at one point is a differentiation indicated. At the end of Chapter IV Moltmann writes: 'The *church* in the power of the Spirit is not yet the kingdom of God, but is its anticipation in history. *Christianity* is not yet the new creation, but it is the working of the Spirit of the new creation. *Christendom* is not yet the new mankind but it is its vanguard, in resistance to deadly introversion and in self-giving and representation for man's future' (196, my italics; unfortunately this differentiation is largely missed in the published English translation). But is the content of this differentiation convincing? What could 'anticipation' mean if not 'resistance to deadly introversion, self-giving and represen-tation'? So are 'Christianity and Christendom' terms with a wider scope, in so far as they are related to 'new creation' and 'mankind'? This does not seem convincing.

Another contrast plays a very much more incisive role in this messianic ecclesiology, the contrast between 'church' and 'com-munity'. Moltmann leaves no doubt that the New Testament *ekklesia* comes very close in substance to 'gathered community', just as he also refers the ecclesiological interpretation of the honorific titles of Christ to the community. Therefore he speaks of the 'exodus community', the 'community of the cross', etc. And therefore he also leaves no doubt that the renewal of the church must follow from the 'principle of the community' (thus first in the Preface, xiv). He sums up the purpose of this book in terms of praxis and church reform in theses in his Preface as follows: 'from the pastoral church, which looks after the people, to the people's own communal church among the people'. As we have seen, the 'communal church' is developed from the principle of the gathered church, whereas the pastoral church that looks after people is associated with the 'official church', the 'mainstream church' and the 'established church'.

It is precisely at this point that the lack of confessional questions and questions about the sociology of the church proves to be a notable disadvantage. The community principle which Moltmann prefers is clearly rooted in the Reformed congregationalist tradition.[61] It remains hard to see how this principle of the 'gathered community' is now to be envisaged locally. Is the author thinking of the parishes which already exist? Or does he envisage local communities which have formed from different confessional communities that celebrate the Lord's supper together, baptize the members of their community together and attempt to represent a messianic fellowship of service for the world around them? How does this model of the church relate to the living conditions of a society which is extremely mobile both in work and in leisure? How does this 'fellowship church' organize itself? How does it organize its networks and tasks which extend beyond regions, for example in the training of the women and men to whom it entrusts its special ministries and offices? Can theology go on undisturbed in state universities? After all, this is quite manifestly a relic of the ordinances of a state church. What would a theology have to look like which developed from, or was necessitated by, the 'fellowship church of the people in the people'?

One detail is a characteristic indication of the failure of this approach. In his introductory comment on the index of names (!, not in the English text), Moltmann says: 'A theological treatment of the works of the church like diaconia, academies, the care of the sick, development aid, etc., would have gone beyond the framework of this book. It is left for later publications' (German, 389). Quite apart from the fact that no such publication has yet appeared, the argument is not convincing either for technical reasons – why should an ecclesiology not be 100 pages longer? – or for substantive reasons. The fields of church work mentioned are all to be understood as forms of solidarity of a church which is messianically involved in modern and mobile industrial society. At least they have mostly arisen out of such a spirit, whereas the local congregations with a parochial constitution 'under the word' have consolidated themselves largely as 'life-style enclaves', unwilling to be reformed, from which forces of life and renewal emerge only very rarely. There is no overlooking the fact that the base communities and community work, both according to Moltmann original aspects of a renewal of the community from below, have largely been rejected by the established parish communities, so that they have to create for themselves an independent ecclesiological value in para-community networks. And what would the World Council of Churches itself be without these committed groups and their networks?

To take another example, what would have become of the feminist renewal movement had there not been the Evangelical Academies? They were the bodies which reacted very much more flexibly to this theme, which is extraordinarily relevant for both theology and the church, than the parish communities on the one hand and the theological faculties on the other. Something similar could also be said about the institutions which have established development aid, development policy and educational work related to development. Only after these world-wide networks had been established could individual parishes or church circles build up relationships of partnership with other churches.

(d) Ecclesiology and ethics

In my view one aspect needs to be emphasized which follows from the concept of the church as a 'messianic fellowship of service', but at the same time also entails a substantive difficulty. It is the relationship between ecclesiology and ethics. These two aspects come very close together, but without fusing. The church, understood theologically as a 'fellowship of service', is as responsible for its life-style, in other words for its importance in social ethics, as it is for its life of worship, since after all its life-style in particular is its 'reasonable service of God' (Rom.12.1). It follows from this that the 'gathered' community is also the sphere in which there is not only responsible liturgical action but also the formation of an ethical awareness. Where else are future generations to learn the meaning of life in solidarity? To put it another way: ethics and education come very close together. The church is not least the place in which 'ethical learning' goes on.

But this learning must have a network which is open to the world, global and ecumenical. It needs ecumenical structures of communication and supportive authorities (which again ends up in creating agencies that go beyond the local communities).

On the other hand, we have to ask, does not an ethical aware-ness, particularly in the face of the complex emergencies of our time, draw on other sources than the Christian tradition? Do not viewpoints come to bear here to a heightened degree which derive from the wisdom traditions of all humankind (which paradoxically have been suppressed by the Christian churches in particular), or which are owed to scientific insights? The fields of learning and the constellations in which ethical awareness is learned today thus extend far beyond the church. How are we to think of this relationship which is so full of tension? Unfortunately there are no references in Moltmann's 'messianic ecclesiology' to the extensive discussion of the key term 'ecumenical learning'. Educational questions are left untouched, and consequently the same is also true of questions about religious education.

This has brought us to concerns which go beyond *The Church in the Power of the Spirit*. Once again they confront us anew with the question of the scope of Moltmann's three (or four) programmatic writings. So the next chapter will be about his ethical notions and proposals.

6

On Being a Christian –
The Messianic Fragment

1. Introduction: Why there is no 'ethic'

'At that time,' observes Moltmann, referring to the time around 1968, 'I was attempting to write an *Ethics of Hope* as a sequel to the *Theology of Hope*. It failed because I did not know whether reforms or revolution would improve circumstances. In the "political theology" movement I attempted to work with a twofold strategy of the "great alternative' and the many "little alternatives", on the model of a Christianity of order there and a Christianity of the world here. But I did not have a detailed knowledge of the different fields of action and spheres of life. So nothing came of the *Ethics*.'[62]

This observation from 1997 is a late but by no means exhaustive answer to a question which Jürgen Moltmann kept hearing: What's happened to your ethics? If it is true that God's history of promise permeates and renews the histories of our people, indeed the history of this cosmos, than it must be possible to note – and describe – the changes in a concrete way! If the 'crucified God' breaks through the 'vicious circles of death', then it must be possible to trace and feel the great liberations of human beings here and now. And finally, if the 'church' experiences its life and its mission in the power of the divine Spirit, then the dynamic of this messianic empowerment must be lived out in the fullness and the presence of the Spirit. Therefore the programmatic writings almost inevitably point towards confirmation in ethical discussion.

That is doubtless correct, and Moltmann would be the last to dispute it. Rather, he would say: precisely because that is the case, an 'ethic' can no longer be fitted between two covers of a book. Precisely because the horizon and scope of the kingdom of God must be understood universally and cosmically, ecumenically and in terms of humankind, ethics must extend to all spheres of life. But think what that would mean! The world-wide ecological crises and their complicated interdependencies must be treated, along with the world economy with its dependencies, and tendencies towards enrichment and impoverishment. The sciences with their economic dependencies and interdisciplinary ramifications which are becoming increasingly complex would need to be treated along with the media and their networks which are becoming ever more global and totalitarian. It would be necessary to note that the peoples and nations have to fight with their own historical inheritances and violations, that their quest for identity and power in the structure of states sets out from the most varied initial conditions and therefore priorities. And finally, all these considerations would have to end up with human beings. But what are human beings? Each one of them is a microcosm in which macrocosmic possibilities and torments are reflected, this 'unestablished' being who experiences happiness and suffering in the world!

This in outline is the great complex of problems which an 'ethic' would have to cope with today. Who could manage that?[63]

It is clear that no individual, however learned, could possess the necessary detailed knowledge on these different fields and areas. They are far too complex for an all-embracing encyclopaedic ethic to be conceivable. Moreover the factors conditioning ethical decisions and options change so quickly that false assessments would be inevitable.

Nevertheless Moltmann was clear that this awareness of the complexity must not lead to a renunciation of ethical reflection. He therefore limited himself to the option of grasping the 'great alternative' in outline form and at the same time in practice furthering the 'little alternatives'. This is an approach which structurally recalls the slogan that could often be heard in the 1970s and 1980s: 'Think globally, act locally'.

In what follows I shall try to make this twofold approach clear by means of examples. In this way I also want to demonstrate in outline the diversity of ethically relevant but unfortunately very scattered published contributions. Even if there is no 'great' ethics, there are many relevant statements which are easily over-looked. And in this chapter I also want to show that with a certain intrinsic necessity Moltmann's approach leads beyond the project of an 'ethic' in the classical sense. (Which could also be one of the reasons why it could not succeed.) He is in fact concerned not only with the (ethical) question 'What must I do?' or 'How do I have to behave?' but with the more comprehensive existential question, 'How am I to live? What (still) gives life meaning?' Now this question goes beyond ethical discussion and seeks a supportive spirituality. Consequently reflections appear which one would not look for in a 'classical ethics', for example on joy in life, feast and celebration, prayer and contemplation. This is therefore in a comprehensive sense the 'art of life'.[64]

But that does not yet exhaust the tasks that we have to consider in this chapter. 'Ethics', 'the art of life' and 'spirituality' always also involve a question of the subject. Certainly, first of all individual Christians must be regarded and addressed as subjects, since they are the ones who have to take responsibility for their lives. Nevertheless both the ethical responsibility of men and women and their efforts to shape their life in a spiritual way cannot just be understood in individualistic terms. They also have a social and a collective side. Much as men and women are responsible for their lives, they cannot detach this task from the communities to which they owe their lives, in which and for which they lead them. Accordingly families, firms, associations, peoples and states are to be addressed as 'subjects'; indeed ultimately humanity as a whole must be addressed as a 'subject' about its safeguarding of life, since through the nuclear and ecological threat it has become a common object of annihilation.

The same is also true of the churches. Their quality of life, i.e. their denseness and vitality, their burden-sharing capacity and their influence, are not only existentially important for shaping a Christian life but turn it into a corporate subject of its own. Churches must be regarded as 'moral communities'. Therefore ecclesiology belongs in ethics or ethics in ecclesiology. That was discussed briefly at the end of Chapter 5. But this makes the task even more complicated, for the church as 'moral community' can exist always only in the plural, because there the most varied factors (like history, culture, traditions and economic conditions) play a determinative role. Moltmann has therefore quite deliberately insisted that the 'community' is the common subject of questions of ethics and lifestyle. As a further stage, some remarks will have to be made about this.

One more question by way of anticipation: is it fair to focus on a part of Moltmann's work which he himself manifestly has not put on the same level as his great books? I think that it is indispensable for understanding his work as a whole to leave the 'main line' of the great books and investigate some of the 'branch lines'. It is precisely in these writings, often based on addresses, sermons, talks on the radio and in churches, that the basic pastoral features of Moltmann's theology become visible. For in the last resort Moltmann understands his work as a contribution of one Christian for other Christians, of one member of the community for other members, and less as the statements of an academic teacher turning to his students, or a scholar who is required to participate in academic discussion. For him theology is primarily an expression of the life of the community, in which he wants to take place in his own way and with his own forces.

Precisely because in this chapter we have to do with approaches, outlines, proposals and statements, I want to set over these remarks a key word which Moltmann himself uses. The word is 'fragment'. He writes: 'Our life is a fragment, naturally, a fragment of death. The life which is reborn to a living hope also remains a fragment. But it now becomes a *fragment of the coming beauty of the kingdom of God*.'[65]

The search for ethical criteria and guidelines, for a lifestyle and spirituality, for vital and viable Christian communities, cannot be other than fragmentary. But the key question is whether in them 'the coming beauty of the kingdom of God' is delineated, in other words, whether they can be experienced as *messianic fragments*.

2. *The passion for the kingdom – ethical approaches*

If we are to understand Moltmann's ethical approach, it is worth referring back to the 'double strategy of the "great alternatives" and the many "little alternatives"' mentioned at the beginning. What do the 'great' alternatives look like? And the 'little ones'?

If there is a code word in the great programmatic writings, it is 'kingdom of freedom'. God's rule opens up freedom.[66] Consequently God's rule is effective in history as liberation. 'In the resurrection of Christ a new freedom in history can be recognized which is not only liberation from historical tyranny but also a liberation from the tyranny of history itself . . . Therefore for faith Christ becomes the focal point of the comprehensive hope of the new world in which God is. In the midst of the open experimental field of history, therefore for Christian faith the future comes to dominate the past and hope to dominate fear.'[67]

The messianic power of the coming kingdom represents a radical – and therefore in nucleus a revolutionary – opening up of history. It becomes the experimental field of freedom. Thus it also loses the character of the fatalistic return of what is eternally the same and its dependence on the fearful and despairing ties to transitoriness and nothingness. God's 'new world' enters the 'old world' of death in a renewing way. To avoid the impression of a sterile dualism here we would do better to say that the 'new world' is of course the 'old' in that it frees this from its remoteness from God and thus from the diverse forms of slavery, alienation and annihilation.

Thus the freedom of the kingdom discloses itself in the *praxis of liberation*; that is the starting point for ethical reflection. In Moltmann's words, 'From this comprehensive vision of God against the nothingness which threatens everywhere we arrive at . . . concrete utopias for historical initiatives against the negative that is experienced historically.'[68]

Behind the formula 'initiatives against the negative' we recognize an approach which sees the new, that which does not yet exist, as a negation of the negative. Suffering over the negative presents itself as the other side of what is expected positively. 'Hope for the positive is alive in suffering over the negative.'[69]

Since freedom is the (positive) leading concept, a lack of freedom becomes the codeword for the negative. *The fight for freedom arises out of suffering over a lack of freedom*: the hope for liberation rubs up against the figures of alienation.

In a 1969 lecture Moltmann mentions three forms of alien-ation: economic, political and racial.[70] Overcoming economic alienation means liberation from hunger, and at the end of the 1960s that meant a resolute yes to world-wide development aid and a criticism of the increasing discrepancies in the world-wide interdependencies of industrialization. Moltmann translates overcoming political alienation into the goal of 'democratizing society and international relationships';[71] here 'liberation' means the end of the oppression of human beings by others. Here too the world-wide perspective plays a determinative role. Basing himself on C.F.von Weizsäcker, Moltmann mentions 'world domestic policy' as the goal of the necessary processes of demo-cratization. Finally, the overcoming of racial alienation is so important because it means liberation from humiliation. The racist split in humankind represents an explosive mixture of complexes of superiority and inferiority, arising out of suppressed feelings of guilt and hurt. But because humankind as a whole must become the subject of its future if it is not to come to grief by being torn apart and because of its increasing arsenals of destruction, it needs a corporate identity and thus an end to racial discrimination.

There are thus three great spheres in which the messianic praxis of liberation presses for realization: *economics, politics and sociality or culture*. Over the years and under the impact of new problems Moltmann has worked in more detail on the content of these *three spheres of action*. The field of economics has been expanded by the aspect of ecology. In the middle of the 1970s, in *The Church in the Power of the Spirit*, the key concept of 'sym-biosis' crops up, which would have to replace the concept of the growth of the (world) economy. At the end of the 1980s this problem appears once again in a more comprehensive perspec-tive as the 'crisis of our whole "scientific and technological civilization"'.[72] The term 'symbiosis' is replaced or qualified by the terms *'community of creation'* and *'community under law'*.[73] They are meant to replace the 'aggressive ethics of the modern world', which is the basis of the project of the absolutist control and exploitation of nature, with 'defensive preservation of life and productive furthering of life'.[74] This includes further development in legal thinking which progresses from human dignity to the dignity of creation, from human rights to animal rights.[75] Perspectives from the theology of rights also emerge in the second great testing field, namely politics. Here Moltmann is determined by a proposal from the Reformed World Alliance, which is devoted to the theological justification of *human rights*.[76] Liberation from slavery, servitude and dependence remains illusory as long as it does not lead to equality before the law and, as a presupposition for this, to generally accepted legal guarantees. This work on rights itself has a history. It takes concrete form in the 1948 Universal Declaration of Human Rights and its social extensions, as far as the 'animal rights' which have already been mentioned. Efforts at justice are not limited to social state goals, but must strive towards what K.Bosselmann has called the 'ecological legal state'. Here a network between the generations is also important. The rights of the generations living today must be shaped in such a way that they do not restrict the expectation of coming generations to rights and dignity.

It is also illuminating in this connection that Moltmann takes up the ethical preoccupation with the modern *concept of property*. As the idea of private property represents the centre of the tendencies towards enrichment and impoverishment which have become a threat all over the world, a critical revision is urgently necessary. Moltmann brings three criteria to bear. First the social wholesomeness of property. This is already rooted in the constitution of the Federal Republic of Germany. However, for Moltmann, secondly, it must be supplemented by the criterion of 'hereditary obligations' so that the 'contract between the generations' can be safeguarded.[77] Thirdly and finally, 'environmental compatibility' is to be brought to bear, for 'ecological justice, which is the basis of a symbiosis of humankind and nature capable of survival',[78] is of equal weight to the other forms of justice.

If we now turn to the third group of themes, namely culture or sociality, the first of Moltmann's comments to be mentioned are, as I have already said, those on the problem of *racism*.[79] Racism is a foolish and destructive crime against the unity and dignity of all human beings: foolish, because it makes the external characteristic of skin colour the criterion of essential differences, and destructive, because it tends to legitimate ethnic, economic or political claims to rule. The resistance against racism is thus at the same time a plea for emancipatory processes.

This emancipatory approach also plays an important role in another complex of themes, the attack on *sexism*. If my perception is correct, this theme comes more clearly into the foreground in the course of the 1970s,[80] whereas the preoccupation with racism fades into the background. Here of course theological collaboration with Elisabeth Moltmann-Wendel is tangible. Frau Moltmann-Wendel discovered feminist theology in the USA at the beginning of the 1970s, and then made a decisive personal contribution towards its establishment in Germany. One of the best known books that she wrote at that time was *The Women around Jesus*.[81] It is a testimony to liberation from the roles and constraints in which many women are imprisoned, and at the same time a testimony to a new partnership of men and women apart from sexist dependencies.

'Not least I was helped by the interest and curiosity of my husband in questions which had previously been unknown in the theological sphere,' remarks Elisabeth Moltmann-Wendel.[82] And Jürgen Moltmann maintains: 'Since I came to know my wife during our study together in Göttingen, I have ceased to feel that I am an "individual". Our shared life began with a theological dialogue, and our marriage since then has been accompanied by a theological dialogue. This has brought a great depth of friendship to our marriage . . . I want to draw attention to the constant and fundamental conversation from which my theological work derives and without which it cannot be understood.'[83] No wonder that the two of them played an important role in the World Council of Churches study project on the 'Community of Women and Men in the Church'.[84]

It could be objected that preoccupation with racism and sexism was one of the 'fashionable' themes of the 1970s and 1980s. Therefore I think it necessary to point to the complex of themes with which Moltmann has time and again been preoccupied and in which his liberation theology approach is very clearly evident. These are *aspects of medical ethics* and especially the relationship between handicapped and 'healthy' people.[85] Time and again Moltmann has made himself available for working parties on medical ethics or diaconia. He sees the everyday exclusion of persons with disabilities from the modern society of competition and success as the notorious denial of the crucified Christ and thus a threatening loss of humanity. 'The Son of man . . . transcends other human beings by understanding himself in the sickness and transgressions of the inhuman. He is the Son of man in that he accepts the lost and the untouchables . . . His rule has nothing to do with the nature of the world ruler. It consists in the reversal of rule to become service, of power to become love, and of demands to become vicarious suffering,' Moltmann wrote in his book on 'Man' which appeared in 1971.[86]

I return once again to the opening question about the 'great alternative' and the 'many little alternatives'. Even this fragmentary survey shows Moltmann's concern to bring the universality of the kingdom of freedom to the many places where servitude is suffered and liberation is necessary for the sake of human beings and the whole of enslaved nature. Time and again his concern is to introduce into petrified and fixed situations the category of the 'new' which is contained in the message of the coming kingdom, as a renewing and mobilizing energy. Thus it is an ethical approach which does not argue with the 'you must' and 'you shall' of an idealistic catalogue of virtues, but rather with the allure of the possible and the provocation of a fantasy which comes from longing for a world in which we are no longer alien and wretched, but can be at home and secure.

3. Friendship in a messianic light

In the introduction to this chapter I pointed out that Moltmann's liberation-theological approach extends beyond ethical reflection in the narrower sense and embraces questions of life-style and spirituality. I want to shed light on this from a theme which is particularly illuminating, that of friendship.

I have already pointed out that friendship is a key term for Moltmann's ecclesiology. Consequently friendship is also a decisive category for his understanding of being a Christian. He recalls that for Jewish thought Abraham and Moses were regarded as 'friends of God'. In showing himself to be a 'friend of toll collectors and sinners' and calling the disciples his friends, Jesus brings them from remoteness of God into a proximity to God, from a state of servile or didactic dependence into the status of friendship with God. That becomes particularly clear in prayer. This is no longer the slavish begging of a servant, nor the grateful stammering and begging of a child, but familiar and open talk of the kind that one has with one's friends. Therefore for Moltmann prayer is to be understood 'as the highest expression of human freedom in God'.[87] It joins God's friendship with human beings to their friendship with God. It creates a climate of joy and friendliness.

If then joy and friendliness are the elixir of life for friendship, they also describe something like the messianic warmth in our relationships. 'It would be well if the church, church officials and those taken care of by them finally recalled that together they are no more and no less than the "fellowship of the friends of Jesus".'[88]

Now it is also clear to Moltmann that the current understanding of friendship is in danger of being narrowed down to exclusiveness, because it largely designates the intimate relationship between people of like mind. Therefore he recalls that in earlier times friendship had something to do with public support and protective alliances. His demand is that 'friendship must once again receive the character of public protection of and public respect for others'[89] of the kind that can be found among the Quakers, who call themselves the *Society of Friends*. Their commitment to the abolition of slavery in the USA or to the peaceful resolution of conflicts demonstrates *how friendship can serve to create relationships which are friendly towards others*. It has a great deal to do with advocacy for oppressed people and takes shape in effective alliances in solidarity. So friendship is not a random matter, but an expression of faithfulness to the covenant. 'Open friendship prepares the ground for a friendlier world . . . It achieves duration and is the abiding, the dependable, in the ups and downs of life.' [90]

If friendship is understood in this way it combines ethical, spiritual and ecclesiological-ecumenical aspects. I want to clarify this in two respects, first in the direction of the *ecumene* and secondly in relation to *worship*.

Moltmann quotes the Korean Cardinal Kim, who speaks of 'the good white bread of friendship', and adds: 'there is also the black bread of suffering, of loneliness and of poverty'.[91] This black bread too is a bread of friendship, and where it is shared, ecumene begins. 'True ecumenical unity begins precisely where we mutually share our poverty, our sickness, our inhibiting obstacles and our stagnations.'[92] So it is this 'community in the negative', the communal negation of the negative, which leads to shared joy. The fellowship of the friends of Jesus has a share in his mission; it therefore also has a share in the suffering that goes with the apostolate. Therefore the martyrs belong to the whole church and may not be claimed by an individual confession. This shared suffering is a fruit of 'the messianic passion of Christ'.[93]

It is clear that the ecumenical movement is a movement of friendship. For Moltmann, ecumenicity is an expression of the fellowship of the friends of Christ. It forms the horizon for their faithfulness to the covenant and the sphere in which the scope of their messianic com-passion is demonstrated. Ecumenicity finds its basis where it is the 'church under the cross'. 'True and lasting ecumenical unity will be lived on the basis of united endurance and shared suffering.'[94] Here the parable of the judgment of the world plays a basic role: 'Matthew 25 tells us that and how "the least of these" are already subjects before the missionaries and the helpers come. They are the brothers of Christ, the brothers of the world judge.'[95]

Where the black bread of suffering is divided, the white bread of joy may also be eaten. Bonhoeffer once said that only those who cry out for the Jews may sing Gregorian chant. That sounds like a legalistic conditioning of worship and festival. Of course Moltmann emphasizes that for the fellowship of the friends of Christ worship may not become a pious niche into which they creep to avoid the torments of the world. However, it is also more than the mere 'refreshing' of exhausted forces or a time of relaxation for the soul; it is the space to express 'joy in the freedom of Christ'.[96] It is not a matter of compensating for the experience of a lack of freedom with the dreamed-of freedom of another world, but of 'encouraging the liberations of this world'.[97] This evaluation of the liturgical feast means two things. First of all Moltmann emphasizes the importance of the sabbath. 'It stands in the cycle of time and yet is a sign of freedom from the cycle of time, for it anticipates the victory over time and death,' he maintains.[98] This also gives the Christian Sunday a sabbath discipline which it has to regain if 'earthly pleasure in God' is to be given its right place.

Secondly, the development of worship as a feast presupposes a fellowship which no longer allows itself to be 'cared for' by (ordained) liturgical experts but understands itself as the subject of its history with God and seeks ways and means of expressing this in a spontaneous and mature way.

4. The quest for the subject: community – people – humankind

That brings us to the third aspect of this chapter, namely the question of the subject of ethics and life-style. Here too, if we take the notion of friendship as a starting point, it immediately becomes clear than no one can be a 'friend' by himself or herself. Friendship is a relational concept: it is constituted in and through community. Thus if the 'community of believers' is really to be understood as the 'fellowship of the friends of Christ', the question of the subject of ethical and spiritual life is possible for individual Christians always only in and with the communities which support them. That is one of the decisive reasons why the 'community' comes into the centre of Moltmann's ecclesiology; for only in its midst can Christians attain their maturity. The basic insight of the Reformation, that faith alone justifies and that therefore all Christians participate in the universal priest-hood, is attained only if there is this 'mature, responsible com-munity'.[99] Moltmann therefore does not disguise his conviction that the free-church movements must be strengthened in Protestantism. He states categorically: 'The future of the church of Christ lies in principle on this wing of the Reformation, because the widely unknown and uninhabited land of the congre-gation is found there.'[100]

It is only consistent that an approach should be made to reforming the established churches which still predominate. The churches which look after the people must become community churches of the people.[101] These must form the area in which both the 'black bread' of the suffering accepted in ecumenical participation and the 'good white bread' of liturgical festivals have their place.

This is to name a communal subject for ethics and spirituality. But Moltmann does not stop here. He has made remarks in which not only the community church of the people but the 'people' itself becomes the subject of ethical decisions. By 'people' he under-stands the oppressed masses, robbed of their power and exploited, who are called '*ochlos*' in the New Testament.[102] On a visit to Mathare Valley, a slum region in Nairobi, he was reminded of his experiences in the prisoner-of-war camp. 'When I saw the insensi-ble, expressionless faces and the stooped gait of the hungry people in the shanty towns, it all came back to me. I must also have looked like that.'[103] In this definition of 'people' notions play a role which are common in liberation theology. 'People' is under-stood to denote the poor and oppressed, not only because they represent that part of the world population which is growing increasingly large, but because the judge of the world and Son of man identifies himself messianically with them and manifests himself in them. By virtue of this identification 'the people discover their own identity and worth of which no ruler can rob them'.[104]

In this messianic perspective the people becomes the subject of its liberation, and the question is how the community can take its side in order to participate in this option. In Moltmann's view that happens primarily through involvement in the base community. If we now ask what the content of this option is, key words which have already been mentioned crop up: democratization, human rights, democratic socialism.[105] This understanding of 'people' is on the one hand clearly governed by the New Testament concept of the *ochlos*, the 'people who walk in darkness'; so it is a theological category. Secondly, the use of this term also reflects a certain romantic socialist glorification of the 'poor people' which was widespread in the 1970s. Therefore we need to ask whether and to what extent the 'people' can be regarded as the subject of ethical decisions. If, for example, we have in view the ethical goal of 'democratization', this concept of 'people' is no longer usable. In that case it would be necessary to talk of 'people' as the people of the state, which would then of course also include rich and poor strata of the population. It would be necessary to talk of constitution and parliamentarianism, of the distribution of power and the state monopoly of violence, of parties and lobby groups. In short, without incorporating political, legal, sociological and economic aspects it would be impossible to envisage 'people' at all and it would very soon prove that the role of the 'subject' in the course of democratic decisions would have to take on different forms.

At the end of the 1980s, yet another 'subject' appears in Moltmann's ethical reflections, namely humankind.[106] His starting point is the insight that since Hiroshima, humankind has become the corporate object of nuclear annihilation. Moreover current ecological developments and most recently developments in gene technology could wipe out the whole population of the earth. 'In this situation the survival of humankind is conceivable only if the nations organize themselves into a collective subject of action for survival,' Moltmann states, and adds: 'If humankind is to be united in the age of nuclear threat in order to save life, what is needed is a relativization of the individual interests of nations, the democratization of ideologies which lead to conflict, tolerance of the different religions and a general subordination of all to the common interest in life.'[107]

Now it is certainly correct that humankind has become the common object of annihilation. But it is questionable whether the adoption of a collective subject role results from this insight, simply because it must be doubted whether this insight has really reached the majority of people on this earth. It would seem that the discrepancies in the specific circumstances in which people live, the inequalities in the perception of the problems, and the techniques for repressing diffuse global threats are far too powerful.

Oppressive though the problem is, no further work can be done on it in this context. Here it is important for me to point out that the question of the subject of ethics and the art of life leads to aporias. We have discovered various 'subjects' in Moltmann's thought, the 'community', the 'people' and 'humankind', but how these relate to one another remains a dilemma.

5. *Fragment as chance*

I emphasized right at the beginning that Moltmann's reflections on ethics, life-style and spirituality are fragmentary. It is more than understandable that this should be so, given the complexity of the problems. To conclude, I would like to draw attention to one aspect which puts the messianic quality of the fragmentary in yet another light.

When I said earlier that humankind is the common object of its own power of annihilation, what was meant is this: human beings have become *faber sui futuri*, makers of their own future. The future is no longer what it once was, namely the lap of the gods that we take for granted. Since the formulae with which all human life on this planet can be ended have become known, this time has become an '*end-time*'. All time has a limit; its duration depends on whether and how long people are capable of keeping their own potential for destruction under control. 'Humankind as a whole has become mortal.' [108]

Paradoxically, this tremendous power, if it is not to destroy itself, calls for a new form of omnipotence, namely the omnipotence of inerrancy. For example no mistakes may be made in controlling and storing radioactive material, for full-blown nuclear disasters would be fatal. There may be no errors in the command centres of military power which have to decide on the production, storage and use of nuclear missiles, no treachery, no neglect, for one mistake could spark off a nuclear conflagration. And this compulsion to inerrancy applies not only to people living today but to the whole future.

'To err is human,' people have said so far. Therefore humanity has defined itself not least by its capacity for trial and error. Consequently the dictate of human inerrancy condemns human beings to inhumanity. It condemns them to an omnipotence which they cannot attain. To want to be like God is the age-old Faustian temptation. To have to be like God is a titanic torment.

How good it is to be allowed to be fragmentary! How human and rightly human! It is in keeping with human beings and their life/survival to be a fragment and to know the necessity of the fragmentary. Precisely in order that the world can remain the field of experiment for free men and women, the fragmentary nature of the attempts at liberation must be accepted and endured. 'Once the decisions are final, irrevocable and unrepeatable, then we no longer have experiments . . . But in this way we come to the end of time and into the eternal presence of what was traditionally called "the Last Judgment".'[109]

If Christians understand themselves as a 'messianic fragment', then they leave the Last Judgment to him who is higher than all their reason. Then it leads their messianic longing for the freedom of the kingdom of God to a way of life which combines work on the liberation of human beings with the confession of their mortality. The overcoming of death is God's affair, but love for fragile life in the circle of death is the legacy of messianic hope and the fruit of messianic patience.

7

Liberation Theology for the First World? The 1977 Turning Point

1. Where is nowhere?

'It was at a conference in October 1977 in Mexico City with liberation theologians, black theologians and feminist theologians that I suddenly discovered: "I don't belong anywhere, since I'm not oppressed, not black and not a woman. I can support these liberation movements and learn from them, but my existence is not in them ... So what should I do?" At that time I reflected on my regular business of systematic theology and between 1980 and 1995 wrote a series of "systematic contributions to theology". I wanted to overcome my "one-sidedness" and concentrate on long-term problems of theology. I no longer wanted to be so controversial.' That is how Moltmann describes in 1997, with the ironic understatement typical of him, a critical turning point in his life.[110]

At another point he indicates that this experience of not properly belonging anywhere had its painful side, until with his decision to write the 'Contributions' he was also able to experience the liberating side of this crisis.[111]

Nevertheless it seems to me necessary to dwell on this crisis for a moment. In 1977 Moltmann had been travelling in Latin America giving lectures and engaging in discussions before he met a group of liberation theologians in Mexico City. There he was sharply attacked – 'crucified', was what James Cone called it.

For Moltmann that was a depressing experience. Certainly he was not black, not a woman, not oppressed. But wasn't it enough to be 'pro-black', 'pro-woman' and 'pro-oppressed' to be accepted as a partner in liberation theology? Evidently not, or not for all. But why not?

When Moltmann got to know the books by James Cone and Gustavo Gutiérrez he gained the impression that he had found the friends and companions whom he had sought with his 'political theology'. What was more natural than to dream of all those of like mind being shoulder to shoulder all over the world? With the slogan, 'Liberation theologians of the world, unite!'

The trip to Latin America made him realize that his longing for integration was premature. From that he drew the conclusion that he belonged 'nowhere', because he was not black, not a woman and not oppressed. But where is 'nowhere'? Is a chair of systematic theology in the venerable and influential University of Tübingen nowhere? Certainly not!

Basically the remark is wrong. 'Nowhere' is of course somewhere. The frustrating experiences of his visit to Latin America compelled Moltmann to accept his own place, his own history and his own role as part of the white First World, controlled by men. His commitment to liberation theology had been so to speak subjected to a 'hardness test'. From now on he had to learn *what liberation theology can look like in the midst of the conditions of the First World.*

This was a long, exciting and laborious way. We may probably also conjecture moments of resignation and withdrawal in Moltmann's remark that he concentrated on the 'regular business of systematic theology'. The remark that he no longer wanted to be so 'controversial' also indicates a degree of exhaustion. But it would certainly be a mistake to want to regard Moltmann's experiences in 1977 as a mid-life crisis. I would prefer to avoid such psychologizing labels. On the other hand, it is appropriate to make a reference to the burdens and demands there were on Moltmann at that time. In the 1970s the Tübingen Faculty was overflowing with students. The attendance at lectures and seminars was equally great. The pressure of examinations increased. And the number of those who wanted to do their doctorate with Moltmann increased. On top of the regular work in Tübingen there were ecumenical obligations, for

example in the Faith and Order Commission of the World
Council of Churches. Involvement in scholarly bodies and journals
like *Concilium, Evangelische Theologie* and *Evangelische
Kommentare* also swallowed up time and energy.

When Moltmann called the turning point which forced itself
upon him in 1977 a 'productive disengagement',[112] it becomes
clear that this was not a U-turn, but a concession that a man who
is past fifty can no longer play with all possible options but has
to find his place and then accept it as a given. And this place was
Tübingen, it was the Faculty of Protestant Theology, and in it the
chair of Systematic Theology.

That is how I understand a remark from 1985, which is taken
from an autobiographical account of 'My Theological Career':
'I must be honest with myself and my limitations, for only then
will it become possible for me to overcome these limitations . . .
One can go beyond them only by recognizing a wider fellowship
of mutual hearing and speaking, receiving and giving, and enter
into it. This is what I have attempted to do since 1980 in my
series of "Contributions to Theology".'[113]

It is therefore appropriate to understand the move towards the
Contributions as the acceptance of a quite particular place and a
quite particular role and at the same time as *the quest for a more
comprehensive community*. The hearing and speaking, taking
and giving, which Moltmann mentions in the account of his
career focus on a conversation which also includes old positions
and concepts that were thought to be obsolete. That is true espe
cially of the acceptance of trinitarian theology and the conceptuality associated with it. As Moltmann remarks, 'it caused some
head-shaking among practical and political theologians, but also
attracted Orthodox and feminist theologians'.[114] The *communio
sanctorum* embraces not only the conversation partners of today
but also the men and women who sometimes have lived long
before us.

The turn from the programmatic writings to the systematic
'Contributions' can therefore also be recognized as a deliberate
inclusion of classical questions. Granted, Moltmann has always
refused to call this project a 'dogmatics', but in its layout it has

all the features of a classical systematic theology. First comes the doctrine of God (1980). Then comes the doctrine of creation (1985) and after that the christology (1989). Next comes a pneumatology (1991) followed by an eschatology (1995). A discussion of method forms the conclusion (1999).

When I survey Moltmann's creative periods I am struck by a remarkable symmetry: the first period, which could also be called '*programmatic*', comprises around two decades (from 1959 to 1979). The second, which I would like to call '*classic*', similarly comprises around twenty years (from 1980 to 1999). Consequently the 'turning point' that we are talking about here can be described as the end of a great swing of the pendulum which is now followed by another swing of the pendulum. If the theological eschatology of *Theology of Hope* stood at the beginning of the first swing, eschatology again stands at the end of the second.

2. *Liberation theology for the First World*

Once again, Mexico 1977. Does the 'productive disengagement' mean the end of involvement in liberation theology? Is the move towards the 'Contributions' also the end of the impulse towards liberation theology which forms the nucleus of the programmatic books? Not at all. In going through the five volumes of the 'Contributions' we shall note that the orientation on liberation theology is maintained and that dialogue with the liberation theological schemes in Asia, North and South America is also always present. But now it is present in a more sophisticated way. That is developed once more at length in the concluding volume *Experiences in Theology*.[115] Therefore here at this early stage I want to take up an important part of this book which (for the moment) is Moltmann's last work. It bears the title 'Mirror Images of Liberating Theology'.

In it Moltmann investigates the question what the schemes of liberating theology which have been worked out on the 'shadow side' of world society mean for the Christians and churches on the 'sunny side'. In other words, the self-critical question of the relevance of developments in liberation theology for the white and oppressive world is discussed explicitly and in detail.

These mirror images comprise four areas: black theology for whites (189ff.), Latin American liberation theology for the First World (217ff.), minjung theology for the ruling classes (249ff.) and feminist theology for men (268ff.).

In all four cases Moltmann follows a method which begins with biographical narrative references, goes on to systematic and analytical conclusions and ends with 'questions'. That makes the learning process in each case specific in a highly vivid way. How exciting such processes are is shown by the chapter on feminist theology, since here it was his own wife, Elisabeth Moltmann-Wendel, who taught him to think again: 'I did not come to feminist theology. It came to me through the discoveries of my wife . . . It was not always easy for me personally to understand the necessity for taking this road. Often enough I became the test case and prime example of "typical male thinking" and of academic "objectivity" without "subjectivity". . . It took some time for me to realize how I had been turned from a young human being into "a man" . . . This process of change brought great pain' (268, 269, 270).

The introductory reminiscences in the chapter on liberation theology also make it clear that such learning processes could be accompanied with severe disappointments and hurts: 'It began so hopefully,' run the first words (217). Then Moltmann describes his enthusiasm for Gustavo Gutiérrez's *Theology of Liberation*, the spiritual affinity with his own *Theology of Hope*, the nearness to the 'political theology' which he had developed together with Johann Baptist Metz. 'So those of us belonging to the political-theology camp thought initially of a new "wonderful friendship" with the new Latin American theology of this new departure. But that proved to be an error.' (218).

The 'error' was that Moltmann and others with him were thinking of integration, whereas the theologians of the Third World were concerned with detachment, since they were afraid of being taken over. What else had their peoples experienced in the whole history since their 'discovery' and colonialization than annexation, exploitation and plundering? The history of their alienations and dispossessions had begun with their objectification: they had never been taken seriously as persons on their own. Therefore the liberation theologians had first and vehemently to insist on going their way alone, thinking their theological thought independently, and thus – finally – becoming the subjects of their own history.

(a) The first step: separation

Therefore 'separation' is a necessary step. It applies equally to the four theological spheres which Moltmann describes. Black theology must separate itself from white culture, above all from structural racism, in order not only to get free of economic and social humiliation but above all to shake off the chains of self-hatred and a sense of inferiority. It must learn, laboriously enough, to perceive its blackness as something beautiful and well-pleasing to God. Therefore here it is said that 'black is beautiful' and that God is black. That stands at the centre of any true black theology.

Separation also applies to the Korean minjung theology, because and in that it promises the poor people the messianic dignity of being the true community of Christ. It raises the constantly humiliated people from its dependence on the ruling classes and makes it a subject in the fight for right, freedom and democracy. Feminist theology, too, must first stress its independence, since for all too long women were defined by men as defective and second-rate beings. The omnipotence of the patriarchate stamped them as second-class people. Therefore their own thought must be developed first and resolutely in contradiction to men, particularly well-meaning men.

Those who do not understand this element of separation and distancing have still not really grasped the injurious massiveness of this history of oppression. And those who are amazed at the sometimes aggressive passion with which this distancing is formulated have not yet taken the trouble to note the extent of historical guilt that binds the European powers to the people whom they have enslaved or that binds the beneficiaries of the patriarchate to the women. For every oppression has two sides, that of the oppressed and that of the oppressors. Where there is a slave there is also a master. Where the poor people are tormented, the tormentors are not far away. And where women suffer violence, violent men are always nearby. Therefore it is particularly important that in the four chapters Moltmann discusses this historical dimension of the oppression at relative length. People have been and still are fond of suppressing the fact that the mass enslavement of the Africans between 1518 and 1888 has been the cruel downside of the building up of the modern Western world. 'Luther took no notice of the "discovery of America", nor did Schleiermacher consider the culmination of the slave trade in his time. Nor was this a theological topic for Barth, Bultmann and Tillich' (191).

No less cruel is the exploitation of the American continent which began with the 'discovery' of America as one of the substantial foundations for the building up of the great European powers. Who in Europe knows about the extent of the annihilation of the 'Indian' peoples? Basing himself on Todorov, Moltmann writes: 'The decimation of the population in seventy years (between 1500 and 1570) by around 70 million may without "black legend" be regarded as the greatest genocide in the history of humankind. The reasons . . . subjection, slavery, conversion and smallpox' (204). At the latest since Eduardo Galeano's *The Open Veins of Latin America* people even in Europe know rather more about the ever new waves of plundering to which the 'New World' has been exposed. First it was gold, then silver, then cotton and sugar, coffee and tobacco. Today the continent is exhausted and consequently uninteresting for the First World; there is nothing more to get.

Despite the great difference between cultures, the patriarchate dominates the whole world. Moltmann calls it an 'institutionalized system of a hierarchy of the sexes and a psychological mechanism' which proves the justification for men being born and trained to rule and women to serve (244). And this is certainly not because of some special merits or capacities; the reasons are purely gender-specific. That is why the concept of sexism takes on such central importance in parallel to racism. This sexism produces the different variants of male vanity, legitimates the privileges of men in family, business, culture and politics, justifies the systematic exploitation of women, and in large parts of the world keeps serving to excuse the notorious violence against women and their mutilation, not only physically and mentally, but also socially and politically.

Whereas black theology, Latin American liberation theology and feminist theology are directed against oppressive mechanisms which are already centuries old – in the case of sexism we must talk of millennia – minjung theology is to be understood as a Christian reaction to the oppressive component of the forced industrialization of South Korea in the 1960s and 1970s. The Urban Industrial Mission is one of the most important instruments of this resistance movement. It is not disputed that this also appeals to old traditions of resistance in Korea; nevertheless this political theology has come into being in the current conflict with forced industrialization, which was introduced with anti-democratic repression. It is not a 'theology that has been made culturally indigenous, like "yellow theology" before it. It is a contextual theology of the suffering people in Korea, and is therefore open for the people all over the world, the people of God's Kingdom whom Jesus called blessed' (252).

To sum up this first train of thought: the moment of 'separation' certainly does not mean that theology in the First World must carry on its business as usual in splendid isolation. Rather, it contains the implicit invitation to perceive and work out one's own share in the world-wide interdependence of the processes of impoverishment. It is not a sign of theological maturity if concerns with the 'Third World' and the theological currents in it are diverted into the field of 'ecumenics and mission' and are increasingly starved out there. The systematic underestimation of the importance of ecumenical questions in German theological faculties is a further indication of the tendency which is increasingly emerging, namely that German theology has withdrawn into an academic niche. The same is true of feminist theology. That it is kept away from the theological faculties is more than an indication of a stubborn lack of understanding. It is a sign of blindness.

(b) The second step: identity

Liberation is a quest. Those who want to shake off the chains of slavery, impoverishment, oppression and sexism must seek the form of humanity which was really intended for them. The humiliated want to raise themselves, those who are bowed down to stand upright, and the people who walk in darkness want to see light. Elisabeth Moltmann-Wendel's book *The Women around Jesus* was published in Germany under the title 'Becoming One's Own Person';[116] this title can be seen as the programmatic formula for all approaches to liberation theology. Becoming one's own person means no longer defining oneself or allowing oneself to be defined by others, but perceiving and affirming a valid form of humanity in oneself. 'Black is beautiful' is therefore an important slogan by which people who by a long history of oppression have been led to regard their blackness as a stigma of inferiority. 'Late have I learned to like being a woman', confesses Marga Bührig in the title of her book[117] – a statement which reflects the long history of the patriarchal degradation of women.

The concept of 'identity' marks a second stage for Moltmann in the processes of liberation theology (cf. 269). What is the theological basis for this struggle for one's own identity? For the liberation theology of Latin America this new identity is based on the '*opción preferential de Dios para los pobres*', on God's preferential option for the poor. In a comparable way minjung theology is based on the special nearness of the *ochlos*, the poor people, to Jesus. Feminist theologians develop their own dignity among other things from the discovery of the *ruach* and Sophia, i.e. female 'figures', in the biblical image of God. For James Cone, Christ is 'the Oppressed One' in whom all those who are oppressed rediscover themselves. 'The slaves understood the suffering Christ, and knew that he understood them. In this sense Christ is "the black Messiah" of the humiliated blacks' (214).

A common point of reference is Matthew 25. 'Here the Son of man *identifies* himself with the poor and suffering in this world' (235). He is present hidden in them. Where they are loved, he is loved; where they are despised, he is despised. This messianic identification gives the quest for identity its real centre. Thus the project of 'liberation' is not just about the overcoming of certain political, cultural or social structures of injustice; it is about the grounding of the identity of the 'underman' in the experience of the merciful and just God. 'The "preferential option for the poor" is the option for Christ, who is present in them' (235).

Now it is this particular moulding of the understanding of identity which raises the question: and what about the identity of the oppressor? If God wills to be known and loved in the poor, then are the rich god-less? Indeed, that oppressive wealth must be paid for by remoteness from God is one of the insights of all liberation theology, and therefore the question arises whether and how the rich can find God. Moltmann has given a thorough summary of this question: the term 'preferential' does not mean 'exclusive'. It is to be seen as 'one-sidedly inclusive'. How is that to be understood? 'God has mercy on the poor so as also to save the rich through them' (233). However, this is a deliverance through judgment and repentance, for if God is present in the poor, the rich must leave their house of slavery and give up their exploitative privileges in order to gain the identity that is also intended for them by God.

For one of the most noteworthy results of the processes of liberation theology discussed here is that, since they fight for the identity of the poor and oppressed and therefore for their humanity, at the same time they also show how distorted and twisted is the identity and humanity of the rich and oppressors. 'The oppressor acts inhumanly and the victims are dehumanized.' Inhumanity is the other side of dehumanization. But both are a betrayal of true humanity. In feminist theology the relationship is put like this: where the woman is robbed of her head (because the man is alleged to be her 'head'), the man is robbed of his body (because the woman is alleged to be his 'body'). The one is paid for with the other (cf. 286). In both cases humanity is distorted, caricatured, incomplete. So where women have learned to gain their own heads in the process of their liberation, the possibility arises for men of regaining their crippled corporeality and caricatured sensuality.

Why do so many people (men) in the rich world reject the creative and renewing impulses which the liberation theologies also open up for them? For Moltmann it is not just a matter of being thoughtlessly accustomed to power, but also of a far-reaching repression of guilt. 'That theologians in the West should do no more than shrink back from black theology, Latin American theology, Korean minjung theology and feminist theology, or allow themselves to be entertained by them, without having the faintest perception of the changes in themselves which are required, is a reflection of "hardness of heart" in the biblical sense . . . It is easy to be liberal when it doesn't cost too much, and through this very attitude we waste the chances for our own liberation from structures incompatible with human dignity, a liberation which would free us for community with the people in the lands of the Third World' (188).

If one is ready to take its biblical meaning seriously, 'hardening' is an explosive word, since it means more than voluntary hardening, just as the word 'blinding' means more than blindness one causes oneself. It means no less than a preliminary stage of damnation which comes from God, an 'objective' lack of capacity for conversion and renewal. Unfortunately Moltmann does not go more deeply into these implications. He stops at the demand for conversion and does not reflect further on the practical consequences which would necessarily follow from this for economics and life-style, for politics and culture.

(c) The third step: integration

'At the end of these two processes (i.e. separation and identity, GMF), we may then one day arrive at a new common theology in reciprocity and with equal rights in the shaping of this community. But this *integration* must not be looked for before the goal of the liberation process has been reached' (269). What can happen 'then one day', and therefore has yet to come, is present today, at least in embryo. This is the proviso with which Moltmann discusses steps in the direction of integration.

In the context of his preoccupation with feminist theology, Moltmann indicates that the 'theological overcoming of patri- archal monotheism' lies in the 'theology of the Trinity'. In the following chapters we shall have the occasion to get to know Moltmann's trinitarian thinking in detail. Therefore here I shall only draw attention to this aspect, that he understands the triunity of God as the space and the history of a fullness of living relationships. This helps him to overcome the usual pictures of an omnipotent 'Lord God' who works hierarchically. 'The solitary, powerful man may be an imitation of the Almighty; the image of the triune God can only be a human community in which free and equal persons are there with each other and for each other in the difference of their characteristics and gifts' (259). Thus the theology of the Trinity represents the theological point of reference. The christological point of reference (i.e. Christ's hidden presence in the poor according to Matt.25) has already been mentioned. In addition, as an eschatological horizon there is the notion of the kingdom of God; for the kingdom of God and the creation of all things new transcends all processes of liberation, even if it does not of course detract from their historical urgency.

On the basis of these perspectives, at the end of this part Moltmann formulates four questions which would need to be discussed in the interest of an 'integration' still to come. They are: 1. 'If praxis is the criterion of theory , what is the criterion of praxis?' (294). 2. 'If the crucified people are to redeem the world, who then redeems the people? (295). 'If the goal of liberation is to make the people the determining subject of their own history, what is the goal of that history?' (297) and 4. 'Does liberation theology lead to the liberation of the poor and the women from Christian theology?' (298).

These are basically cautious and anxious questions about aspects to be found above all in Latin American liberation the- ology and in minjung theology, where the 'poor' or the 'people' seem to take on a kind of messianic quality themselves because of their nearness to Christ. These questions are justified. Nevertheless I find it regrettable that Moltmann concludes this large part of his book with these 'unanswered questions'. Important as they are, from the perspective of the First World the last word should have been probably directed to it in self-criticism. All I will say is this: if the project of liberation is specifically concerned also with the liberation of the First World from hardening and blindness, how would theological education and research then have to be changed? What consequences would follow for the traditional canon of theological disciplines? What consequences would have to be drawn not least for the status of academic teachers as employees of the state and their salaries?

What applies to the theological faculties applies *mutatis mutandis* to the state churches. What would liberation have to mean for their parochial service structures, for the civil-servant type status of ministers and their defensive insistence on privileged salary systems?

And we might not stop at these self-critical questions to theology and the church. Would we also talk of 'hardening' when we look at the way in which world economic 'interests' are established and world-wide processes of impoverishment are taken for granted? What kind of an applied political theology is needed to free the peoples from the vicious circles of debt, which fundamentally represents the present-day form of collective enslavement? How do we deal with the new forms of warfare? What attitude do we develop towards the selective and manipulative power of the electronic media? Will we bow to the oligarchization of banks, of genetic engineering or the food industry? Do we want to bow to monopolization in the computer industry?

This is by no means an exhaustive list of the 'unanswered questions'. But it already clearly indicates that 'liberation theology' is not a theological 'theme' which merely serves the interest of particular sectors or regions. The perspectives that Moltmann opens up with his 'mirror images' of departures in liberation theology ought to occupy theology far more broadly and decisively than has been the case so far. 'Liberation' will remain the fundamental dimension of theological work as long as humankind is in the house of slavery and as long as Christianity is moved by hope of the kingdom of freedom.

In his review of the second volume of *Mysterium Liberationis*, Moltmann sums up the alternatives with which we are confronted like this: 'Either social justice or growing criminality and ever more expensive security. Either international justice or revolts in the poor countries caused by famine. Ether long-term investment today for the future of life together or short-term gain today and the calculated bankruptcy of humankind in the near future.'[118]

So it is not a matter of what theological 'school' has the say. To assume or to fear that is foolish and careless. The issue is no less than a 'culture of life'.

We can note that the second period of Moltmann's creative activity, which is expressed in the six volumes of the 'Contributions', is also to be seen from the perspective of liberation theology. However, now his own context comes more strongly into view. In this way the long-term problems posed over almost two thousand years of the history of theology are taken up. The 'classical' questions of theology occupy a great deal of space. We shall have to note whether the self-critical perspective which liberation theology offers to the First World are worked on with the necessary urgency and sharpness. What becomes of theology and the church if they stand in the shadow of hardening and blindness? Can they still serve life? Or are they already doomed to destruction?

8

On Unification – The Theology
of the Trinity as a Retelling
# of God's History of Love

1. Convergences

Is it really necessary to shut up the good news of the revelation of God in Jesus of Nazareth in the concept of the triunity of God? It is not just in our days that Christians have felt that the notion of the unity and trinity of God is difficult to understand. No wonder that the feast of the Trinity in the church's year has become a meaningless appendix to the great feasts like Christmas, Easter and Pentecost.

Yes, says Moltmann, it is absolutely necessary to understand the Christian belief in God in a trinitarian way. Without the notion of the Trinity the peculiar character of the Christian concept of God and the significance of the good news cannot be understood appropriately at all. It is clear to him that in some ways this is asking too much of people. 'It is difficult enough to believe that there is a God at all and to live accordingly. Does belief in the Trinity not make the religious life even more difficult, and quite uneccessarily?',[119] he writes, and points out that the theological schemes of our time, from political theology to process theology, dispense with a trinitarian basis.

In contrast to this, Moltmann claims that the biblical anchoring of the Christian faith leads to a trinitarian understanding of God: 'We understand the scriptures as the testimony to the history of the *Trinity's relations of fellowship*, which are open to men and women, and open to the world' (19). This reference to the Bible takes up the prejudice that the theology of the Trinity is a subsequent construct, which has more to do with Greek philosophy than with the Bible.

I want to take two examples to show how Moltmann seeks to develop his trinitarian thinking from the Bible and thus to give it a biblical basis.

(a) 'Unification of God' – an argument for trinitarian thinking from Jewish belief in God

Is not the Hebrew Bible in particular stamped by faith in the one and only God? 'Hear, Israel, the Lord is our God, the Lord alone' (Deut.6.4). This famous and central 'shema Israel' after all seems to emphasize that the 'alone' is also stating an 'all-one'. So must a trinitarian concept of God be understood as a typical expression of Christianity which finds no support in Jewish thinking? Now Moltmann is particularly interested in developing the common roots of Jewish and Christian faith, also and specifically in the concept of God. Therefore a passage appears in *The Church in the Power of the Spirit* in which Moltmann makes the attempt to connect his understanding of the doctrine of the Trinity with the Old Testament-Jewish understanding of the unity of God.[120] There we read: 'Franz Rosenzweig interprets the Shema Israel as follows: "To acknowledge God's unity – the Jew calls this uniting God. For this unity is, in that it becomes; it is Becoming Unity. And this Becoming is laid on the soul of man and in his hands." Rosenzweig relates this "divine union" in prayer to that "cutting off of God from himself" which is suggested in the mystical doctrine of the Shekinah: "God himself cuts himself off from himself, he gives himself away to his people, he suffers with their sufferings, he goes with them into the misery of the foreign land."' After this quotation Moltmann asks: 'Is not what is here, according to Rosenzweig, entrusted to Israel, *in an analogous way* entrusted by Christian thinking to the Holy Spirit, who through believers "unites" God by glorifying him? Does not God's separation from himself in order to suffer with his people correspond *on another level* to the separation of God the Father from his Son in the cross, in order that he might suffer with the godforsakenness of the godless and so vicariously abolish it?'[121]

The question is, what is the 'level' on which this comparability is claimed? Is it compelling in substance or is it more of a typological figure? We can probably conclude from the fact that Moltmann puts this parallelism in the form of a question that he is not quite certain. But then follows a sentence in which Moltmann moves from a pure question to a supposition: 'How much more could the glorifying of the Son and the Father in the Spirit of liberation and of fellowship then be understood as the "union" of the triune God?!"' Here, interestingly, question-mark and exclamation-mark stand side by side (not, unfortunately, in the English translation). Thus the two questions are all at once turned into a supposition. And then suddenly in the next sentence this becomes a thesis: 'The unity of the triune God is the goal of the uniting of man and creation with the Father and the Son *in* the Spirit.' And then follows the categorical assertion: 'The history of the kingdom of God on earth is *nothing other* than the history of the uniting of what is separated and the freeing of what is broken, in this being the history of the glorification of God.'[122]

I have my doubts whether Jewish theologians could regard Moltmann's argument, which all too quickly moves from questions through a supposition to conclusive statements, as a compelling exegesis of the *shema Israel*. When Rosenzweig introduces the Shekinah tradition, then what follows from it is at all events something like a duality in the concept of God. The Shekinah would then be the divine force which accompanies the people in its wandering, in exile and suffering. But can this tradition be applied in Christian interpretation on the one hand to the Spirit and on the other to the Son, so that a Trinity can be derived from the duality?

I would want to add that in his reference to Rosenzweig, Moltmann leaves untouched one aspect which seems to me to be extraordinarily important. If the Shekinah tradition is rooted in Jewish mysticism, then that must also apply to the concept of the 'unification' of God. Consequently the adoption and use of this notion in the theology of the Trinity should also be designated a mystical approach. This kind of analogy would then have to lead to the far-reaching question: *is trinitarian thinking a form of mystical thinking?* And what role does such thinking play in Moltmann's theology? I shall return to this question at the end of the chapter.

(b) The Abba mystery

The common trinitarian formulas run 'God the Father, Son and Holy Spirit'. Thus they give the impression that God the Father, whom the Apostles' Creed also calls the 'Almighty, maker of heaven and earth', is the foundation and starting-point of faith. Consequently, first the unity of the Creator and Father God has been asserted, and after that the trinity of Father, Son and Spirit has been arrived at, as if this was a later development. Likewise, the heavenly almighty Father has also become the basis and start-ing point of patriarchal paternal power in the family, the church and society.

Moltmann refers back to the preaching of Jeus to show that this patriarchalism cannot have a biblical basis, but rather repre-sents the consequences of a 'fusion of the Christian and the Roman concept of God'.[123] He points out that Jesus always addressed God as 'Abba' (the only exception is his cry on the cross). In Jesus' Aramaic mother tongue, 'Abba' is a term of affection, a familiar, intimate and tender name for father. It is manifest that this form of addressing God is very closely con-nected with the form of Jesus' preaching. The fact that Jesus spoke of God – and to him – in intimate terms as a father is reflected in his unconditional nearness to the suffering and outcast. 'Abba' is the God who is near, who surrounds his children with protection and looks after them. (It is quite mani-fest that experiences of both father and mother are fused in this name Abba![124]).Thus both Jesus' preaching of the kingdom which has come near and Jesus' revelation of the 'Abba God' belong together. 'One can address God as "Abba" only in the presence of his liberating and healing kingdom.'[125] If the kingdom has come near, then that only means that 'Abba' is very near, and conversely that in the messianic age God himself is near.[126]

Here Moltmann speaks of the 'Abba mystery' of Jesus and sees in it 'the liberating nucleus of his messianic message'.[127] The invocation of the Abba God and the cry for the 'Maranatha' of the kingdom belong together. And it is no coincidence that where the 'Maranatha', i.e. the beseeching cry for the imminent kingdom, falls dumb, the near Abba-God is removed to the distance of a heavenly almighty Father.

So a Christian theology of the Trinity is grounded in the 'Abba-mystery' of Jesus. To put it differently: if the 'Abba-mystery' forms the centre of Jesus' 'messianic mystery', then a trinitarian form of Christian faith follows. 'The formation of a doctrine of the Trinity was always also an attempt to express this child-relationship without ideas of patriarchal rule.'[128] Here we have the description of community relationships; for a father – or mother – is never separate, but an adult becomes a father or mother through children. Parenthood and childhood are relational concepts, and they embrace all the happiness and suffering, hope and disappointment that is experienced in such relations. And parenthood and childhood cannot be understood statically, any more than they can be understood as ontological concepts. As they express relationships, they are also historically changeable. Relations between parents and children change in and with time.

If we refer these reflections on the relationship of childhood revealed by Jesus to a Abba-God, we see why Moltmann wants to understand *the theology of the Trinity as a history of relations in God*. But that turns our ordinary images of God on their head. And so we understand why Moltmann says, 'The doctrine of the Trinity is a *critical doctrine of God* in a specifically Christian sense.'[129]

2. Developments

The doctrine of the Trinity is basically not a 'doctrine', if we understand by that a generally valid doctrine of the eternal nature of God; rather, it is about the telling, or better *the retelling, of God's history*. An attempt had been made in the early church to grasp the triunity of God with the formula 'one substance – three persons'. Since Hegel, the formula 'one subject – three modes of being' had been brought into play. For Moltmann, both the concept of substance and the concept of subject lead to the logical priority of the unity of the Trinity, with the result that the doctrine of the Trinity is reduced to monotheism. 'In distinction to the trinity of substance and to the trinity of subject we shall be attempting to develop *a social doctrine of the Trinity*. We understand the scriptures as the testimony to the history of the *Trinity's relations of fellowship*, which are open to men and women, and open to the world' (35). And scripture may not be subsumed under allegedly presuppositionless, abstract concepts – 'heresies lie in abstractions, as history shows' (190) – but must be retold and relived.

(a) God's passion narrative

What does the 'history of God's relations of fellowship' look like? Is it possible at all to speak in God of past, present and future, as we do in the case of human history? To put the question differently: is there something in God's history that is still to come, a *telos*, a goal, a consummation?

As is well known, Joachim of Fiore had combined the doctrine of the Trinity and salvation in such a way as to assume a sequence between the kingdom of the Father, the kingdom of the Son and the kingdom of the Spirit. Moltmann remarks that here Joachim was describing 'a historical dynamic which seeks to reconcile human history eschatologically with the eternal history of God'.[130] He himself undertakes a similar attempt which he seeks to achieve in 'conversations' with Thomas Aquinas, Karl Rahner, Karl Barth and Ernst Bloch.[131] He too sees reality as a history with an eschatological goal. And therefore he thinks it meaningful also to assume in God's history 'a movement from the initial creation through historical reconciliation to eschato-logical consummation . . . The kingdom of nature, the kingdom of grace and the kingdom of glory are not three aspects of the one kingdom of God, but *three stages on the way* of its consumma-tion.'[132] Thus we have to understand Moltmann's *doctrine of the Trinity as God's history of consummation.*

So God is not 'finished'. As long as God is not finished with the world, and as long as this creation is not yet finished with itself and with God, God cannot come to rest. That is the 'Passion of God', the title of Chapter II (36ff.). In contrast to the axiom of the impassibility of God, as this is to be found in classical Greek antiquity, Moltmann keeps to the biblical concept of the passionate, suffering and compassionate God. We already came across this notion in the survey of *The Crucified God*. In *The Trinity and the Kingdom of God* Moltmann once again explicitly emphasizes his proximity to the Jewish theologian Abraham Heschel and his 'theology of the divine pathos' (25ff.). In this context he also take up the mystical-kabbalistic reflections of the Shekinah of God with the help of which it became possible for Jewish thought to grasp this pathos as God's 'being outside himself'. The indwelling of God in his people is then an expres-sion of the Shekinah, and likewise the condescension of the Eternal One in the history of his creation and the anticipation of coming glory.

Moltmann does not find allies for his 'theopathy' only in Jewish thought. He refers to the theological discussion of the passibility of God in English theology in the nineteenth and early twentieth century. He refers to the Spanish passion mysticism which is taken up again in Miguel de Unamuno's work *The Tragic Sense of Life*. Another support for him is the Russian 'theosophist' Berdyaev, for whom trinitarian thought is closely linked with God's 'story of suffering'.

Why should God have to suffer? Because God is love. Therefore God suffers in and with all that experiences suffering. 'The experience of suffering reaches as far as love itself' (51). Therefore God's compassion reaches into all the realms and times of creation. That is the only way in which the question of theodicy can be endured, as it cannot be answered.

Does God's pathos put limits to his freedom? Only if we develop God's freedom against the background of rule, and thus regard it as something like the control of a sovereign or an absolutist freedom of choice. But if freedom is thought of against the background of communal relations, aspects like hospitality, friendliness and friendship come to the centre.

Love wants to give. But love also wants to be loved. And love is blessed only when it is eternally united with the beloved. The concept of 'communal relationships' becomes evident in this concept of love. 'If God is love he is at once the lover, the beloved and the love itself' (57). Here Moltmann again refers to the Jewish Shekinah tradition and says: 'The theology of love is a theology of the Shekinah, a theology of the holy Spirit. This means that it is not patriarchal, but rather feministic. For the Shekinah and the Holy Spirit are "the feminine principle of the Godhead"' (57). Therefore God's love is a being in suffering, as long as the beloved creation is not wholly and eternally re-conciled with God. 'In this sense, not only does God suffer with and for the world; liberated men and women suffer with God and for him. The theology of God's passion . . . also has to arrive at the idea of God's eschatological self-deliverance' (60). We shall meet this notion again at the end of the 'Contributions', in *The Coming of God*.

(b) The salvation of the world in the passion of God

Under the heading 'convergences' I have already indicated that Moltmann regards the 'Abba-mystery' of Jesus as the central point of reference for his trinitarian thinking. In *The Crucified God* we have seen that the theology of the cross issues with a inner logic in the theology of the Trinity. Both references illus-trate that christology forms the starting point of the possibility of being able to think in a trinitarian way at all in the Christian sense. However, this must be an 'open christology', 'open to the knowledge of the creation of the world by the Father of Jesus

Christ and open to the knowledge of the transformation of the world through the Holy Spirit, who proceeds from the Father of the Son Jesus' (106).

This 'openness', understood as a wealth of relationships, is developed in Chapter IV of *The Trinity and the Kingdom of God* under the title 'The World of the Trinity'. Moltmann attaches great importance to overcoming the classical links according to which the 'work' of creation is associated with the 'Father', the 'work' of redemption with the 'Son', and the 'work' of sanctification or transfiguration with the 'Holy Spirit'. In general he finds the term 'work' too masculine and technical. The theology of creation, christology and pneumatology are always about relationships and reciprocal influences. A striking key word for this is the term 'indwelling' (104, etc.).

After this clarification Moltmann then speaks in three stages of the 'creation of the Father', the 'incarnation of the Son' and 'the transfiguration of the Spirit'; each step ends with a characterization of the Trinity. So here there is a 'trinitarian creation', a 'trinitarian incarnation' and a 'trinitarian glorification'.

The term 'glorification' which appears in the context of pneumatology is illuminating. The outpouring of the Spirit of God can be called both 'transfiguration' and 'glorification' because the end-time begins with it. The goal of the work begins to become clear in the indwelling; the messianic time dawns, the glory of God comes to light. Precisely a term like 'glorification' shows the way in which the trinitarian history of God proceeds. The wealth of relations in God is not an eternal game but a work which is not yet finished, a battle which is carried forward by the messianic longing for fulfilment. If *Trinity is a code word for the history of God's love with his world,* then its historical character becomes understandable, for as long as love is alive, in it there is wooing and longing, losing and suffering, seeking and finding. 'Love never ends,' says Paul. That also means that it never stops loving. Love never comes to an end.

(c) Perichoresis and movement

But how these relationships and 'works' of God are to be thought of has caused many headaches from the beginning. Moltmann goes into them in Chapter V of *The Trinity and the Kingdom of God* (129ff.). He shows here how time-conditioned patterns of thought, like monotheistic and monarchian notions, have an influence on the development of the theology of the Trinity. There is no room in the present book to follow these discussions, nor is it necessary to introduce Moltmann's reflections on 'immanent' and 'economic' Trinity or to go into the questions of which movements are to be put within the Trinity and which outside it, or in which way one may or must speak of God's three modes of appearance as 'persons'. What is important to me in this context is that Moltmann takes up a notion which has been developed in the theology of the Orthodox churches, namely that of 'perichoresis'. It goes back to John of Damascus (c.670–750) and describes the continual cycle of the divine life and the constant exchange of the divine energies. 'The Father exists in the Son, the Son in the Father, and both of them in the Spirit, just as the Spirit exists in both . . . It is a process of most perfect and intense empathy . . . In the perichoresis, the very thing that divides them becomes that which binds them together' (174f.). According to Moltmann, this is a 'brilliant way' of combining trinity and unity without reducing the trinity to the unity or dissolving the unity in the trinity.

In the preface to *The Trinity and the Kingdom of God* Moltmann reports that a reproduction of the famous icon of the Holy Trinity by Andrei Rublev (fifteenth century) inspired him when working on this book: 'Through their tenderly intimate inclination towards one another, the three Persons show the profound unity joining them, in which they are one' (xvi). Rublev's icon is thus an image of the notion of perichoresis, because it shows that this inclination can be thought of only between two beings of the Godhead of equal importance. Thus the concept of perichoresis contributes to avoiding all forms of subordinationism in the doctrine of the Trinity.

Important as Moltmann's basing himself on Orthodox theology is ecumenically,[133] he does not content himself with mere reception. The Orthodox conception of perichoresis is so to speak 'dynamized' by being combined with the messianic-historical feature of his thought. For him it is no longer an eternal cycle of the divine life which repeats itself eternally, but a movement which brings in God's world and draws everything together into the kingdom of glory that is still to come.

We can also say that the Orthodox concept of perichoresis is given a panentheistic and process 'loading', so that it becomes a basic structure of life generally. All life, and also all spiritual life, is understood in perichoretic terms, i.e. as life in relationships, and conversely as a structure of relationship which makes life possible at all. So what happens in the Trinity of God in the truest sense of the word embraces all that happens in the word. What is 'played out' in God embraces the great 'play' of creation and the 'world theatre' that is so full of suffering.

Thus the theology of the Trinity becomes more than one topic of theology alongside others. It is a particular way of thinking. *Thinking in a trinitarian way means thinking in terms of relationships on an equal footing*; it means considering all developments in their relationships, pursuing the way in which they are conditioned and their historicity. If we do that seriously, the practical and critical function of trinitarian theology is disclosed.

3. *The practical relevance of trinitarian thinking*

The perichoretic structure of Moltmann's theology of the Trinity produces eminently critical perspectives. The most important of them seems to me to be the 'Criticism of political and clerical monotheism', to quote the heading of the first section of the last chapter, Chapter 6, of *The Trinity and the Kingdom of God* (191ff.). By the key term 'political monotheism' Moltmann understands the notion going back to classical Greece of a hierarchically divided world order which has both cosmological and political features. If creation is ruled by a single 'Lord God', it is likely that a dominating superiority and subordination will also be accepted and established in the governments of states and in the direction of businesses and even in the ordering of marriage and family. That leads to a hierarchy in relationships. It is then almost a matter of course that these are as a rule dominated by patriarchalism. This way of thinking penetrates Western history. It can be found in theocratic patterns of order from the time of the apologists and in monarchical doctrines of the state down to the European absolutism which Moltmann describes as 'the final form of political monotheism in its religiously legitimated form' (196). It follows from this that: 'It is only when the doctrine of the Trinity vanquishes the monotheistic notion of the great universal monarch in heaven, and his divine patriarchs in the world, that earthly rulers, dictators and tyrants cease to find any justifying religious archetypes any more' (197). A trinitarian way of thinking, i.e. a thinking in terms of relationships of equal importance and equal value, therefore entails participatory, communal and thus democratic structures.

The same then of course applies to the clerical sphere. There, too, since the time of the apostolic fathers, theological hierarchies have become established. One God – one Christ – one bishop – one community, this principle laid the foundation for a monarchical episcopate that culminates in the theology of the papacy.[134] But where thinking is in resolutely trinitarian terms, these structures of subordination and power cannot be maintained. With the Orthodox theologians Moltmann states: 'The trinitarian principle replaces the principle of power by the principle of concord. Authority and obedience are replaced by dialogue, consensus and harmony' (202). It is evident that 'the presbyteral and synodical church order and the leadership based on brotherly advice are the forms of organization that best correspond to the *doctrine of the social Trinity*' (202).[135]

Secondly, the messianic unfolding of the Trinity of God as a history of love leads to a decided link between the kingdom of

God and freedom. Following Joachim of Fiore, Moltmann understands the inner dynamic of the Trinity as a 'trinitarian doctrine of the kingdom' (202ff.), though he rejects the chronological narrowing of Joachim's theory of three kingdoms. Rather, he wants to understand the kingdoms of the Father and of the Son and of the Spirit as 'continually present strata and transitions in the kingdom's history' (209).

In this connection it is also important to note that Moltmann interprets Joachim's doctrine of the three kingdoms as a 'doctrine of four kingdoms' (207). According to this, the kingdom of the Spirit will be the sabbath day of world history, and thus describes the consummation of history. But that may not be understood as the end of history. Consummation is not the same as end. 'The forms and eras of the kingdom of the Father, the Son and the Spirit again point beyond themselves to that *kingdom of glory* which replaces this history' (207). So the 'consummation' is to consist in 'the eternal kingdom of glory'. Later we shall have to consider the question what kind of thinking characterizes this 'doctrine'. But the structure of this approach is a help in emphasizing the fundamental openness of history. As the 'strata and transitions' in God's history always point beyond themselves, the real *quality of the kingdom of God can be described as freedom*. Consequently Moltmann's doctrine of the Trinity culminates in the concept of the 'trinitarian doctrine of freedom' (212ff.).

But to understand this freedom rightly we must always extract it from the history of the effect of monarchical and patriarchal distortions. It is then no longer the freedom which rages as the arbitrariness of the absolutist ruler who relies on violence to his subjects or as the liberalism of the 'winner' towards the host of 'losers', but is to be understood as the expression of community, as 'creative passion for the possible' (217), as a combination of sociality and creativity, the inner nucleus and truth of which is love. Again we come upon the concept of 'friendship' as the 'concrete concept of freedom', as Hegel had said. Thus servants become the children of God in the brotherhood of the Son, and these in turn in the power of the Spirit become friends of God, who are then once again exalted into the 'kingdom of glory' in the bliss of the unselfish and unquestioning vision of God.

Thus trinitarian thinking, thinking in relationships, presents itself as the 'theological history of freedom'. The God who is not yet finished is the incessant and inexhaustible ground of the freedom of all his creatures.

Thus the history of God becomes the time and space of free unfolding. In the urgent messianic power of the kingdom, time is no longer an indifferent or fateful flow which carries all with it. Time points beyond itself to the homeland of God in the kingdom of glory. And in this way our time becomes open and fruitful. It is the time of our visitations, and it is the place of our homecoming. *The promise of a homeland embraces the course of the world.*

4. *Is trinitarian thinking a form of mysticism?*

At the beginning of this chapter we discovered that Moltmann calls the Shekinah tradition an element of Jewish mysticism, and I therefore raised the question whether the adoption of such a notion for the theology of the Trinity would not mean that this also takes on mystical features. I want to take up this consideration once again.

It is indeed striking that Moltmann not only refers back to Jewish mysticism but also takes up other mystical traditions. In *The Trinity and the Kingdom of God* we find, for example, references to Spanish passion mysticism (36ff.), to Meister Eckhart (236) or to Jakob Böhme (237). That Ernst Bloch calls the 'kingdom' a 'mystically democratic' figure of thought is quoted with approval (203). On the other hand Moltmann refers to notions which he had presented in 1979 in his short book *Experiences of God*.[136] Therefore his theology of the Trinity also contains passages which not only 'sound' mystical but are beyond doubt of a mystical kind. Here is an example: 'Time is an interval in eternity, finitude is a space in infinity, and freedom is a concession of the eternal love. God withdraws himself in order to go out of himself. Eternity breathes itself in, so as to breathe out the Spirit of life' (111). Many statements of this kind can be found. Are they fortuitous, or can one 'think in a trinitarian way' only when one is prepared to think 'mystically'?

In the preface to *Experiences of God*, mentioned in the previous paragraph, Moltmann notes, 'The sequence of the themes of *hope, anxiety and mysticism* is meant to indicate the direction of the journey and the goal of the experiences which lead to God.'[137] I understand this reference to mean that our journey or way through life is always governed by hope and fear, but that the *goal of the experiences* can only be described mystically. What leads to God is always governed by hope and fear, but what is at the goal of these 'guidances' of God can only be 'seen' or anticipated mystically. *From this perspective, mysticism would be the only possible form of expression and approach to that which transcends all experience.* That is true especially of the theology of the Trinity, which claims to describe relationships which are in God. But as God dwells in light which no one can approach, silence about God is basically the only possible way of speaking of God. The mystics have always known that. In the presence of God there is really only mystical silence, the *silentium mysticum*. But to make this known one must speak. And mystics do this often by describing the way of their approximations to the deity as 'stages' or 'stations'. Moltmann writes: 'This can be understood to take place so simply that, from the *gifts of grace* for which it prays and for which it gives thanks, faith finds and grasps the gracious *hand of God*, from which these gifts come. From this gracious hand of God, faith moves to the *open heart* of God; so that it finally loves God no longer for his gifts of grace, or for his gracious hand, or even for the living indulgence with which he bestows these things; it loves him *simply for his own sake*.'[138] The key words 'gifts of grace', 'hand of God', 'heart of God', 'God himself', describe the goal of the ways taken by faith which ultimately culminate in the mystical vision. But if, as Moltmann keeps saying, the doctrine of the Trinity is a rethinking of the history of the relationships of God, the goal of which is consummation in the kingdom of glory, how could this be anything other than mystical theology?

I shall be returning once more to this basic feature of Moltmann's theology at the end of my survey of the 'Contributions'.

9

Creation: The Wonder of Existence

Five years after *The Trinity and the Kingdom of God*, the doctrine of creation appeared as the second volume in the 'Systematic Contributions to Theology'.[139] Its beginnings go back to lectures which Moltmann had been giving at regular intervals since 1973. However, in the form presented in 1985 they essentially represent the Gifford Lectures which Moltmann gave in the University of Edinburgh in 1984/1985. In the Anglo-Saxon world, to give the Gifford Lectures is like being elevated to the peerage. Moltmann is the only German-speaking theologian of his generation to have been singled out in this way.[140]

The twelve[141] parts of the doctrine of creation discuss such a diverse and textbook-like wealth of questions and positions that it is impossible to present them in detail. I have therefore decided to describe only a few characteristic features in order to show the inner logic of this work and its connection with the doctrine of God.

1. *Creation as indwelling*

Moltmann calls his doctrine of creation 'ecological'. In the preface he also uses the adjective 'pneumatological' as an additional description.[142] What is the connection between 'ecological' and 'pneumatological'?

First of all, Moltmann is clear that reflection on the theology of creation, which claims to be at the level of time, has to take note of the far-reaching danger to nature and the threat of the collapse of essential systems of life on this planet. The ecological crisis is concerning more and more people (though still not enough, above all those in power). And the fact that this crisis has its starting point and still its centre in the regions of the earth influenced by Christianity sheds a significant light on traditional biblical creation faith. Probably no sentence is better known than that of Gen. 1.28, which runs 'Subdue the earth!' That has been understood as divine permission to exploit nature, to plunder the earth and to dominate others, above all the 'pagan' peoples. 'The Christian belief in creation as it has been maintained in the European and American Christianity of the Western churches is therefore not guiltless of the crisis in the world today' (21).

That Moltmann begins his doctrine of creation with a description of the ecological crisis – he calls it a 'crisis of the whole life system of the modern industrial world' (23) – sheds light on a basic feature of his theological thinking that we have often noted. It is his effort to be recognized as a committed man of his day. Theologians who want to be taken seriously today must be open and accessible to the doubters and opponents before coming to speak to their sources and engaging in conversation with the various theological partners.

Nevertheless, for Moltmann the adjective 'ecological' has another and deeper sense. It points to the Greek *oikos*, which also emerges in terms like economy and ecumene and means 'house', 'household' or 'dwelling'. The creation is also 'ecological' in so far as it represents the 'house' and 'dwelling' of God. It therefore goes with 'indwelling'. And that brings us to the point at which the adjectives 'ecological' and 'pneumatological' touch on and explain each other. If we recall what was said on the theology of the Trinity, this interlocking of the theology of the Spirit and the doctrine of creation becomes clear. There trinitarian thought had been brought to us as thinking in relationships of equal importance and on an equal footing, and it follows from this that reflection on God as Creator must also be governed by this basic feature of perichoresis. Therefore Moltmann says, 'If we understand the Creator, his creation and the goal of that creation in a trinitarian sense, the Creator, through his Spirit, dwells in his creation as a whole, and in every individual created being, by virtue of his Spirit holding them together and keeping them in life' (12).

Therefore this ecological and pneumatological doctrine of creation is entitled *God in Creation*. The 'in' is rich in associations. It makes clear that God by no means regards the world as an external 'work' which could function without him, but God is present as the energy of life in creation, and so to speak constantly 'animates' it. What is traditionally described as continuous creation is emphasized with this description of the relationship. Here we find what we got to know in the previous chapters as God's 'history of love' as an infinitely creative, inexhaustibly inventive history of what is living.

On the basis of the doctrine of God the doctrine of creation logically presents itself as a description of relationships. 'Creation' presupposes what we descriptively call 'nature', in relation to God. It takes the cosmos into the vital élan of God. Existence, which extends far beyond what is perceptible by human beings, is a 'miracle',[143] a universe through which divine energies pulse.

What is gained by this 'spirit-full' approach to the doctrine of creation? At this point it can already be said positively that cosmology and the natural sciences are again incorporated into theological reflection on God's world. Moltmann describes what Schleiermacher called the 'liberation of freedom by faith', which also emerges e.g. in Gogarten, Bultmann, Ebeling and Barth, as a 'legitimation formula' which appears from the perspective of the modern natural sciences as a 'myth that theology was the ruling party' (36). The concentration on the salvation of the individual's soul resulted in a surrendering of the universal scope of salvation and thus deepened 'the calamitous dichotomy between the subjectivity of human beings and the objective world of "mere things"' (35). In contrast to this, Moltmann wants his doctrine of creation to be understood as an 'ecological theology of nature' (37), here emphasizing that he is not associating any claim to totality with it, but wants to encourage a process of understanding between theology and the natural sciences which recognizes 'silenced and dying nature' as a secret 'third partner' (51), i.e. as a common structure of conditioning. We find an interesting example of this dialogue in Chapter VIII, which is concerned with the 'evolution of creation' (185ff.).

Now a doctrine of creation understood as a knowledge and awareness of relationship also implies a criticism of the thought patterns which issue in a reduction of relations between human beings and nature, reification and objectification. This basic pattern of the modern understanding of the world and corpo-reality, which has been given classic definition by Descartes and Bacon, sets the reason as the subject of knowledge and will over against the *res extensae* of the world. Moltmann quotes with approval Franz Baader, who called this kind of modern dualism a 'non-spiritual view of nature, a non-natural view of the mind and spirit and the godless view of both' (27). Thus it becomes clear that the modern understanding of nature and body is a practical nihilism characterized by a lack of relationship, and that the ecological crisis represents above all and most deeply a crisis in thought. The 'crisis of domination' already begins in the methodological foundations of the modern sciences, is continued in their technological application, and extends as a 'power-shaped' system over all living relationships. An ecological and pneumatological theology of nature must consequently be concerned with an 'integrating and integral thinking' (3). The hermeneutical interest does not consist in the formula 'know in order to dominate', but in the slogan 'know in order to parti-cipate' (3). What this way of thinking means for the image of human beings and for the very way of thinking will concern us in the further course of this chapter. But first we must turn to another striking feature in Moltmann's doctrine of creation.

2. *The crown of creation: God's sabbath*

'The human being is the crown of creation' is a view which has become proverbial, reflecting the violent human control of nature. It is confirmed in the common interpretation of the creation story in Genesis 1 according to which God's 'six-day work' is concluded with the creation of human beings and thus 'crowned'. Does that make human beings the goal of creation?

No, not at all, says Moltmann. Together with all other creatures, human beings too wait for redemption. All creation is subject to the processes of coming into being and passing away and therefore awaits the consummation. Therefore Moltmann interprets the seventh day, the sabbath, as the 'feast of creation' on which everything comes to its consummation. 'The sabbath is the true hallmark of every biblical – every Jewish and also every Christian–doctrine of creation,' he asserts quite unequivocally (6).

What does the sabbath of creation mean? In Chapter IX and thus at the end of the doctrine of creation Moltmann develops this meaning. He refers first to Gen.2.2, which says that God completed the works that he made on the seventh day. How does this completion relate to the statement made shortly beforehand that God looked on all that he made and thought it 'very good'? Can something be added to a creation which is already very good, to improve it or point beyond it? According to Gen. 2.3 that is the 'rest' of God. In the face of his creation God 'celebrates'. He delights in his creatures and incorporates them in good pleasure.

Consequently this 'rest' is not to be understood as a return to a state which could also have existed before the work of creation; it embraces creation. 'After his creation God comes to himself again – only not without his creation but with it' (279). In other words, if God is at work in his creation, God comes to rest only with his creation, and consequently creation is only completed in God's rest. God's good pleasure becomes its joy, God's rest becomes its hope.

'The works of creation show God exoterically and indirectly, as it were, as the creator. But the sabbath, in its peace and silence, manifests the eternal God at once esoterically and directly as the God who rests in his glory. Creation can be seen as God's revelation of his works; but it is only the sabbath that is the revelation of God's self' (280). These remarks become understandable if we associate them with notions which were mentioned in the previous chapter under the heading 'kingdom of glory'. There it became clear that Moltmann understands God's triunity as the development of his being which only comes to itself in this kingdom. Thus the notion of the sabbath serves to incorporate the time and space of creation in the process of the unfolding of God. It is thus also meant to show that all times and spaces of creation are open, that they point beyond themselves, 'and its consummation will be to become the *home* and the *dwelling-place* of God's glory' (5).

For Moltmann, this teleological orientation of creation follows from the messianic quality of the message and history of Jesus. The messianic time which this has opened up is aimed at freeing human beings, making nature peaceful, and redeeming the two from the powers of the negative and of death. Liberation, bringing peace and redemption together, forms, if one may put it that way, *God's messianic project*. Of course this embraces not only human beings and their history but the history of the creation, and therefore only reaches its consummation in God's sabbath.

This approach has far-reaching critical consequences.

1. The sabbatical doctrine of creation takes the ground from under any anthropocentric understanding of salvation. At the same time it gives the Christian image of human beings an interesting stamp, which I shall discuss in the next section.

2. If they are put in the light of their consummation in the sabbath, all systems of life are seen as open and intensively related. That rules out all attempt to prescribe relations in nature or in human history in a deterministic way. Social Darwinism, which speaks of a 'fight over existence' and the 'survival of the fittest', is unmasked for what it is, namely an ideology which attempts to depict and legitimate the destructively competitive fight of modern economies as a 'law of nature'.

3. It also seems important to me that in his reflections on the sabbath Moltmann arrives at the notion of the 'sanctification of time' (283f.). That here he bases himself intensively on Jewish thought does not need much explaining. The sanctification of time means that the world is understood 'predominantly in terms of time, in generations and histories, not in spaces and regions' (284). Following Abraham Heschel, who interpreted Judaism as 'the religion of time', Moltmann emphasizes that a messianic-sabbatical understanding should also be governed by the sanctification of time. But what does sanctification mean? Not only that the sabbath interrupts and orders the course

of human working time, nor even that it prevents a lapse into cyclical and thus closed concepts of time, but that it represents 'the sign of the coming freedom from time's cyclical course' (286).

The way in which Moltmann relates the two archetypal symbols of liberation which the world owes to the Jewish faith, namely exodus and sabbath, is very impressive. 'The exodus from slavery into the land of liberty is the symbol of external freedom; it is efficacious, operative. The sabbath is the symbol of inner liberty; it is rest and quietude. The exodus is the elemental experience of God's *history*. The sabbath is the elemental experience of God's *creation*. The exodus is the elemental experience of the God who *acts*. The sabbath is the elemental experience of the God who is, and *is present*' (287).

In the next chapter we shall see that this notion of the sanctification of time has critical and constructive implications for the way in which people deal with time.

4. Finally, the chiliastic and thus teleological basic structure of Moltmann's concept of time[144] also influences his understanding of evolution. Accordingly, the structure of evolution follows the sequence which begins with elementary particles, and goes through atoms, molecules, macro-molecular cells and multi-cellular organisms to living populations, living beings and animals, to human beings, to human populations and finally to the community of humankind (cf. 203). Here Moltmann understands evolution not only as spreading out like a fan in the sphere of creation, but also as an ever more complex extension of what lives into the 'spheres of possibility for the future' (202). Thus increasing intention and communication are closely related to their openness in time, i.e. their power to transcend existing conditions. Therefore open systems are 'anticipatory systems' (205) and so 'the world in its different parts and as a whole is a *system open to God*' (205). The original creation moves over through continuous creation to the new creation. Consequently this concept of time knows no end but keeps pointing beyond itself. The openness of the world to God and of God to the world condition each other. Thus Moltmann arrives at a theological

qualification of the concept of evolution when he states: 'We have to see the concept of evolution as a basic concept of the *self-movement* of the divine Spirit of creation' (19).

However, that raises a question which has to be asked despite its speculative character. If the 'consummation in the realm of glory' is not an end and a conclusion but represents the eternal rest of the Creator, then certainly we can think of a beginning of creation in and with time, but not of an end in and with time. Is this theological understanding of the concept of evolution a theological expression of the teleological structure of evolution? Could there not also be an understanding of evolution which connects teleology with finitude or is understood as an expression of finitude? If I understand the cosmological scenarios of our time rightly, the extension of our universe in time which is still going on is not compelling evidence that it must keep going on like this. It would also be conceivable for the élan of this extension to be exhausted, so that a 'backward movement' or implosion of the universe took place. Theologically speaking, this would then run back to the 'original creation'. In other words, must the self-movement of the divine Spirit by its very nature be assumed to be pointing forward? Are the expressions 'forwards' and 'backwards' still suitable at all as cosmological concepts?

3. *Human beings as the image of the Trinity*

It has already been said that human beings ought not to regard themselves as the crown of creation. But how is the special role of human beings within the framework of creation to be understood?

Here, too, in the understanding of anthropology, the perichoretic structure of Moltmann's doctrine of God becomes established. The hierarchical subordination of life to the Spirit and the drift towards power which is connected with it, and which results in the devaluation and instrumentalization of the corporeal, is rejected. It does not correspond to the notion of the constitutive reciprocity of all relationships. Therefore following

Benedict Baader, Moltmann speaks emphatically of embodiment as the highest human goal. His critical intention is clear. He wants to get beyond the tendency to spirtualize the soul while at the same time materializing the body, which has become normative for Western anthropological theories. 'The theology of the patristic church was pervaded by the Platonic idea of the liberation of the soul from the body; mediaeval theology was determined by the Aristotelian view that the body is formed by the soul; and modern European anthropology is dominated by the will to give the conscious mind power over the instrument of the body' (245). But what gain is there in knowledge if we begin from embodiment as the goal and end of the works of God?

Moltmann shows that God's creation is aimed at the embodiment of human beings. In order to see the 'image' of God one must take into view the whole human being, sensual and creatively fertile. The same is also true of the reconciliation of human beings in the 'flesh'. They not only are 'flesh' but also assume broken, sinful and suffering flesh in order to heal it and give it dignity. Finally, redemption also aims at the 'transfiguration' of the body. It does not cast off the body as something unworthy, but takes it up into the 'vision' of the glory of God.

Thus the trinitarian dimensions of creation, reconciliation and redemption also stamp the 'living character of created, reconciled and redeemed men and women' (246); they give them the 'span' which extends from their bodily creation to the resurrection of the flesh.

Now it is precisely this bodily nature which binds us human beings together and with the world around us. Embodiment is inconceivable without sociality. As 'open systems' we human beings are dependent on the most diverse communal relationships. That begins with the air that we breathe and extends to the most intimate union in love. Need, exchange and the capacity to communicate govern one another. And precisely in this form of community we are *imago Trinitatis*.[145]

The critical and constructive significance of this approach is obvious. The human being is the image of God not as the isolated monad; human beings who are deeply grounded in sharing and receptive relationships reflect the triune God. That is true both of our 'external relationships' in the human environment and also of our inner life, our spirit-body field, where it is always vital for the unconscious, the deliberate and the involuntary to come to an agreement and permeate one another. Therefore the subjectivity of human beings is reflected in their sociality; their identity stands in direct relationship to their natural and cosmic receptivity; their dignity is most closely connected to their value of the reality which is around them. The ethical relevance of this approach is obvious.

Finally, it is in keeping with the eschatological and teleological structure in the concept of the Trinity that Moltmann also adopts a teleological orientation in his understanding of human beings. 'When we talk about people's spirit, we do not mean their reflective subjectivity or their fixed, static identity. We mean the anticipatory structure of their whole physical, mental and spiritual existence' (265). Accordingly being human is a kind of orientation. 'Human beings are in becoming' (265). The human life-history is stamped by their expectation of life. People attempt to realize the project of their life.

Such an approach of course immediately raises the question: And what becomes of us when we fail? If we do not recognize the 'project' of our life, or even have no chance of realizing it? What about failure, sickness and meaninglessness? In a separate section headed 'Life in health and sickness' (270), Moltmann goes into questions of this kind. He interprets health as 'the strength to be human' and therefore as a strength which is proved 'in a person's acceptance of life's joy and the grief of death' (273). Consequently a concentration on an undisturbed well-being and attractive youthfulness would be a sign of sickness, because it contains within it a rejection of fragility and death.

It is also in keeping with Moltmann's eschatological thinking in terms of process that he by no means interprets death as total loss of relationship but as a 'transition to a different kind of being and a metamorphosis into a different form' (278). What 'kind of being' and 'form' that could be is, however, left open.[146]

Here Moltmann is not (just) concerned with the question what becomes of our life when we die. But he *is* concerned with the question what we make of our life before we die. Is the perspective of the sanctification of time which is to be consummated in the glory of God also a ground and motive for sanctifying our concrete life? To take just one example, what has sanctification to do with work? Here Moltmann's remarks on the sanctification of Sunday are illuminating. He shows that, for Christians, the regaining of the dignity of Sunday must be closely connected with the degree to which they again make connection with the experiences of the sabbath in Judaism. Therefore his suggestion of combining Saturday evening with Sunday morning into a time of sabbath and Sunday rest and celebration is interesting. In this way the sabbath evening would commemorate the 'rest of the presence of God' whereas worship on Sunday morning could be 'set wholly in the liberty of Christ's resurrection for the new creation'. So this time would need to be understood as an 'ecological day of rest' which consequently would have to be 'a day without pollution of the environment – a day when we leave our automobiles at home, so that nature too can celebrate its sabbath' (296). If we see that it is precisely at the weekends that the idol of the 'automobile' can mobilize its adherents most effectively but at the same time also calls for its greatest sacrifice, then the rebellious nature of Moltmann's proposal immediately becomes evident. We are miles away from such a sanctification of time.

4. *The partners and the opponents*

In the chapter on Moltmann's doctrine of God I already pointed out that he takes up the Jewish Shekinah tradition as he came to know it above all from Rosenzweig. This closeness to the mystical patterns of thought in Judaism also reappears in the doctrine of creation. As an example I would just cite the kabbalistic theory of *zimzum*, which helps to explain the notion of creation *ex nihilo*. Thus the question where there would be space for creation if God is all is answered with the notion of the self-limitation of God. By withdrawing into himself, God leaves a place for creation outside himself. Thus while creation comes from God, it moves in God's space and thus has its own freedom.

Kabbalistic mysticism is like an underground river system which comes to the surface in many ways and at different points. That is true of Judaism, but it is also true of Christianity. An important instance here is Friedrich Oetinger, who referred back both to kabbalistic witnesses and to the writings of Jakob Böhme[147] for his *philosophia sacra*. Oetinger in turn was influential in many directions; his influence on pietism must have been most important. On the Catholic side Benedict F.X.Baader was influenced by these traditions. His 'theosophy' influenced idealistic philosophy.

It is no coincidence that these patterns of thought emerge at decisive points in Moltmann's doctrine of creation. As I already said at the beginning of this chapter, Moltmann is in search of an 'integrating and integral thinking' (4). Therefore he takes up traditions which are indebted to this approach. Alongside the mystical traditions these also include the Orthodox notion of perichoresis. But mention should also be made of organic, evolutionary and panentheistic currents which can be found above all in the English-speaking world.[148] The option for thought following an approach in terms of process that is rich in relationships and integrative implies criticism of theological and philosophical schools which have developed the doctrine of creation predominantly in monarchical or dualizing thought patterns. This becomes clear from extended critical discussions of Augustine,[149] Thomas Aquinas[150] or Karl Barth.[151]

It seems to me particularly important that the dualistic opposition between creation (as the mere 'stage') and human redemption (as the real 'drama') should be overcome. This understanding is to be found in many variants in Christian theology and spirituality and encourages an anthropocentric egotism of salvation for which the good and ill of creation is indifferent.

5. For a habitable world

The ethical and political implications of Moltmann's doctrine of creation are only hinted at. I have also pointed out above how the emphasis on the sabbatical structure of creation leads to a new evaluation of Sunday, not just as a day of liturgical concentration on God but also as the time when nature rests.

It would be interesting to develop the notion of indwelling ethically. Moltmann has indicated the direction that he would take here by using the key term 'habitable existence' (xii). A habitable world would presuppose a relationship between human beings and nature which was no longer stamped by exploitation but aimed at a 'viable symbiosis' (xiii). The mechanistic and materialistic modern view of the world would have to be replaced by an ecological one. The patriarchal structures of life and society would have to be replaced by 'new egalitarian forms of society' and 'comradely communities' (320). The movements towards concentration in the world economy which are becoming increasingly clear as a result of the mechanistic model of the world need to be replaced by networks in which mutual relationships on an equal footing emerge. Moltmann is not concerned to replace a patriarchal world order with a matriarchal one, but to describe the two socially and co-operatively in the messianic perspective of friendship with God.

I regard Moltmann's ecological doctrine of creation as a foundation for ethical considerations which will also occupy us in the twenty-first century. When his book appeared in 1985 it was in the trend, and corresponded with many schemes for the ecological redirection of the world economy. If I see things rightly, barely fifteen years later this trend has turned round again. Influential circles in the Western world, above all in the United States of America, are celebrating 'globalization' as proof of the boundless vitality of a model of the world which combines networking with control, which links together the economically strong regions of the earth in incessant streams of capital and goods, while at the same time leaving ever-greater zones of the world to chaos and impoverishment.

Moltmann's doctrine of creation is ecumenical in that it seeks dialogue with Jewish, Orthodox, Catholic, Anglican and Reformation positions. But at the same time its practical and political consequences still have to be worked out. It is far from being demonstrated that this earth will remain or become 'habitable'. 'Ecumene' means the 'inhabited world'. The goal of the ecumene needs to be the fight to make the world habitable. To do that it will be necessary to develop diverse but mutually compatible models of liveability. The model which is concealed behind the programme of 'globalization' is so destructive because it is far too centralistic and one-dimensional. Over against that we should not only recall the slogan 'small is beautiful', but supplement it by the slogan 'diversity is essential'. A 'spirit-full' ecological doctrine of creation could help us here to combine diversity and a wealth of relationships. The ecumenical movement is not at an end as many people think; it is only at a beginning, for we still face work for the goal of the habitability of the earth. That sounds like a tantalizing demand. But it becomes possible if it feeds on the trust that God dwells with all his power in his creation and therefore also gives our struggles for a habitable world their inner dynamic.

10

Under Way on the Way
of the Messiah

1. *The messianic*

What is the messianic? It is the unrest which cannot be content with history as it is. With such unrest in one's heart, one thinks back and says, 'It can't have been that!' So memory seeks in the past for unsettled and unfulfilled moments; it looks for what has not yet had its future and attempts to give it a chance. But can the messianic unrest be content with what is there in the present? There must be still more life in life, it says. There must be more than everything.

What else does this mean than that 'it' must still come? Thus one is intent on the future. What has not yet happened today can happen tomorrow. Such expectation does not remain inactive; it does not just fold its hands. It exerts its strength and works on the fulfilment of what has not been lived out. So the messianic is the source of revolutionary impatience and therefore of course is also always in danger of sacrificing the present to what is expected. Therefore it is a sign of messianic wisdom to reckon that tomorrow the longing will be still there, albeit in a way which cannot yet be foreseen. Even if an urgent need has been satisfied today, another will arise tomorrow and spur the expectation to take new steps.

The expectation extends wider and wider. It does not stop at personal fortunes, but embraces the people, the human world, indeed nature. So it covers ever wider areas. One day even death must find its master. The futile must not have the last word.

But why does the messianic hope? Why is it not content with what is there? Why does it assume that our fate must be not only changeable but also capable of improvement? Because the messianic is inspired by the confidence that all human fate and all human history is borne up and willed by a power which is greater, better and more purposive than anything that human beings can think. Or, to put it in negatively, because in the light of such a trust one cannot be content with the sufferings and the torments of history. Without the experience of a basically gracious God the messianic loses its real motivation, its passion for successful life. It is grounded in the confidence that the spirit of mercy and justice dwells at the heart of the world. Therefore it consumes itself in restless expectation and only finds rest when God himself has found rest.

Where does the messianic come from? How did it arise? Martin Buber said that messianism is 'the most deeply original idea of Judaism'. He also put forward the thesis that the messianic hope came into being with the institution and the downfall of the hereditary kingship in Israel. The true king of Israel is Yahweh, and his rule serves to give justice to the poor, to protect the weak and to give the oppressed their rights. Inspired by trust in this merciful God, the messianic hope gains criteria to criticize its kings and lords. Accordingly even in the catastrophe of the exile, it goes by this trust and particularly under the experiences of historical collapses it develops an awareness of the ever greater extent of the messianic expectation.

Moltmann follows Buber and Scholem when he says that the prophets form the figure of the messiah, for example when Isaiah speaks of the 'Immanuel' and thus goes beyond the memory of king David with the image of the expected messiah king. The figure of the 'suffering Servant' spoken of in Deutero-Isaiah (Isa.40–55) also belongs on this line. It is in keeping with this tradition that in Jewish apocalyptic, say in the prophet David, the figure of the 'Son of man' emerges, to whom, after the bestial powers of chaos, all power is given, whom the peoples will serve, and whose kingdom knows no end: 'In the apocalyptic hope, Israel's messianic hope apparently becomes so universal that its special promise and its own history disappear, and the original horizon of creation is reached.'[152]

To the present day, Jewish faith consists in the expectation of the messiah. From this follows an understanding of life as 'deferred' and 'in anticipation' (26). This is celebrated, recalled and practised in the celebration of the sabbath. The sabbatical ordinances of Israel, the sabbath day and the sabbatical year, give time 'messianic rhythms' (44) and thus at the same time provide an orientation. For there are excesses of messianic expectation which bring violence and frustration. 'Beside the noisy messianism of the apocalyptic of catastrophe, and the wild messianism of revolutionary utopianism, the sabbath is a still but steady, and thus lasting, messianism' (27).

'Are you he who is to come, or shall we look for another?' This question which John the Baptist in prison puts to Jesus of Nazareth (Matt.11.3) is the central question which separates Christianity from Judaism. The Christians have answered this question in the affirmative, the Jews in the negative. At this point a history has begun which has caused the Jews unspeakable suffering. Nevertheless, or rather precisely because of this, Moltmann begins his christology at this point. The sub-title indicates this starting point, 'Christology in Messianic Dimensions'. He maintains that the messianic hope leads 'us', Christians, to Jesus. But it is the same messianic hope which prevents the Jews from recognizing in Jesus the expected messiah. 'The gospels understand his (i.e. Jesus') whole coming and ministry in the context of Israel's messianic hope. Yet it is the very same messianic hope which apparently makes it impossible for "all Israel" to see Jesus as being already the messiah. Because earliest christology grew up in this field of tension, every Christian christology is forced to come back to this conflict, and has to struggle and come to terms with the Jewish "no". This is the fundamental question at the centre of Christian christology: Is the Jewish "no" anti-Christian? Is the Christian "yes" anti-Jewish? Are the "no" and the "yes" final or provisional?' (28).

If we recall that for Moltmann it is possible to know God only by following the trinitarian 'history of God's love for the creation', then it immediately becomes clear that in this question he must opt for the 'provisional' in the truest sense of the word. The question of the no and the yes goes before us; it remains a question for us, since it will be resolved only in the parousia of the Messiah. Jesus is and remains the messiah of Israel. But the church is called to take this messianic expectation of Israel into the 'Gentile' word of nations. It stands in the *praeparatio messianica*, the term used by Maimonides and other mediaeval Jewish theologians, and thus in the 'messianic preparation' of the world of the Gentiles, so that these come to God's Zion and the heavenly Jerusalem. 'Just because the gospel has come to the Gentiles as a result of the Jewish "no", it will return – indeed it must return – to Israel. The first shall be last. Israel is "the last" towards which everything else draws' (35). In other words, a final no would be possible only over the betrayal of the messianic in the messiah Jesus. That is manifestly an impossibility; for what would Jesus be were he not the messiah? What kind of 'Christ' could he be if he was no longer grounded in the messianic hope of Israel? Perhaps a Gnostic redeemer figure, but he would no longer have anything to do with Jesus.

2. The 'way' of Jesus Christ

A christology in messianic dimensions can describe Christ Jesus only in process categories. He must be understood 'dynamically in the forward movement of God's history with the world' and not abstractly and statically as 'one person in two natures or as a historical personality' (xiii). Words like 'process' or 'forward' indicate movement, and therefore Moltmann describes the movement of Christ in God's history with the symbol of the 'way'. His christology is meant to be a 'christology of the way' and thus at the same time a 'christology of those on the way' (xiii). Consequently the symbol 'way' contains three elements.

First, it communicates an impression of the orientation and the goal of christology. It describes 'Christ's way from his birth in the Spirit and his baptism in the spirit to his self-surrender on Golgotha', and then also 'the way leading from his resurrection to his parousia – the way he takes in the Spirit to Israel, to the nations, and into the breadth and depth of the cosmos' (xiv). This reference helps us to recognize the lay-out of Moltmann's christology. After the two introductory chapters, Chapter III is about the 'messianic mission of Christ', and thus describes the way and the activity of the 'historical' Jesus in the light of his messiahship. Chapter IV turns to the passion and cross of Christ and describes it against 'the apocalyptic horizon of world history'. Chapter V is about the resurrection of Christ. This should really have been followed by a chapter on the 'presence of Christ', discussing the apostolic presence of Christ in the church and in the poor. That would be as it were Christ's 'way to the peoples'. But this part is missing. Instead Moltmann refers to the relevant passages in his book *The Church in the Power of the Spirit,* another impression of which appeared at the same time as the 'christology'. So in the present form of the christology in Chapter VI we have the way of Christ into the breadth and depth of the cosmos, until Chapter VII speaks of the destination of the way, the parousia of Christ. 'The earthly – the crucified – the raised – the present – the coming One: these are the stages of God's eschatological history with Jesus. It is these stages[153] which the title "Christ" gathers together, and it is these which should interpenetrate christology and provide its framework' (33).

Secondly, Moltmann uses the symbol of the way to bring out the 'historical conditioning of any human christology'. Like any activity of a Christian, theological reflection about Christ, too, is an element of discipleship. We can reflect on the messiah only by sharing the way with him and reflecting on his movement – in the strict sense of the word. Thus reflection is a form of discipleship. A 'christology of the way' is not yet a 'christology of the homeland'. By its nature it is on the way and 'provisional' and therefore dependent on critical conversation with others on the way.

Finally, taking the way of Christ and the call to discipleship also addresses an ethical category. 'Christology and christopraxis find one another in the full and completed knowledge of Christ' (xiv). This approach means that there are constant reference to ethics throughout Chapters III to VI of Moltmann's christology.

3. A 'postmodern' christology

I have referred to the ecological dimension in Moltmann's doctrine of creation and pointed out that this not only follows from the present-day emphasis on the ecological crisis but is also rooted in the 'economy' of the divine Trinity. The ecological interest – like the social and relational interest – is thus already there in the theology of the Trinity. It must therefore also reappear in the christology. Furthermore, precisely in the christology it must develop its central significance if reflection on Christ Jesus is to be prevented from being distorted into an anthropocentric or even an ecclesiocentric belief in salvation. This theological approach, which 'will be in a position to relate human history to the nature of the earth, and to reconcile the two' (xvi), must also be carried through in the christology. Therefore in his Preface Moltmann says programmatically that for his christology there must be 'the transition from the metaphysical christology of the "ancients" to the historical christology of modern times'; this christology must 'make the *now necessary transition from the historical christology of modern times to a post-modern christology, which places human history ecologically in the framework of nature*' (xvi, my italics). The 'old metaphysical thought about cosmology' (xvi) must be taken up again under the conditions of modern thought. But in what does the 'post-modern' peculiarity of Moltmann's christology consist? By attempting to keep combining the history of humankind with the framework provided by nature, it draws attention to 'Christ's bodily nature and its significance for earthly nature', 'because embodiment is the existential point of intersection between history and nature in human beings' (xvi).

Now the key words 'embodiment' and 'existential' could give the impression that Moltmann's christology was 'existentialistic', say in a decidedly personalistic and subjectivistic sense. The opposite is the case. Both concepts must be seen in the context of the rich relationships of sociality and ecumenicity which mark out Moltmann's theology, and especially his trinitarian thinking. That means that it is about the bodily and existential intersections of human life in the comprehensive crisis of the modern industrial and technological world and is concerned with the question of what Jesus Christ means at these intersections. What has the messiah Jesus to do with the misery which spreads all over the world in and with the 'major project of scientific and techno-logical civilization' (63)? Therefore an embodied ecumenical christology asks about the victims in this major project: 'Who is Christ for these "surplus" masses of people today?' (66). In addi-tion, in the face of the potential for nuclear self-destruction it asks, 'Who really is Christ for us today, threatened as we are by the nuclear inferno?' (67). And finally, in view of imminent nuclear catastrophes, it asks, 'Who really is Christ for dying nature and ourselves today?' (87). It is these global dangers which represent the existential urgency for a cosmological christology.

In my view these 'post-modern' questions are expressed most evocatively in Chapter VI, entitled 'The Cosmic Christ'. Therefore I want to concentrate on the reflections in this chapter.[154]

In the traditional theology and piety of the Western churches the conviction predominates that Christ became man to save us human beings. This anthropocentric emphasis in the doctrine of human salvation and sanctification then also often leads to a disparaging of nature, as if this were completely indifferent to the Messiah of God. By contrast, at the beginning of Chapter VI Moltmann emphasizes that there could be no salvation for human beings without a 'healing of nature'. He continues: 'Today a cosmic christology has to confront Christ the redeemer with a nature which human beings have plunged into chaos, infected with poisonous waste and condemned to universal death; for it is only this Christ who can save men and women from their despair and preserve nature from annihilation' (275). This sentence is an evocative description of the concern of christology and soteriology. This is not the deliverance of human beings kerygmatically and pastorally from despair, which must be understood both actively as destructive rage and passively as fear of destruction. Nor is it just ethical concern about the preser-vation of nature from the threat of a return to chaos. A cosmic christology is about Christ himself and the manifestation of his universal mission of reconciliation.

Therefore we read: 'Christology can only arrive at its completion at all in a cosmic christology. All other christologies fall
short and do not provide an adequate content for the experiences
of the Easter witnesses with the risen Christ' (278). For if the
Risen One is called the 'firstborn from the dead', then that may
refer not only to humankind but also to all creatures. Why?
Because they are all in need of reconciliation and because they
are all to be transformed into eternal glory. Therefore Moltmann
can also say with Teilhard de Chardin that the Risen One dwells
in 'the heart of creation' (279). He quotes with approval a
mystical Advent hymn which goes, 'O earth spring forth, spring
forth, O earth, that hill and valley all become green.[155] O earth,
bring forth this flow, O saviour, spring from the earth.' And then
he continues: 'In the final "greening of the earth" the cosmic
Wisdom Christ will come forth from the heart of creation,
setting that creation in the light of God's glory' (280). That is the
messianic expectation in the garb of purest mysticism.

How is this 'post-modern' cosmic christology grounded?
Moltmann finds the biblical orientation first in the cosmic
passages of I Corinthians (1.15–20) and of Colossians and
Ephesians, and also in the texts which identify Christ as mediator
at creation and 'Logos' with 'Wisdom' (I Cor.8.1–3, but above
all John 1.1–3, etc.). 'Logos christology is originally Wisdom
christology, and is as such cosmic christology' (282).

So Moltmann is working with the two 'historical titles of
Christ', 'Son of God' and 'Son of man', to describe the 'way' of
Christ from his birth and baptism in the Spirit to his resurrection;
he takes up as a third title the 'Logos' or 'Wisdom' or even 'Life'
to be able to cover the 'cosmic' dimension.[156]

In terms of the history of dogma Moltmann refers to the
cosmocrator motif, which since the early church has exercised
great influence on Christian thought and Christian piety. But he
gives it a place in the old Protestant doctrine of the threefold
office of Christ and thus arrives at a threefold *officium* of
Wisdom-Christ: 'Christ rules in the kingdom of nature (*regnum
naturae*), in the kingdom of grace (*regnum gratiae*) and in the
kingdom of glory (*regnum gloriae)*' (286f.). On the basis of this

systematic ordering he can first describe Christ as the 'ground of creation' (311). Here he understands 'ground' not one-sidedly as 'primal ground' or beginning but as the inner and 'immanent unity' of creation, as the power of life which sustains it and holds it together. This brings out the aspects of the consolidation, preservation and renewal of the world.

This perspective leads Moltmann to a discussion with the French mystic Teilhard de Chardin, who has spoken of the 'Christ of evolution', *Christus evolutor* (292ff.). He first shows that Teilhard has attempted to see the process of evolution in eucharistic categories. 'Ultimately his christology of evolution is nothing less than the vision of the cosmic eucharist through which God becomes part of the world and the world part of God' (294). Much as Moltmann is inclined to agree with this vision, he resolutely criticizes the uncritical acceptance of the theory of evolution which has led Teilhard to overlook the terrors of evolution, its breaks and catastrophes. In that case the *Christus evolutor* is none other than a 'cruel, unfeeling *Christus selector*' (296). But so that the weak and those excluded in the process of evolution get their due, Moltmann speaks of the *Christus redemptor*, the redeemer of evolution.

Moltmann also makes a similar criticism of Karl Rahner's notion of the 'self-transcendence' of evolution. By 'self-transcendence' he means the self-communication of God indwelling matter. Thus matter and spirit are not artificially separated, but interlocked and understood as the history of ever higher and more complex forms of life. In such a development Christ stands at the end as a culmination, but he cannot be regarded as the redeemer who liberates evolution from its deep ambivalences. There is not only a theodicy problem in respect of human guilt. The 'evolutionary world-view' also raises the question of theodicy, because 'physical evil', i.e. the deep breaks and rejections in the process of evolution, calls for an answer. This problem 'can be overcome only through an eternal new creation of all temporal things' (301).

If the cosmic Christ also rules in the 'kingdom of glory', this means that all that is temporal will be brought into eternal rest, into God's sabbath. Here we keep coming up against ideas which we have already encountered in the doctrine of creation. God's sabbath is the kingdom of consummation. Consummation does not mean the end of the process of creation. In that case eschatology would end in teleology. 'What is eschatological is the raising of the body and the whole of nature. What is eschatological is that eternity of the new creation which all things in time will experience simultaneously when time ends. To put it simply: God forgets nothing that he has created. Nothing is lost to him. He will restore it all' (303).

He will restore it all. Thus cosmic christology ends in and with the restoration of all things. It insists that 'the reconciliation of all things, whether on earth or in heaven (Col.1.20) and their redemption from the fetters of the transience of the times leads to the gathering together of all things in the messiah and therefore to the completion of creation' (304). I will return to this 'resolution' of all the questions of theology when discussing Moltmann's eschatology in *The Coming of God*.[157] Therefore here it must be enough to point out that the doctrine of the restoration of all things and their 'universal reconciliation' in the kingdom of glory is of course vigorously disputed. For many assailed Christians this does not seem to be a reconciling solution of their unresolved question but an ultimate attack on their sense of justice. If God does not forget anything that he has created, how is God then to think of guilt and evil? Moltmann's statement 'He will restore it all' must become 'He will put it all right'. That means that God brings down the mighty from their thrones and puts them in their real place, among all the others. 'The reconciliation of all things' is not a designation for a universal turning of a blind eye to everything, but designates a putting right of all things which have been distorted by guilt and evil. What are the ethical consequences of a cosmic christology?

Precisely because the theory of evolution has degenerated into an aggressive social Darwinism which has the effect of making the persistence of the natural conditions of life a virtual chaos, a cosmic christology must strive for an *ethic of putting things right*. Moltmann's first concern is the 'reconciliation of human beings with nature' (306). This is aimed at reconciling 'the requirements of human civilization with the conditions and regenerative powers of nature' and shaping them towards 'a productive co-operation in the interests of common survival' (307). For this, it is quite vital to regard the relations between human beings, animals and plants as a 'community based on law' (307). Not only human beings have rights and are subjects in law. The same is also true of God's other creatures. In this connection Moltmann refers to the 'Universal Declaration on Animal Rights' which has existed since 1978 (380). I also think important the remark that as the 'owner of creation' God alone should have disposal over his creation, and that accordingly all creatures could only be accorded 'a right of use' (311). 'The extermination of whole plant and animal species must therefore be viewed as sacrilege, and punished' (311).

Such a statement indicates the scope of the change that would come about if our right to property were turned into a right of use. However, if we take it not only as an expression of ethical indignation but as a guideline for concrete ethics, then serious problems arise. For basically this demand calls for a global theocracy with a corresponding court of justice and effective world-wide mechanisms of punishment. It is immediately obvious that this would lead to far-reaching questions in the philosophy of law, politics and religion, not to mention the practical problems of implementation. That brings us back to a point which already occupied us in Chapter 7. Moltmann's systematic theology leads on to ethical tasks but does not go into their complexity. On the other hand we must grant that there is also no provision for a developed ethics in the lay-out of the 'Systematic Contributions'.

4. *In conclusion: two impressions of a reader*

When I got hold of Moltmann's *The Way of Jesus Christ* shortly after it appeared I was living as a university professor in Costa Rica, as it were 'on the way and far from home'. I still remember clearly how much the book affected me and 'edified' me in the truest sense of the word. Beyond doubt everyday life in Costa Rica had a major influence on this reading. It was the everyday life of a 'Third World' country or, as we might perhaps say better, the 'underworld' of the rich world. The students came from all the countries of Central America, the Caribbean and the Andean states of South America. Most of them had to struggle under the most onerous economic conditions to study. Some of them had fled to Costa Rica from the repression which dominated in their homelands, for example in Guatemala. The meaning of impoverishment and dependence, humiliation and persecution was present in an oppressive way at every encounter and in every seminar.

In that context, above all Chapters III to V spoke to me, the gospel of the 'way of Jesus Christ' as the 'brother of men and women' and 'friend of the poor' (94). The messianic mission of this brother of men and women really was 'good news' for the outcast and the wretched. The gospel was about their dignity (99ff.), their salvation was unfolded as 'healing' (105ff.). 'Jesus celebrates the feast of the messianic times with those who are discriminated against in his own time' (115). That was more than a historical and exegetical reference, it was directly relevant. 'The one who brings to the poor the dignity of the kingdom of God and reveals to sinners and tax collectors the righteousness of God which itself makes righteous, is also the messianic "host" who invites the hungry to eat and drink in the kingdom of God' (116). This christology translated itself almost automatically into 'christopraxis'. That God's messiah brings sabbath ordinances was developed, for example, as a programme of social and political relief from debt. And Moltmann's statement that the 'community of Jesus which lives and acts messianically . . . practises the great alternative to the world's present system', and 'through its existence it calls in question the systems of violence and injustice' (122), served to mobilize us.

It was the same in Chapter IV, which discussed the 'apocalyptic sufferings of Christ' (151ff.). That the 'community of the sufferings of Christ' also suffers in this time helped us to understand everyday testimony. Oscar Arnulfo Romero, the Archbishop of

El Salvador who was murdered at the altar, was for us a living witness to the alternative of radical change which has come into the world with the crucified Jesus. That Moltmann described him alongside Paul Schneider and Dietrich Bonhoeffer as a typical and significant martyr of our time (202f.) made this christology gripping and immediately illuminating.

I could cite many other examples to emphasize the immediate relevance of this outline. These included not least the wealth of biblical references and motifs and the intensive preoccupation with Jewish traditions and insights. Nevertheless I have to confess that even if at that time I read Moltmann's christology through from beginning to end, I certainly read it selectively. I understood it as a helpful example of pastoral support. Through the book a contemporary spoke to us who wanted to be a 'professor' in the original meaning of the word, namely a confessor, a witness, a 'comrade' of the kingdom.

When now, ten years later, I attempt to go back to *The Way of Jesus Christ*, the positive experiences of that time return. But my perception has shifted. I recognize more clearly than then the ecological interest which connects this christology very closely with the doctrine of creation and thus with the doctrine of the Trinity (around which at that time I made a great detour). Thus the systematic architecture stands out more clearly, the 'blueprint' of the work is more evident, and an impression is made which differs from the first.

Two points above all make me think today.

First, I ask myself whether it is in keeping with the inner meaning of the honorific titles that we find in the New Testament to understand them as 'stages' on the 'way' of Christ. Moltmann calls his christology a 'narrative christology' 'which seeks to link remembrances of Christ with expectations of him' (xv). But is it really the case that the remembrance of the historical Jesus, his activity and his death, lie on the same narrative level as the expectation of the one who is to return or the hope that this Christ is also the wisdom of the cosmos? Why do the Gopsels with their narrative remembrances stop precisely at the threshold of the resurrection? In other words, is the meaning of the earthly

Jesus to be described in precisely the same way as the meaning of the Risen One and the Christ of the parousia? It seems to me that it is by no means a coincidence that the New Testament speaks in very different ways about the different messianic dimensions of the Christ. That is demanded by the subject matter. The New Testament narrates his career in the Gospels until Easter morning. It attests his kergymatic presence in the Spirit in the letters of the apostles. It reports the power of the Present One in the preaching of the apostles and in the appearance of the first communities throughout the 'ecumene'. It celebrates his cosmic significance in songs and hymns. With the images and language of apocalyptic it grasps after the meaning of his parousia. That means that wherever there is something to tell it is told. Wherever something is expected it is imagined, sung, longed for, prayed for metaphorically.

In my view these different forms of language are not unimportant when it comes to describing the effect of the messiah. But that this in particular happens in Moltmann's christology makes me think. It suggests that it is the preconceived salvation-historical theology of the Trinity which leads him to treat remembrances and expectations as the same and to put the 'messianic dimensions' of Christ in one 'chronological sequence'. That becomes clear in the following sentences. 'We shall *begin* with the messianic mission of Jesus, the prophet of the poor, *go on* to the apocalyptic passion of Jesus, the Son of the Father *and then* arrive at the transfiguring raising of Jesus from the dead. We shall devote particular attention to his reconciliation of the cosmos, as the Wisdom of creation. In the future of Christ in judgment and kingdom, *we then find* the completion of salvation in the glory of God, and the fulfilment of the promise of reconciliation in the redemption of the world. *In accordance with the different situations of this divine eschatological history, the person of Jesus Christ changes and expands,* until he is seen "face to face"' (72, my italics).

Let me try to put my objection again in another way. Over the gospels there lies the tension of knowing and not-knowing, of belief and unbelief, of acceptance and rejection, as this is expressed in exemplary fashion at the beginning of the Gospel of John: 'He came into his own and his own received him not.' This tension has occasionally been called 'the messianic secret'. It seems to me that taking note of this secret ought also to govern all the 'stages' or 'situations' or dimensions of the messiah which we think we know. For after all there is a messianic secret not just in respect of the 'historical' Jesus. Is there not also the 'secret rule' of the risen Christ? In putting the emphasis on the term 'secret' I do not want to mystify the word. But I would have liked an account which left more room for doubt and tribulations, which underlined the experimental and the provisional. And as I do not find this sufficiently differentiated in *The Way of Jesus Christ*, for me it comes close to a triumphalism which claims to see more than we might be given to see. 'Now we see through a glass darkly, but then face to face', says Paul (I Cor.13.12). To be mindful of this is important for me, for it relates deeply to the experience that our hoping is troubled by tormenting doubts. Our messianic expectations are overshadowed by nagging temptations.

11

The Superabundance
of the Power of God

A pneumatology was not foreseen in the original scheme of the 'Contributions'.[158] But after all it appeared relatively quickly. Two years later the christology was followed by *The Spirit of Life*, which in the subtitle, changed in the English edition, was presented as a 'holistic pneumatology'.[159] That is also logical in terms of its content, for what would a systematic development of the theology of the Trinity look like if it did not contain an extended doctrine of the Spirit of God?

Now that we have already made the acquaintance of three volumes of the 'Contributions', of course the basic structure of this book does not present any great surprises. We are already familiar with the perichoretic form in which Father, Son and Spirit are related to each other and with each other. If for Moltmann trinitarian thought means spelling out the history of the communal relationships of the divine 'persons' as a single 'history of love', then pneumatological aspects were already present in the doctrine of creation and in the christology, just as now creation and redemption must again become a theme from the perspective of the 'third' person of the Trinity. Consequently a doctrine of the Spirit of God was a logical development of the systematic programme.

Nevertheless the historical context plays an important role. In his preface Moltmann has acknowledged that *The Spirit of Life* was stimulated by the works of his doctoral students Lyle Dabney, Donald Claybrook, Hong-Hsin Lin, Peter Zimmerling and Adelbert Schloz-Dürr. Here it is made clear in a practical way that he really wants his 'Contributions' to be understood as parts of a great conversation and not just as an enclosed and unassailable system.

Moreover the interest of this group of young theologians in pneumatology[160] once again points beyond itself to the ecumenical climate. Among other things one could point out that an increasing number of Pentecostal churches are growing rapidly and that many people find them far more attractive than both the traditional Catholic and Reformation churches. Moreover the Seventh General Assembly of the World Council of Churches took place in Canberra in 1991 under the slogan 'Come, Holy Spirit, and renew the face of the earth'.

This prayer shows that reflection on the Spirit of God is by no means a fashionable phenomenon of the time or a matter of opportunistic ecumenical politics. Behind it stands a problem of the utmost urgency. With the beginning of the 1990s people had become so massively and clearly aware of the ecological danger to all life on this planet, and not just human life, that they risked being overwhelmed by it. 'Whether humanity has a future or whether it is going to become extinct in the next few centuries depends on our will to live and that means our absolute will for our one, indivisible life' (xii). But where is this will to come from? On what sources should it or could it feed? Not all religions know how to move ahead. Some fall back on attitudes which are *de facto* distanced, orientated on the beyond.

This brief reference to the historical context already makes the programmatic content of the title clear: 'The Spirit of Life' is the origin and source, the means of salvation and goal of all that lives. It is cosmic and universal. This is expressed very aptly in the English sub-title, which speaks of 'A Universal Affirmation'. Moltmann is in fact concerned to make a universal confession of God who calls everything into existence so that it delights in this life and in so doing delights in God. The book is the unfolding of belief in the power of this God who gives breath and soul to all that lives, so that it can become whole and holy.

'Where can we find the religion which Albert Schweitzer sought for, the religion of an unconditional affirmation of life, and a comprehensive "reverence for life"? I have in mind a theology which springs from the experience of life, a theology similar to the one which Friedrich Christoph Oetinger conceived in 1765, when he wrote his *Theologia ex idea vitae deducta* as a counter-blast to the mechanistic philosophy of the Enlightenment' (xii). But what can be meant by the 'idea of life'?

1. God's ruach – *creative power and power of life*

As in all his other books, here too Moltmann first investigates the biblical basis. Spirit, the Old Testament *ruach*, is the 'divine energy of life' (40). If we are to grasp the full meaning of this term we must forget meanings which have attached themselves to the word 'spirit' (*pneuma, spiritus, esprit*) in the Western tradition, since these always have associations of the incorporeal, immaterial and supernatural. By contrast *ruach* is breeze and hurricane, breath and soul, the creative energy which holds every atom in tension and makes every nerve vibrate in us. 'The Western cleavage between spirit and body, spirituality and sensuousness is so deeply rooted in our languages that we must have recourse to other translations if we want to arrive at a more or less adequate rendering of the word *ruach*' (40). I ask myself why Moltmann nevertheless retains the word 'spirit'. Would it have not made more sense to use the Hebrew word *ruach* and thus work at establishing it in German and other languages, as has already happened with a considerable degree of success in the case of the word *shalom*? Furthermore *ruach* is feminine in German; it is the motherly energy, the soul of the whole. This *feminine maternal dimension* would also be important to correct the male associations in the Trinity (the Father, the Son and the Holy Spirit).

So the *ruach* is the divine creative energy. To the degree that it is divine energy it remains transcendent to all that is created. In that it has an effect in all that is created, it is immanent in it. 'The creative power of God is the transcendent side of the *ruach*. The power to live enjoyed by everything that lives is its immanent side' (42). Thus Moltmann arrives at the paradoxical sounding designation 'immanent transcendence' (31ff.) for God's Spirit. However, it loses its paradoxical ring when we remember that in Moltmann all terms are to be understood in the light of forward movement and process. 'Because the forward direction allows us to perceive the time element – the irretrievability of every event, the irreversibility of future and past, and the partial indeterminacy of that sphere of possibility which we call future – we can then grasp the temporal rhythms of life, which vibrate between transcendence and immanence, and fan out the network of life's relationship into the spheres of the possible' (227).

What applies to the creaturely process of what lives, also applies to the properties of soul and 'spirit'. In biblical thinking the *ruach* is also 'wisdom', the ensouling power of ordering in all things and thus also the ensouling force in human awareness. It is important that Moltmann combines the notions of *ruach* in the Bible with the Jewish notion of the Shekinah. Thus the *ruach*-Shekinah becomes the 'presence of God' which travels with us (48). This Shekinah theology (51) is important for three reasons. 1. It emphasizes the 'personal character of the Spirit'. 'The Spirit is the efficacious presence of God himself' (51). 2. This tradition emphasizes the sensibility of God, for the Shekinah also suffers in all the suffering which comes upon creatures just as it also rejoices in all that is joyful. And finally, 3. It brings the kenotic aspect to bear. God becomes capable of suffering; his indwelling in the world of the created makes God vulnerable. I have already mentioned on several occasions that this Shekinah theology is the bridge which is to root Moltmann's trinitarian thought in the Bible and to associate it with Jewish notions. Similarly, it has also been demonstrated that it is the bridge which forms links with the messianic understanding of Jesus Christ. 'To be filled with the Spirit is God's Shekinah' (55), Moltmann remarks, referring to the vision in Ezek.37, the subject of which is the raising up of the people. It is precisely this divine power which also raised the crucified from the dead.

I have first emphasized the continuity in the biblical understanding of *ruach*, since in my view it cannot be emphasized often enough that it is this understanding of *ruach* which associates the experience of the Spirit in the Christian community with the experience of the Spirit in Israel. The *ruach* is the bond which links the two Testaments. It is of course part of this that the Spirit which ensouls the life and mission of Jesus to his death is none other than this *ruach* which from the beginning is with God. The Gospels show, albeit with different accents, that Jesus lived and worked in the power of the *ruach*. 'What begins with his baptism through the operation of the Spirit ends with his passion through the operation of the Spirit' (64). This kenotic aspect is as central as the other, that the resurrection of the Crucified One also took place in the power of the pneuma. 'Christ was raised through Yahweh's *ruach*, the divine energy of life, so that his raising and his presence as "the Living One" is the manifestation *of the Spirit*, which will transform this transitory world into the new world of eternal life' (66). In this connection it is highly significant that many early Christian communities spoke of the Spirit of God as 'mother'. The 'Paraclete' whom Jesus promises to send according to the Johannine farewell discourses comforts 'as a mother comforts one' (John 14.26). These maternal traits in the concept of the Spirit are then fought against as Gnostic and sectarian by the church with a patriarchal and episcopal constitution which is establishing itself in the Roman empire. However, they have been preserved in the mystical literature, for example in the fifty homilies of Makarios, which go back to Symeon of Mesopotamia. Moltmann shows that these homilies were adopted in the seventeenth century by rising Pietism and became influential there. It is in keeping with this line that in 1741 Count Zinzendorf proclaimed the 'motherly office of the Holy Spirit' as official community doctrine (159).[161]

2. *Experience – the medium of* ruach

If God's *ruach* is present in every phase of our life and in every expression of our existence, then it is manifestly not enough to speak of the knowledge of the Spirit. A term must be found which reflects the perception of the divine energy as holistically as possible. Moltmann finds it in the term 'experience'. Here he sets himself apart from Karl Barth, who on the basis of his narrow understanding of revelation repudiated any theology of experience as an inappropriate mastering of the 'Word' of God which in principle cannot be experienced. 'By setting up this antithesis between revelation and experience, Barth merely replaced the theological immanentism which he complained about by a theological transcendentalism,' Moltmann judges. In the basis of his dynamized concept of transcendent immanence he then says, 'Because God's Spirit is present in human beings, the human spirit is self-transcendentally aligned towards God' (7). However, that is again a dangerous sentence, because it suggests an ontic self-evidence which is difficult to defend, particularly against the background of everyday human experience. When and how is this self-transcendence orientated on God to express itself? What Moltmann has in mind is not an ontic self-evidence but an eschatological self-evidence.[162] In that case it must be said that because God's Spirit is the power of the raising of the dead, the new creation of all that is made and the restoration of all things, this power is also at work in human beings as the power of rebirth, sanctification and glorification and thus is aimed at the transformation of human beings in the kingdom of God.

Is the concept of experience subjective, chance and arbitrary? Is it suitable for designating the different forms of human discernment, which range from the creaturely unconscious to highly complex sophistication? At the beginning of Part I, which is about the 'experiences of the Spirit', Moltmann states: 'By experience of the Spirit I mean an awareness of God in, with and beneath the experience of life, which gives us assurance of God's fellowship, friendship and love' (18). Such experience lives on the one hand from the memory of Christ and on the other in the expectation of his kingdom, but it can occasionally also attain an ecstatic experience of the immediate presence of God.

Experiences stamp the lives of all men and women and form their particular subjectivity. However, such subjectivity is always at the same time moulded as intersubjectivity, because the creating and receiving of experiences always take place in relationships. These include not only interpersonal relationships but also experiences of community and nature. If we remember this diversity of experiences, we may not start from modern consciousness of the self but must allow a 'many-dimensioned concept of experience' (34). Here it is important to replace the exclusive reference to personal experience ('What does this or that mean for me?') with the inclusive question of the different effects of experience. Then the 'relating of things to the horizon' would take the place of 'perception related to the subject' (36). By relationship to the horizon I understand the perception (by intimation, feeling, intuition, reflection) of the infinite networks in which all things communicate with one another and in which we are caught as beings who perceive. Such an understanding of totality then sets itself critically over against modern tendencies to contrast the perceiving human subject categorically with 'objects', i.e. the body and nature. This exaltation of reason over the body and nature has encouraged an anthropocentrism and a thinking in splits which by now can be seen quite manifestly to inflict violent destruction upon nature. Consequently a Christian doctrine of the Spirit must break out of the narrow circle of an approach orientated on immediate consciousness of self so that it is in a position to know God as the 'lover of life'. The holistic programme thus follows from this many-dimensioned concept of experience, and this corresponds appropriately to the biblical concept of *ruach*.

3. *Living in the Spirit – the dynamic of grace*

Moltmann's doctrine of the Spirit has three main parts. The first opens the discussion of the theme, especially in respect of the concept of experience. Part III, entitled 'The Fellowship and Person of the Spirit', is essentially concerned with classical theological problems arising from pneumatology, particularly in relation to ecclesiology and the theology of the Trinity, here above all the problem of the spirit as person. (As we shall see, this is done in a very 'unclassical' way.) But the central part is the core of the book, and not just by virtue of its extent. Its seven chapters are about 'Life in the Spirit', and what is discussed here moved me most. This used to be called the *ordo salutis*, the 'orderly way' of salvation; today people are fond of talking about 'spirituality'. But neither term approaches the range and diversity of the aspects on which Moltmann works in this major part. The key words are liberation, justification, rebirth, sanctification, charismatic powers and mystical experience. These terms still sound quite ecclesiastical and traditional, but the way in which they are developed shows that this is no introverted piety of the heart but is about the question 'How can we live in the presence of the Spirit today? What is the meaning of the presence of the power of God for the world of today, which seems to have been taken over by the powers of evil?'

So in what follows I want to go on to speak in rather more detail about the themes of this central part.

(a) Liberation

How far is God's *ruach* a power of liberation? Many modern men and women say with Ernst Bloch, 'Where the great Lord of the world reigns, there is no room for liberty, not even for the liberty of the children of God.' In his view "Liberty, equality and fraternity" is a vision that can be upheld only without God and contrary to the earthly authorities who reign "by the grace of God"'(105). Moltmann asserts against this that the modern alternative, 'God or freedom', is fundamentally the alternative between a revolutionary concept of freedom and a conservative understanding of authority, between an egalitarian principle of relationships and a hierarchical pattern of order. Moltmann does conceal the fact that Christianity has often taken the side of conservative, hierarchical thought. But he emphasizes that the Bible speaks of a God whose rule is 'the wide free space he gives for the freedom of his people' (100). To experience God means to experience the promising and dangerous happiness of freedom; for freedom is not as simple as that. Who can really live in freedom without becoming anxious, without suffering the chains of a lack of freedom or longing for the security and protection of preconceived opinions? 'The liberation theology of Latin America is the first convincing outline to combine belief in God with the will to be free,' Moltmann remarks (109). It has understood history 'as the space of God's revelation and the place where human beings encounter God', and has replaced 'the world in relation to the cosmos' with the 'future orientation of history' (110), thus at the same time laying the foundation for an ethical and political understanding of the history for which human beings are to be responsible. But since in Moltmann the 'orientation on the future' is always related eschatologically to God's kingdom, the experience of historical liberation passes over into the expectation of redemption. Courage to live and comfort in dying come from one and the same source.

Such freedom is 'creative passion for the possible', 'productive fantasy', inspired by the 'messianic daydream about the new life, the whole, healed life, the life that is at last entirely living' (119). Therefore such freedom does not define itself as the power to rule but as social and communal empowerment. 'We discover freedom in the relationship of determining *subjects* to the *project* they share' (119).

'Where the Spirit of the Lord is, there is freedom,' says Paul (II Cor.3.17). Those who allow themselves to be grasped by this freedom are not caught, but released. The Spirit of the Lord Christ constitutes itself as 'free power', 'free space' or 'free place' (121) and thus creates the broad space for the creative and confident presence of the Spirit.

(b) Justification

What is the specific meaning of justification for those who commit sin and those who suffer sin? A universal concept of sin can mislead us into veiling the grave differences between those without rights and the unjust. It is correct that God has mercy on sinners, but this means that God helps those without rights to secure their rights and the unjust to their conversion. Therefore 'the Protestant doctrine about the justification of sinners, and today's theology about the liberation of the oppressed, do not have to be antitheses. They can correct and enrich one another mutually' (128). In his cross Christ is the seal of divine mercy for all, but for that reason this mercy must have different effects on contradictory experiences of sin. 'The liberation of the oppressed from the suffering of oppression requires the liberation of the oppressor form the injustice of oppression' (132). So if we regard justification as an expression of the power of God, we catch sight of its effect in raising up, judging and thus putting right.

The very way in which Moltmann deals with the difficult aspect of atonement in this context is important. 'There is no forgiveness of sins without atonement,' he states, not without adding the question 'Who can atone?'. But as atonement is not a human possibility, God himself must atone. In his mercy he bears (endures) human guilt in suffering. 'As long as the world exists, God 'does not merely carry the world's history of suffering. He carries humanity's history of injustice too' (134).

Fortunately Moltmann does not limit himself to a personalistic concept of sin. He also speaks of sin in structures, for example of the 'progressive destruction of the environment, both the atmosphere and the earth', which is produced by the 'major project of modern society' (139). Here sin appears as the doom in which we human beings experience ourselves both as perpetrators and victims, as producers and products. What does justification mean for people who are in these vicious circles and deadly spirals (139)? Moltmann illuminates merely the legal implications of a solidarity which changes structures. He speaks of the 'justice of compassion' as the highest form of justice and as the 'creative source of justice for every rule of law' (142). However, unfortunately he does not discuss what this must mean in detail.

I think it important that under the key words 'liberation' and 'justification' Moltmann brings the side of the perpetrator and of the victim into place. This makes it clear that the liberating and justifying message addresses perpetrators and victims in different ways and opens up complementary processes of reconciliation and peace. So I find the absence of an explicit discussion of the theme of forgiveness all the more striking. Does not the 'forgiveness of sins' have an extraordinarily striking place in the third

article of the creeds of the early church? Precisely because
Moltmann has left behind the traditional fixation on the perpetrator in the concept of sin, it would have been possible for
him to show the dynamic of forgiveness between victims and
perpetrators which puts things right. Here I shall limit myself to
a few questions.[163] 1. Important though it is to depict atonement
as a dimension which ultimately is only in the power of God,
does that make superfluous any discussion about programmes to
put damage right and to share burdens – I am deliberately avoiding the difficult term 'reparation'? Surely not! 2. The significance
of the law is doubtless central. Nevertheless, in many cases of
violence the law is far too coarse and useless an instrument. One
need only think of the subtle hurts and injuries which do not fall
under the law and yet can seriously damage the shared life of
couples, friends and relations. So are there healing processes
which lie beyond the possibilities that the law opens up?
3. Precisely because I agree with Moltmann that the compassion
of God is the creative source of justice, there should have been
closer reflection on the possibilities and limits of amnesty. 4.
Moltmann rightly emphasizes that federative-democratic ordinances are needed to overcome structural injustices. That makes
it all the more important to work out the relationship between
traumatization (through the collective experience of injustice)
and the capacity for covenant (for avoiding new injustice). Does
not the trend towards violence in many international conflicts lie
in the fact that peoples do not find their way out of the vicious
circles of collective hurts and patterns of retaliation and precisely
because of this remain incapable of entering into reliable
alliances for building up peaceful conditions?

(c) Rebirth

If justification was the core term of the Reformation, 'rebirth'
represents the codeword of Pietism and the revivalist movements
of the eighteenth and nineteenth centuries. Here 'rebirth' is really
a misleading term. What is in fact meant is not *re*generation but
the beginning of a new life. '*Incipit vita nova* – a new life begins,

as the conversation with Nicodemus in John 3.3–5 shows' (145). So a new life begins and therefore it would be better to speak of 'new birth'.

Why does Moltmann have such an interest in 'rebirth'? He clearly thinks it of decisive importance to set up the dimension of hope of the new life in the centre of life that is passing away. 'Rebirth' and 'living hope' belong together. Here too the anchoring in the Trinity is helpful. 'The *eternal foundation* of rebirth is the mercy of God, the Father of Jesus Christ. The *historical foundation* for rebirth is Christ, or to be more exact, the resurrection of Christ from the dead . . . *The medium* of rebirth is the holy Spirit, which is "richly poured out"' (146, my italics).[164] The systematic interest consists in emphasizing the cosmic scope and the process-type dynamic of salvation and thus overcoming a reduction to a forgiveness of sins which is understood only personally or inwardly. '*A coherent process issues* from the rebirth of Christ from death through the Spirit, by way of the rebirth of mortal human beings through the Spirit, to the universal rebirth of the cosmos through the Spirit' (153, my italics). It is this universal undertow of the divine life which leads to a radical affirmation of life, in particular also in all its broken and damaged forms. This has been seen and stated above all by mystics. So it is not surprising that in this context Moltmann takes up Hildegard of Bingen's concept of *viriditas*, the greening power of the Spirit, and refers to the 'maternal office of the Spirit' that has already been mentioned.

Of course the sacramental anchoring of this universal view of rebirth lies in baptism. And in this way Moltmann restores to baptism a meaning which it has often lost in current baptismal practice. Nevertheless this aspect, relevant though it is, denotes only the *incipit*, the beginning, the opening to a new history. And this stands under another leading concept.

(d) Sanctification

What is new born wants to grow. And growth in the power of the holy *ruach* is sanctification. It is significant for German-speaking theology fixated on the Reformation heritage that here Moltmann speaks of John Wesley, from whom the Methodist church derives (163ff.). Because Wesley thought in terms of the 'new man', he regarded sin as 'sickness', so that for him justification appeared as healing and sanctification. 'Holiness' and 'wholeness' thus come close together. The salvation of the world has a therapeutic, a healing function for the sick and injured world.

I think it important that Moltmann speaks enthusiastically of 'sanctification today' (186), for at least in Germany, the churches have become so afraid that they no longer feel able to address the claim of salvation to human life and to a healthy communal life with other people and with nature. Moltmann refers to Albert Schweitzer's 'reverence for life'; he calls for the 'renunciation of violence' (172) and describes 'sanctification today' as the 'search for the harmonies and accords of life' (173). I could have wished that he had given examples relating these creative impulses to human sexuality, for it is there that ethical uncertainty is particularly striking, also in church circles. What would a renunciation of violence mean for a rediscovery of the healing and inspiring power of Eros since love has degenerated into crude 'sex' according to which children are only 'made' and consequently can also be 'unmade'? What does Schweitzer's principle of reverence mean for dealing with human fertility, especially for men? Precisely because Moltmann is not afraid to describe the power of the Spirit as 'eroticizing energy' (196), it would have been worth his while to make even more of a resolute and extended effort to bring the beauty and power of Eros into sexual relations and thus overcome the narrow-mindedness and fears which surround much of the churches' discussion of human sexuality.

(e) Charismatic power

The gifts and endowments which people have can be attuned to the negative; then they develop their destructive power as 'tormenting spirits'. I often think what fabulous gifts the great Mafia bosses have. How inventive and full of energy they are, and how capable their organization! And yet all these powers are put at the service of brutal enrichment, heedless self-benefit and a naked lust for power. But where human gifts and endowments are inspired by the Spirit of life they unfold their constructive and healing powers which serve life. Where grace (Greek *charis*) permeates our lives, our powers become charismata, gifts of grace. Following Paul, Moltmann distinguishes between the everyday charism which includes being a father or a mother, but also faithfulness and reliability in everyday relationships, from the special relationships in the discipleship of Jesus among which he includes the 'kerygmatic', the 'diaconal' and the 'cybernetic' (297). I think it important that he avoids giving the impression that charismatic gifts can be confused with bodily or psychological health. It is important that a handicapped life, too, is or can be charismatic, for the present-day cult of invulnerability leads to an underestimation of people who have to cope with lasting impairments.

It therefore also seems to me important to supplement Moltmann's remarks by saying that charismatic endowments must not be seen as a human trait and consequently a possession. They remain the powers of the Spirit, and therefore are 'loans'. Where they no longer serve to further community, to increase love and to extend respect and faithfulness, they can be withdrawn again. Then we really are forsaken by all the powers of good. It seems to me that this is a perspective which ought to be brought into play more clearly in dialogue with the so-called 'charismatic communities'. There are charismatics who give the impression that they virtually have the Spirit in their hands, whereas others do not trust their 'little power'.

4. *The Holy Spirit as person*

'A more precise discernment of the personhood of the Holy Spirit is the most difficult problem in pneumatology in particular and in the doctrine of the Trinity generally' (268). Moltmann begins the last chapter of his pneumatology with this statement, and precisely because one can only agree with him here one is eager to know what solution he is able to offer.

First of all he dissociates himself from the Western concept of person formulated by Boethius and disseminated by Augustine and Thomas Aquinas. According to this, person is the *rationalis naturae individua substantia*. But the persons of the divine Trinity cannot be encompassed by this definition starting from the human being, or more precisely from the male.

In general Moltmann thinks it inappropriate to want to approach the personality of the Spirit with a preconceived concept of person. Even if one had a concept of person for the 'Father' and the 'Son', that would not comprehend the personality of the Spirit, for each of these three persons is original and unique.

But do notes like 'unique' and 'original' mean that conceptual definitions must be dispensed with? In a sense that is the case. So Moltmann adopts another course. On the basis of the biblical evidence he develops four groups of metaphors in which experiences of the Spirit are described. First he mentions the 'personal metaphors', which describe the Spirit as 'Lord, mother and as judge' (270). These concepts denote a natural subject, a 'subject' whom human beings encounter in one of these capacities. But that does not yet clarify whether and how this 'subject' understands itself personally or what its relationship is to the other persons of the Trinity.

Moltmann then speaks of 'formative metaphors' and mentions 'energy, space and form' (274). These are the formative forces which surround, permeate and shape all that is alive. As creative beings we live by these forces, and therefore we cannot even 'define' them but must leave them in their inexhaustibility. Thirdly Moltmann mentions the 'movement metaphors: tempest – fire – love' (278). Here the points of contact with biblical notions of *ruach* can be recognized particularly clearly. There follow, fourthly, the 'mystical metaphors: light – water – fertility' (281). These also occur often in the biblical writings but suggest an 'organic cohesion' (285) between the divine and the human. We know this 'You in me – I in you' above all from the Johannine writings. It has had a particular attraction for mystics.

Now it is striking that Moltmann quotes mystical texts not only in this fourth group of metaphors, but also in the case of the three others. He mentions Hildegard of Bingen above all with approval. I conclude from this that the mere attempt to approach the nature of the spirit of God with metaphors is mystical. It is typical of the mystical tradition that it speaks of the nearness of God, but also knows of the tormenting experience of the distant God, that it is ensouled and blessed, enflamed and consumed by God's overflowing power of attraction but at the same time knows the absence of God as the 'dark night of the soul'. If God's triune being is a 'history of love' as Moltmann says, then it is the mystics who experience – and endure – this love most intensively. They are the ones who abandon themselves to this history for better or worse. So Moltmann stands more deeply in the mystical tradition than he is prepared to concede.

But what about Moltmann's most difficult question, the personality of the Spirit? He makes the attempt 'to deduce the contours of his (i.e. the Spirit's) personhood'. This is 'a deductive knowing, derived from the operation experienced' (285) to the operator. Therefore the need is to move from experience to understanding. But precisely this is impossible with the Spirit of God, for 'we cannot make whatever encompasses us an object without moving out of it' (287).

There precisely is the problem, and in my view Moltmann does not think its consequences through to the end. If any concept essentially has something to do with conceptualizing, and thus if any conceptualizing has as its presupposition something that is objectified, and if every attempt to understand God's Spirit has to do with the objectification of the Spirit and consequently has to be paid for with a distancing from this Spirit, then para-doxically we are on the way towards becoming spirit-less precisely in conceptualizing the Spirit. It follows from this th conceptual distancing is not only impossible in respect of the Spirit of God but is not even desirable. And indeed Moltmann gets into difficulties with his attempt at a conceptual definition of the *ruach* of God. I honestly confess that I do not know what to make of the term 'the streaming personhood of the divine Spirit' (285) which he proposes. I cannot imagine what 'streaming personality' means. Here again I see a metaphor. And one should not seek anything else in respect of the Spirit of God. For it must be possible to generalize concepts, definitions, if they are not to be incomprehensible. They must by nature remain within the framework of what can be comprehended; they describe limits, and precisely here do not encompass the Spirit of God because that transcends such a framework.

Therefore the mystics were right to maintain that their passionate attempts to approach God were in principle metaphorical and to respect the fact that God dwells in a light that no one can attain. So we can keep with Angelus Silesius, who maintained: 'God is pure nothingness, no now and here touches him. The more you reach after him, the more he escapes you.'[165]

However, Moltmann passes over this reference and also attempts to say something about the inner-trinitarian personality of the Spirit. Can his nature be inferred from the relationships which constitute him and not just from the effect on creatures? 'With all due caution about speculation and over-hasty dogmatizations' (290), Moltmann goes through the thought models of trinitarian theology in the Eastern and Western church and finally concludes that 'trinitarian doxology is the *Sitz im Leben* for the concept of the immanent Trinity' (320). One arrives at this kind of doxology in analogy to the mystical ladder of love. Lovers go from the gift to the giver until finally they no longer think of the gift but come to fulfilment in wonder at the beloved. In this wonderment 'all self-love stops and the wonderer sinks wholly into the selfless contemplation of God' (302). Then the thanksgiving turns into praise: 'Glory be to the Father and to the Son and to the Holy Spirit, as it was in the beginning is now and ever shall be, world without end.'

wanting to comprehend ends in doxology. This no longer

seeks to define, nor in the end does it even want to understand any more, but stands in awe at a fullness which bursts all notions apart. 'Of course in human doxology the Trinity becomes an unfathomable *mystery* which excels all imaginings and concepts' (304). I think it significant that in facing the ungraspable reality of God Moltmann moves from wanting to understand to worship. What he wants to say *about* God thus ultimately becomes what he says *to* God. Theology turns into prayer.

Thus the doxology becomes the final point of theological knowledge; it reveals that theology too is to be a form of prayer. It comes from wonder and culminates in wonderment. All those who pray often find that they must endure the experience of the alien and hidden God and only attain for moments an intimation of the divine glory. But such moments have given wings to the hope that one day the eternal moment will come in which God emerges from his hiddenness, in which all creation loses its rents and darknesses and God will be all in all.

It is therefore certainly no chance that Moltmann ends his pneumatology with the Pentecost hymn of Hrabanus Maurus, since all theological knowledge arises from the invocation of the power of God and in the invocation of the power of God it is fulfilled.

12

What Remains is Expectation:
The Coming of God

The key words which we met in the first four volumes of the 'Contributions' like 'history of love', 'indwelling', 'sabbath of creation', 'messiahship', 'wholeness', also stamp Moltmann's eschatology.[166] His doctrine of the *'eschata'*, the last things, develops in rings which become ever wider. Here I have been reminded of Rilke's well-known lines:

> I live my life in growing rings,
> which spread out over things.
> Perhaps I will not complete the last,
> but I shall attempt it.

These 'growing rings' of Moltmann's eschatology develop from four questions: What will become of me? ('personal eschatology'), What will become of history? ('historical eschatology'), What will become of the cosmos? ('cosmic eschatology') and What will become of God? ('divine eschatology'). These four dimensions of Christian eschatology form the real body of the book in Chapters II-V. (Under the theme 'Eschatology Today', Chapter I offers an analysis of the situation in which Moltmann marks out his own position over against Barth, Althaus and Bultmann, and the 'rebirth of messianic thought in Judaism', i.e. grounded in Bloch, Rosenzweig, Scholem and Benjamin).

When we look at the four parts, it is striking that the second aspect, 'historical eschatology', is the most extensive. Here Moltmann occupies himself in detail with the millenarian and chiliastic currents which have become important for the history of the church and for world history. By contrast, 'cosmic' eschatology turns out much briefer, whereas at seventeen pages 'divine' eschatology is really only a brief 'attempt' (to pick up Rilke's words again).

1. *'He who comes' – time in the advent of God*

To begin with the decisive question: does a Christian eschatology, if it wants to be Christian, really deal with the 'last things'? Is it really concerned with the 'final solution' of world history, as happens in the violent apocalyptic fantasies, the dreams of Armageddon? 'If eschatology were no more than religion's "final solution" to all the questions, a solution allowing it to have the last word, it would undoubtedly be a particularly unpleasant form of theological dogmatism, if not psychological terrorism. And it has in fact been used in just this way by a number of apocalyptic arm-twisters among our contemporaries' (xi). But an eschatology is Christian if it seeks to be none other than 'the remembered hope of the raising of the crucified Christ' (xi) and thus in the *end* – and everything in time moves towards its end – proclaims the *beginning*.

How can it be that a beginning stands over against all that is finite? That this is the case is grounded in the gospel of the coming God. 'Grace be to you and peace from him who is, and who was and who is to come', we read at the beginning of the Revelation of John (1.4). That statement could be the biblical motto of the whole book, since it designates this decisive shift in the understanding of time which Christian faith owes to Jewish faith. Here we have the recognition that time does not consist simply in its ongoing linearity. In that case the future would merely be the past that is not yet past. However, there is not just the 'future' but also the 'advent', that which comes towards us. If the mysterious tetragrammaton YHWH of the Jewish name of God means that God will be who he will be, this means that our God is the coming one, that God is coming towards everything temporal, and thus is futurity – diachronous to all time. Ernst

Bloch had spoken of a God with 'future as the essence of his being'. Moltmann speaks of God with 'futurity as the essence of his being'. That is a decisive difference. '*The God of hope* is himself the *coming God*,' Moltmann writes, and continues: 'The power of the future is his power in time. His eternity is not timeless simultaneity; it is the power of his future over every historical time' (24). 'So if all times and all history are comprehended against this horizon of the futurity of God, there is an inexhaustible added value' (24), which in fact gives us every occasion to hope with the seer of Patmos for 'grace' and 'peace'. That denotes the point from which Moltmann criticizes the 'transposition of eschatology into time' (96), which for example in Albert Schweitzer led to a dropping of eschatology or in Oscar Cullmann to a series of periods in salvation history. From this perspective he also criticizes the 'transposition of eschatology into eternity' in dialectical theology. In his eschatology Moltmann is not concerned with future history but with the future of history. He wants to have as a basis an 'advent concept of the future'. Thus the future is presupposed as the possibility of time generally (26). In other words, the future is understood as the 'origin and source of time' (22). What is gained by this? The perception of time changes. If the power of God is defined as future, then it defines the past as past future, the present as present future and future time as future future. If we take up the image of the source, then we have to assume a flow of time which streams from God's inexhaustible future and forms all world time. In that case all possibilities also flow from this source; everything becomes contingent. God's advent historically takes form in the 'category *Novum*'.[167]

This beginning takes up statements which we have already met in *Theology of Hope*. What is new in *The Coming of God* is the deep anchoring in 'messianic thinking in Judaism' (29ff.). Ernst Bloch's 'Metaphysics from Messianic Sources' is quoted, which can already be recognized in the 1918 *Spirit of Utopia*. Bloch's philosophy of hope, which at the same time was an expression of his abiding indignation at all injustice and suffering, is ultimately rooted in the 'Jewish longing for a return home in the exile of the world' (33). When Moltmann puts the categories of 'advent' and '*novum*' in an eschatological-historical dialectic, this associates him with Franz Rosenzweig, who had combined the category of purpose with 'redemption as a category of the expectation of a total change possible at any moment' (35). With Rosenzweig, Moltmann speaks of the 'reversal' of the relation of the times. It is not the past that determines the course of history. Rather, *the future creates the 'undertow' which 'makes' history*. In Gershom Scholem and his theology of the sabbath Moltmann finds a form of communication of the messianic expectation which makes it present in rhythm and ritual. The celebration of the sabbath is the anchor for a 'deferred life'.

Moltmann finds another source in Walter Benjamin's 'theses on the philosophy of history' because Benjamin had emphasized the 'sudden messianic presence of eternity'. This 'moment' is determined in a way that is both mystical and revolutionary at the same time.

In the thinking of Bloch, Rosenzweig, Scholem and Benjamin the 'moment' seems to be the point at which futurity touches, breaks up and opens temporality. 'Does the moment tower out of time so that in the light of that moment those touched by it can see the future of the redeemed world in God, and God in the redeemed world?' That would then be a 'mystical *nunc stans*' and a 'messianic splinter' in time (45). Therefore Moltmann comes to the conclusion: 'There is evidently this mystical inter-pretation of "the moment" that "leaves nothing more to be desired", and there is the messianic interpretation, which throws open new perspectives, and discloses everything that is to be desired' (45).

Here Moltmann distinguishes between the mystical interpre-tation, which knows that 'nothing' more is to be desired, and the messianic interpretation, which claims that 'everything' is to be desired. But now the 'nothing' and the 'everything' are mystical concepts, words which go beyond what is imaginable and thus also desirable. Not to want anything more or to want everything amount to the same thing. Therefore I think it erroneous to distinguish the mystical in principle from the messianic. There are also links between them. Bloch, Rosenzweig or Scholem are thus to be understood probably only as messianic mystics or mystical 'messianics'. And that would also apply to Moltmann.

2. *What will become of me?*

Personal eschatology is sparked off by the question: what happens at death? How are we to, indeed how can we, imagine that in this end there is a beginning? What should and can the term 'eternal life' mean?

In his 'personal eschatology' (49ff.), Moltmann begins from the insight that death is thought of as being so terrible only because it wounds the love which binds us to life, our own and that of others. The fact that human life is rooted in love makes our death more than a natural phenomenon that we share with all living beings; it transforms death into a collapse of relationships and therefore it can spark off groundless anxiety and inconsolable mourning. Living means learning to love and therefore also learning to mourn. 'But in what we love we also become vulnerable, for in this affirmation of life we open the door to happiness and pain, life and death' (55). Only as those who love do we become consciously alive and consciously mortal. Therefore the death of others, those whom we love, is the real experience of death. In ourselves we experience only the dying. But in others we experience death and having to go on living with this fact.

Therefore it is love from which all these questions come. Is all up with us at death? What happens to those whom we love when they are dead? Will we see each other again? It is wounded love which asks whether life that has fallen short here will one day be put right, whether all the broken, destroyed, unlived life will once again be healed, set upright and fulfilled. It is love which will not be content with being told that 'all is up' at death; for that would be the triumph of the absurd. 'Must we not think the thought of an ongoing history of God's with this life, if – in this world of disappointed, impaired, sick, murdered and destroyed life – we are to be able to affirm life and go on loving it notwithstanding?' (118).[168]

Now if we recall that Moltmann wants his – trinitarian – doctrine of God to be understood as a retelling of 'God's history of love', it becomes clear to us that he sees the future of our mortal lives anchored and transcended in this history of love. It is not only our love which will not stop at the limit of death; it is the love of God, who reaches out beyond the limits of death and snatches all that is transitory and fragmentary into his loving fullness in order to put right what has never achieved its rights. 'So I would think,' Moltmann writes at the conclusion of his 'personal thoughts' (116), 'that eternal life gives the broken and the impaired and those whose lives have been destroyed space and time and strength to live the life for which they were intended, and for which they were born. I think this, not for selfish reasons, for the sake of my personal fulfilment, nor morally, for the sake of some kind of purification; I think it *for the sake of the justice which I believe is God's concern and his first option*' (118, my italics).

From this position we can take up briefly the three major questions which stand at the centre of Moltmann's 'personal eschatology'.

(a) Resurrection of the flesh

First of all the age-old problem of the immortality of the soul and the resurrection of the flesh (58ff.). It is easy to recognize that Moltmann puts the whole emphasis on the resurrection of the flesh, for God's promise of eternal life means the whole person in its undivided identity of soul and body. Furthermore, it means the whole person in its deep bond with 'all flesh', i.e. all that is alive, so that the hope of the resurrection of the dead goes over into the hope of the new creation of all things and relationships. 'Resurrection' is interpreted as 'transformation' and 'metamorphosis' .'What happened to, and with, the dead Christ is a transformation and a transfiguration through and beyond dying and death, a transfiguration of his bodily form (Phil.3.21), a *metamorphosis* from our low estate into the form of glory

(Phil.2.6–11). In analogy to this, believers will see their deaths
too as part of the process to which this whole mortal creation
will be transfigured and be born again to become the kingdom of
glory' (77). Three things are important for me in these sentences.
First, the reference to the death and resurrection of Christ. Time
and again it is this reference to Christ which makes eschatology
'Christian'. Then the concept of analogy, according to which what
happened to Christ will happen to us. And finally the emphasis
on process leading to the 'kingdom of glory'. Here Moltmann is
manifestly thinking not of abstract eternity but of an eternal time
and eternal space into which this whole created world will be
transfigured and transformed and find its new and imperishable
homeland.

(b) Death and sin

The next question is: 'Is death the consequence of sin or life's
natural end?' (77). That death is the 'wages' of sin (Rom.6.23),
and thus that death is the payment for our sin, has had a persistent
effect in the history of the church. Only since the Enlightenment
has the view become established that death is the 'natural end' of
life. Moltmann on the one hand rejects the old idea that our
death is to be regarded as the 'natural end' of life. But on the
other he shows that the 'natural' is not so 'natural' but is 'in need
of redemption' (91). With Hildegard of Bingen he compares the
creation with winter, whereas the new creation is like the 'spring-
time when everything is green and beautiful' (91). Thus Moltmann
leaves behind the modern distinction between person and nature.
It is the bodily nature of human beings which implies their link
with nature. Therefore the death which human beings suffer is
also not to be distinguished categorically from the death which
takes place everywhere in nature. Therefore everything that has
to die consciously or unconsciously waits in mourning and longing for the future world in which death will be no more and
everything that has to suffer under the violence of death is overcome. Here too the personal eschatology logically passes over
into a cosmic eschatology.

(c) Where are the dead?

Finally Moltmann discusses the question 'Where are the dead?' (96ff.). He discusses the Catholic doctrine of purgatory and the Lutheran doctrine of the 'sleep of souls'.[169] Neither is satisfactory because they cannot really be thought of in terms of Christ. If Christ's rule has already begun with the resurrection, then the space and the time and the power in which the living and the dead are kept safe is also opened up. 'Not in us, not in the world, and not in the realm of spirits is the division into this world and the beyond which death brings with it overcome, but assuredly in the risen Christ. So in him we remain indestructibly and unforgettably joined with the dead in love for each other and in a common hope' (106f.). But how we are to think of this 'in' is not discussed.

3. Time itself becomes different

We have seen that 'personal eschatology' logically goes over into 'universal eschatology'. Moltmann calls the 'wider ring' that we now enter 'historical eschatology' (129ff.). Here we are no longer concerned with experiences that human beings have of their own history but with *the experiences that we have of history generally*. If the personal hope of resurrection was designated with the symbol 'eternal' life, Moltmann uses 'kingdom of God' as the symbol of hope for historical eschatology. (And this is in turn taken up into the symbol of the 'new creation of all things' when cosmic eschatology is discussed.)

As I have already indicated, with the 'historical eschatology' we come to the most extensive part of *The Coming of God*. So many notions and ways of understanding church history and politics are discussed under the key words 'messianic eschatology', 'millenarianism' and 'chiliasm' that in this context one cannot think of giving an appropriate account of them. I shall limit myself to discussing the two problems which Moltmann describes as the 'most difficult' and the 'most disputed'. The first is the understanding of time and the second the doctrine of the 'restoration of all things'.

Christian eschatology refers to the biblical witnesses. And as these are extraordinarily open to misunderstanding, it is not surprising either that the history of their exegesis and therefore the development of Christian eschatologies seem extraordinarily ambivalent. Most difficult beyond doubt was the notion derived from Jewish apocalyptic of a thousand-year kingdom which is taken up in Revelation 20 and which led to a variety of interpretations in subsequent periods. 'No eschatological hope has fascinated men and women as much as the idea of a thousand-year empire in which Christ and those who are his will reign on earth before the end of history,' Moltmann also remarks (146). This idea is of messianic origin and is called either 'chiliasm' or 'millenarianism'.[170]

Moltmann describes the 'political millenarianism' which thought that it would recognize Christ's thousand-year reign of peace in the Roman empire with the shift under Constantine. This prepared for a pattern of interpretation in imperial theology which could be applied to very different 'kingdoms'. That is true of 'Byzantinism' and 'Czarism'; it is true of the 'Holy Roman Empire of the German nation' and of the terrifying 'thousand-year empire' of Adolf Hitler. Millennarian notions stamped the consciousness of the mission of the United States and still do. Millenarianism experienced its ecclesiastical variant in the development of the papal church, which inherited the political chiliasm of the Roman empire. By understanding itself as the inspired counter-model of a *societas perfecta* over against the empires of the world which are passing away, this papal monarchy developed an absolutism with a downright murderous abundance of power.

As Moltmann demonstrates very vividly, this messianic model of interpretation also showed its inspiring power as a formative idea in modernity to counter the papal church. Now the world-wide seizure of power by European civilization was to usher in the 'Christian age' and thus the last, golden age of humankind. 'The radiance of glory returns once more: Enlightenment. Now comes the final exodus of human beings from their "self-inflicted tutelage" into the "free and public use of their reason". This is realized chiliasm' (186).

The danger of this model of interpretation does not just lie in the fact that it transforms the 'martyr eschatology' to be found in the Revelation of John into an 'eschatology of rule' and thus turns hope for liberation from the powers of death into permission for oppression, at the same time turning the element of resisting the oppressive powers of death into an oppressive instrument of the legitimation of the maintaining of power. The ease with which this model of explanation can be perverted should make us think twice. However, what in Moltmann's view really causes this inadmissible shift is the transformation of eschatology into teleology. 'Only chiliasm makes eschatology teleology' (186).

But how is this danger to be avoided? Would we not be well advised to take chiliastic imagination out of circulation as an unsuitable mythologoumenon? Moltmann thinks not. However much one must repudiate 'historical chiliasm' as a 'religious theory used to legitimate political or ecclesiastical power' which 'is exposed to acts of messianic violence and the disappointments of history' (192), one must energetically preserve 'eschatological chiliasm . . . as a necessary picture of hope in resistance, in suffering, and in the exiles of this world' (192). But what does such 'eschatological chiliasm' look like?

Here too Moltmann refers to the central point of reference of any Christian eschatology, i.e. to christology. And then the question becomes whether the 'chiliastic hope is based on Christ's coming, his surrender to death on the cross and his resurrection from the dead' (194). Now if it is attested that Christ has come into the world and been manifested in the crucified and risen Jesus, that means no less than that the new aeon has dawned in the midst of the aeon that is passing away. The kingdom of this Christ has appeared in and under the kingdoms of this world, but his rule is still disputed. And those who are on the side of the messiah in this battle may expect for themselves nothing other than what has happened to the 'leader of life'. So messianic mission can always also mean martyrdom, participation in the 'suffering of Christ'. What does this struggle mean for 'eschatological chiliasm'?

This is chiliasm which is concentrated on the 'resurrection *from* the dead' (195). And that brings us to discuss a point which is decisive for Moltmann's argument. 'But what resurrection is meant here? It is the especial and messianic "resurrection from the dead", not the universal and eschatological "resurrection of the dead". But the resurrection from the dead necessarily leads into a reign of Christ before the universal raising of the dead for the Last Judgment. That is to say, it leads into a messianic kingdom in history before the end of the world, or into a transitional kingdom leading from this transitory world-time into the new world that is God's' (195). Accordingly there is to be a kingdom of Christ before he hands all things over to the kingdom of his Father. It is to be a 'kingdom of transition' which is not to be found in world history, but does not yet represent 'God's new world' either. The typically chiliastic feature of this option is that the temporal preposition 'before' still plays a role; however the being outside time is eschatological'.

Moltmann thinks that his theory of a messianic transitional kingdom is in accord with Pauline theology, but I do not find it very convincing. When he himself says that the general resurrection of the dead is 'only the final consequence of that process of new creation which began with the coming of Christ' (196), I do not see why he has to assume a 'kingdom of the Son' before the kingdom of the Father. This is needed simply to rescue the idea of chiliasm.

When Moltmann keeps emphasizing that eschatology in no way represents something new in time but transforms time itself, then constructions which still work as it were in the world of the Trinity with a before and afterwards become superfluous. It looks as if Moltmann wanted still to recognize a qualitative difference between what he calls 'historical eschatology' and 'cosmic eschatology', as if the 'kingdom of God' were still something less than the 'new creation of all things'. But are these not mental games which overstretch terms like 'kingdom' and 'new heaven – new earth' and end up making them meaningless?

So the difficulties with the concept of time remain. Indeed in my view they cannot be overcome at all, since the forms and possibilities of human talk about time are as such time-conditioned and persist within time. So if human beings think beyond time, their language takes them to a limit at which it threatens no longer to be communicable or understandable. They call for an 'imaginative leap' (to use Whitehead's phrase) which takes us to the limit of comprehension. I therefore have the impression that eschatology always and by nature represents the crossing of a boundary and that this should also be brought out in language. The notions which seem to me humanly possible for the crossing of this boundary are those of myth. Indeed it is no coincidence that the Revelation of John works with many mythical images. I find the forms of language which are possible for us in the witness of the mystics and in the language of prayer, i.e. in invocation and doxology.

By contrast, the linguistic form of indicative discourse which progresses systematically suggests a certainty which in my view does not exist. The following sentences make this quite clear: 'The chiliastic expectation mediates between world history here, and the end of the world and the new world there. It makes the end as transition imaginable: christocracy is the transition from the world's present condition to its coming consummation. The transition will be brought about through a series of events and the succession of various different phases' (201). These apparently simple statements suggest a plausibility which I cannot go along with. What is meant by the 'here' and 'there'? What 'series of events' and what 'succession of various different phases' suggest themselves, which 'bring about' a 'transition' from 'the world's present condition' to its 'coming consummation'? I get the impression that these words from our everyday life must inevitably collapse and become meaningless under the burden of chiliastic expectation with which they are loaded.

So I am in no way arguing against the eschatology, but for a more conscious reflection on the appropriate form of language for eschatology. It seems to me absolutely necessary that we retain the notion that our lifetime as human beings and the time of nature and the cosmos are embraced by the time of God, indeed that they flow from his time, as from an inexhaustible source. But precisely for that reason we must find a language that shows people that the interest in eschatology is more than a whim of theological specialists. If 'hope' in Indonesian is the same as 'seeing through the horizon', that gives us an indication of the span of hope, which I regard as indispensable for coping with the terrors in our time.

What becomes of history concerns us all, precisely because we live in an end-time which we have ourselves made and have brought upon ourselves. The date 6 August 1945 stands for this. It marks the dropping of an atomic bomb on Hiroshima. Since then humankind has had the formula to destroy itself.

It is the merit of Moltmann's eschatology that it clearly emphasizes this end-time condition. The means of nuclear mass destruction signal the 'nuclear end-time' (204ff.); the destruction of the earth and its forms of life marks the 'ecological end-time' (208ff.); the socio-political impoverishment of the Third World indicates the 'economic' end-time (211ff.). These conditions of the end-time affect our life with massive violence. They release a negative undertow which Moltmann calls 'exterminism' (216). But that brings us to the question: how are we to cope emotionally and spiritually with the undertow of these powers of death which swallows us up? How can we come to terms conceptually, ethically and politically with the fact that our time is limited? Whence do we get that indestructible love of life which enables us to break free from the fatalistic embrace of a future that is already past and gain time to live? And this should be more than a meagre survival; it should be the preservation of times and spaces in which future generations can lead dignified and enjoyable lives.

This perception that we live in an end-time shows how topical and urgent it is to reflect on eschatology. If and because human beings have become *faber sui futuri*, the makers of their future, it is indispensable to bear witness to the contrary message of the advent God from whose inexhaustible future we can draw new time.

That the fullness of time is the elixir of the gospel becomes clear in the opening verse of the Gospel of John. There we read: 'John bears witness to him, calls and says, "This is he of whom I said, 'After me will come he who was before me; for he was before me. And of his fullness we have all received grace upon grace'"' (1.15f.). That this 'fullness' may also be understood as a fullness of time is a grace which in the straits of the end-time we need more than anything else.

4. *When God is all in all – the restoration of all things*

Dies irae, the 'day of wrath', the last day, the great and last judgment of the world. For centuries many Christians have regarded this, as they still do today, as that fearful, terrifying 'day of reckoning' on which the Almighty opens the great book of life. Then the just will go to him into eternal glory, but the unbelievers into eternal fire. In countless depictions this 'double outcome of judgment', as the theological experts call it, has been presented in a very vivid way, and in countless sermons God's last judgment has been described as a day of the final reckoning. It is hard to assess how much spiritual anxiety this 'day of wrath' has evoked and deepened. At the same time it must be conceded that the thought of such a day of final vengeance corresponds well with the angry need of many people for compensatory 'justice'.

But if we reflect on the matter somewhat more closely, questions arise: if God is really love, how then can he condemn a large part of his humanity? Or if Jesus teaches us in the Sermon on the Mount that it is a sign of our love of God to love even enemies and to do good to those who hate us, how then can God inflict eternally on those who have hated him the worst conceivable evil, namely eternal torment? And how could redeemed beings rejoice in paradise if they knew that so many unredeemed people are suffering in eternal damnation?

So since the beginnings of theology there has always also been the view that the great judgment of the world is the moment of the 'reconciliation of all', the *apokatastasis panton*, the 'restoration of all things'. Granted this view is still not 'official' teaching in the Catholic Church, and even the confessional writings of the Protestant churches reject it. However, time and again there have been church groups and theological teachers, for example the Blumhardts or Karl Barth, who have advocated the reconcilia-

tion of all. Moltmann also takes this direction. He sketches out
the biblical evidence and discusses at length the questions in the
Reformed tradition which associate the notion of the grace of
election with the doctrine of predestination. However, it is not
these considerations which lead him to speak out for the restoration of all things but a concentration on christology. If we want
'to measure the breadth of the Christian hope . . . we must sub-
merge ourselves in the depths of Christ's death on the cross at
Golgotha' (250). Therefore he concludes: 'In the crucified Christ
we recognize the *Judge of the final judgment*, who himself has
become the one condemned, for the accused, in their stead, and
for their benefit. So at the last Judgment we expect on the Judgment
seat the One who was crucified for the reconciliation of the world,
and no other judge' (250). It follows from this that if we really
believe that the Crucified One has reconciled the whole word
with God, then in the end there can be no verdict other than that
of reconciliation; otherwise Christ would have died in vain.

But in that case the question arises: and how does this message
of reconciliation reach all human beings? How does it reach the
generations which have lived before Christ? How does it get to
people who have not yet heard his word or could not hear it and
therefore have died without him? Moltmann's answer is: 'Christ's
descent into hell is the ground for the confidence that nothing
will be lost. but that everything will be brought back again and
gathered into the eternal kingdom of God' (279). However, this
statement immediately provokes the question how we are to
imagine such a 'descent into hell'. In his explanation Moltmann
follows Luther, who did not interpret hell as a separate place but
as an 'existential experience' (252). Therefore Christ's 'descent
into hell' must be understood as the hellish experience of extreme
godforsakenness which he has experienced in his death on the
cross. So Moltmann's thesis is that the hope for the reconciliation of all things is 'the only realistic consequence of the theology
of the cross' (279).

Is that cheap grace, because in the end it seems to be indifferent
to whether someone has been good or evil? On the contrary, it is
'costliest grace' (254), because its 'wages' were the hellish tor-

ments of forsakenness on the cross. Therefore the 'Last Judgment' is no message of terror, but 'in the truth of Christ it is the most wonderful thing that can be proclaimed to men and women' (255).

Only – is not this 'wonderful message' completely out of date? Which of our contemporaries still lives in an awareness of the 'Last Judgment' and of 'hell'? For most of them is not the existential experience of the *Dies irae,* as it is expressed, for example, in Mozart's *Requiem* with oppressive power, simply an aesthetic museum experience? Moltmann's eschatology does not go into this kind of question. Certainly his plea for the reconciliation of all things is still new and controversial within the world of biblical and theological discussions, but if one goes out of this world into the everyday world, such reflections seem remote and alien. That is not an accusation, but a lament. It is regrettable that at the beginning of this century, as 'makers' of our own future we have also become 'makers' of our own judgment and therefore our own judges, and that because we are godless we have also become graceless, as is proved every day by our world economic (dis)order and the anti-social conditions in our world. What message could free us from this blindness?

5. Soli Deo gloria – *in the kingdom of glory*

As I have already indicated, Moltmann's eschatology ends with 'divine eschatology' (350ff.) and this ends with the doxological cry *'soli Deo Gloria'*, 'to God alone be the glory'. Here Moltmann approaches the question 'What becomes of God? If God is the coming one, when does he come wholly to himself?'

Many believers will think such a question completely senseless, because they begin from the presupposition that God is already 'all in all'. But in the context of Moltmann's universal eschatology it is logical that God can come to himself only when God has taken his whole creation out of its alienation and gathered it into himself.

Hence God is not unconcerned about what becomes of creation. Only the new creation of all things also brings the Creator to his completion and eternal rest. To develop these considerations Moltmann goes through approaches which he finds in Hegel and Whitehead, and then returns to the Shekinah theology of Rosenzweig and Scholem. Only when the Shekinah, which is at work as God's self-emptying power in creation, returns to God, does God come to his consummation. Then the final sabbath dawns. Then the fullness develops and in it is contained the 'interplay of all blessing and praising, singing, dancing and rejoicing creatures' (336). What rings out in Easter jubilation in the face of the experience of the risen Christ is completed in the 'feast of God's eternal joy'. That is how God wants to be loved. Thus it becomes clear that for Moltmann eschatology must go over into doxology. Reflection on the ultimate glory of God then changes into a possibility of glorifying God. 'What does it mean to glorify God?' With this mystical category of the enjoyment of God which comes from Augustine, the question what God means for the world and for us is left behind and replaced by the question what the world and what we could mean for God.

For theologians have also reflected on whether God could in any way be dependent on our pitiful praise for his glorification. Is not God blissful in himself? Manifestly the praise of creatures could not add anything to what God already is and has in himself. Yet Moltmann insists that our praise is as little superfluous for God's bliss as the redemption of creation is for God's peace.

Therefore the last sentence in Moltmann's eschatology is: 'The laughter of the universe is God's delight' (339). In this sentence the doxological shift in eschatology is once again manifest. But it also becomes clear that this shift is the purest mysticism. The 'laughter of the universe' is as much an expression of expectant imagination as the phrase 'God's delight' which reflects Augustine's concept of the *fruitio Dei*. And that 'is' which associates the two pictures suggests a present which not yet 'is' but can always be imagined only 'in the coming'. The immersion in that 'is' of the nearness of God and expectation of the coming God coincide. Such a sentence cannot be followed through rationally, but only in the mode of song, dance and exuberant joy.

Here, however, I would like to go a stage further. In the end,

Moltmann's eschatology goes over into doxology. It seems to me that eschatology ought to be understood to be by nature and therefore from beginning to end *a reflexive form of praying*. 'Thy kingdom come,' says Jesus' prayer. I understand this to mean that we can reflect on the kingdom of God only by praying for its coming. God's kingdom does not 'come' otherwise than in prayer, i.e. in incessant expectation. Nor does it come to consciousness otherwise than in a reflection which regards itself as meditative prayer. In this remark I am basically very close to what is also dear to Moltmann's heart. Thus in 1997, two years after the appearance of his eschatology, he said of his theological 'method': 'A person with different theological views should also be able to say *to* God what he or she says *about* God. It should also be possible to use theology for praying, lamenting or praising.'[171] What follows from that? Only such a theology as has emerged from lamentation and praise, invocation and imploration, can be 'used' for praise and lamentation, for prayer and worship. Theology is prayer developed in reflection: it grows out of it and leads back to it.

However, we understand praying not as a ritual activity for which one occasionally takes a few moments, but as ceaseless awareness, as constant receptivity for God.

The prayer 'Thy kingdom come' reflects the incessant 'work of hope'; it asserts itself as the power of the expectation of God's world in the midst of the constant tribulation of the graceless state of a world which is bordering on its end. So eschatology stands between the cry of need, 'Thy kingdom come', and the doxological praise, 'for thine is the kingdom'. Thus it must go through the long tunnel of despair and drink the bitter water of exile and enmity. It must attempt to endure the suffering of tormented creation. But what is said about 'the coming of God' must also be said to the one who comes. Thus eschatology can go over into doxology, if it allows itself to be recognized as developed prayer from the beginning.

I believe that large stretches of Moltmann's eschatology would have caused me less trouble had I been able more clearly to perceive this nearness to prayer, this constant state of being assailed. I have already pointed out that his indicative sentences suggest a plausibility which is conceivable only within specifically theological discourse and on the presupposition of statements of faith.

Moltmann is aware of this difficulty when in his Preface to *The Coming of God* he concedes: 'Some people think that I say too much theologically, and more about God than we can know' (xiv). That is also my impression. In many passages I have kept asking myself, 'How does he know that? Where does he get the certainty to say things that one cannot say at all?' For example: 'The *end of time* is the converse of time's beginning. Just as the primordial moment springs from God's creative resolve and from the divine *self-restriction* on which God determined in that resolve, so the eschatological moment will spring from the resolve to redeem and the 'self-restriction' of God determined upon in that . . . the primordial time and the primordial space of creation will end when creation becomes the temple for God's eternal Shekinah' (294).

In the passage in the Preface which I have quoted, Moltmann says: 'I feel profoundly humble in the face of the mystery that we cannot know, so I say everything I think I know' (xiv). I can only understand this 'so' like this. Precisely because Moltmann is aware of the deep mystery which we cannot fathom with our knowledge, he says everything that he thinks as he thinks it, trusting that in the community of seeking and questioning Christians this may be accepted as his voice and his contribution. What he offers is 'imagination for the kingdom of God' (xiv). Therefore it is dependent on the imagination of others and remains in dialogue with other 'fantasts' on the way through a barren land. 'My image is the exodus of the people, and I await theological Reed Sea miracles,' he says (xiv).

Therefore the great eschatology, too, remains an expression of expectation. The 'Reed Sea miracle', that overwhelming experience of liberation, is still to come. What remains is expectation.

13

Contemporary and Comrade
of the Kingdom

We have followed Jürgen Moltmann's way over half a century. I have attempted to give a view of his most important books. Now we must sum up the essential contours of this work once again. At the same time I want to bring together the critical observations and remarks that I have made here and there. This is not a matter of 'evaluating' Moltmann's life's work. First, I am not the right person for that, and secondly, it is premature to speak of a 'life's work', for who knows what is yet to come from Moltmann's workshop?

My concern is to demonstrate the main motives which have stamped Moltmann's work over the decades and to elucidate some questions which have come to mind when reading it.

1. *The contemporary*

First of all it should be recalled that Moltmann develops his theology and offers it for discussion as a committed contemporary. Thus the decisive political and social problems which have dogged us since the end of the Second World War are present in his books. Alongside Johann Baptist Metz he has become the most important German representative of a 'left-wing' political theology. Thus it was no more surprising that he was open to Christian-Marxist dialogue in the 1960s than that he was resolute in seeking conversation with liberation theologians all over the world. His tasks as an academic teacher did not prevent him from working in ecumenical commissions. He has never limited himself to his 'chair', but time and again set out to seek an encounter with Christians outside the academic world. Therefore alongside his learned academic works there is a whole series of books with sermons, addresses and more popular discussions.

In Moltmann's books we find statements and proposals on the critical problems of the last four decades. I might mention human rights, racism and sexism, the ecological dangers and the nuclear threat, but I would also refer to the impulses towards church reform, to his commitment to disabled persons and his interest in Sigmund Freud.

I would guess that this *resolute involvement in contemporary affairs* has to do with the place of origin of Moltmann's theology. This consists in the catastrophe of the Second World War, the years in a prisoner-of-war camp, but above all the horror which is associated with Auschwitz. Moltmann's theology came into being near to and in the shadow of personal and collective experiences of death, not in the protected world of a parish community or a monastery. It came into being 'outside the gates'. Here he is very near to his Hamburg contemporary Wolfgang Borchardt, whose play *Outside the Gates* created a big stir in the early years after the Second World War.

Another characteristic of this involvement in contemporary affairs can be described with the key word *ecumenicity*. Here too a reference to the years in an English prisoner-of-war camp is appropriate. His theological work not only came into being in encounter with influential ecumenical figures like Mott and Visser't Hooft, but was also grounded in the experience of reconciliation, the gift of freedom and many proofs of a matter-of-fact solidarity which leaves behind it all frontiers of nations and peoples. It is from this kind of initiation that his curiosity about themes and positions, wherever they present themselves, arises. Confessional provisos and fears of contact are unknown to him. Therefore he is as open to Gustavo Gutiérrez from Peru as to James Cone from New York or Dimitru Staniloe from Romania and many others.

But this profound ecumenicity is by no means limited to academic contacts. Because it is rooted in the experience of a prisoner-of-war camp, it also preserves the memory of the experiences of humiliation, poverty, oppression and dishonour. Half a century later these memories are as alive as ever: they form the mirror in which Moltmann perceives the humiliation and poverty, the oppression and dishonour of ever larger parts of humankind and makes it his cause. Therefore he does not withdraw from the oppressive reality of impoverishment and dependence wherever it manifests itself. His strong commitment to the Protestant Christians in Nicaragua is only one example of the way in which the 'people who walks in darkness' lives in his soul.

2. *The comrade of the kingdom*

Yet it would be wrong to define Moltmann's involvement in contemporary affairs only by the circumstances of his biography or as a consequence of the traumatic experiences of his youth. This commitment is only the other side of what I would want to designate with the pietistic term 'comrade of the kingdom'. Comrades of the kingdom are those Christians who owe themselves to the kingdom of God and attempt to live in its advent power. According to the famous chorale by Johann Rist the comrades of the kingdom live in the expectation of the approaching king. They are 'much tormented' and 'disheartened', but they take comfort in the morning star which has risen before them. They are the poor who are supported by God's mercy, the 'deeply troubled' to whom God's love is directed.

Moltmann's theology is tuned to this key. Christian life arises and exists in the approaching power of the kingdom of God. Christian hope is directed towards citizenship in the sphere of rule of the God who encounters us with his mercy.

Of course other theologians speak of the kingdom of God, too. However, for Moltmann it is a fundamental category. 'Kingdom of God' is the basic symbol for the eschatological dimension which shapes his theology. Because it is the kingdom of the coming God, it has a critical effect on the kingdoms of this world and draws people from the many forms of imprisonment with which they are fettered to their conditions. Therefore the kingdom of God is also called 'the kingdom of freedom'. Its undertow and power of attraction consist in liberation. The advent kingdom has liberating power.

So we can understand *Moltmann's theology as a single great exploratio liberationis dei*, as an investigation of liberation by God, as a single great process in which the scope of God's liberating power is investigated and described. At the centre of these investigations stands Christ, the Crucified One as the Risen One, the Risen One as the Crucified One. These two dimensions must be emphasized; for as much as the resurrection describes the scope of the kingdom, so the cross describes the quality of this kingdom. The Pantocrator is the Son of man who on the cross suffered the whole burden of remoteness from God. The one who 'sits at the right hand of God and intercedes for us', as the creed says, is the one who has suffered and died for us.

Investigating the scope of the kingdom has directed Moltmann's gaze to the dimensions of universal history and the cosmos. If and when the kingdom of the Risen Christ goes out, it not only goes beyond the death of the individual human beings but also transcends the 'death' of human histories and the 'death' of the universe, for its goal is the new creation of all things. Moltmann has emphasized time and again that the kingdom of the coming God is not a new possibility within history but a new possibility for history itself. It has 'turned round' the direction of time. For him, time comes from the future of God, as a river springs from a source. Therefore the transitory nature of all creaturely life puts no limits to this future, although it defines our life, our experiences and our thoughts. The imagination of hope lives by the power of the emanation of the future of God that extends into our temporality. Anyone who is a 'comrade' of this kingdom lives in messianic expectation and waits expectantly for the redemption of all creatures from everything that oppresses and torments them.

However, if one wanted to emphasize only this dimension of the kingdom, one would quickly get near to enthusiastic arrogance and untroubled forgetfulness of the massive torments of our historicity. Therefore Moltmann has time and again directed his attention to the cross of Jesus Christ. For it is the suffering

God whose kingdom comes to us. Therefore the 'comrades' of the kingdom attempt to see the world with the eyes of the suffering God. And therefore they become particularly 'clear-sighted' and sensitive to the suffering of the creatures of God. They are drawn into *messianic compassion*.

That is the inner reason why the suffering of our time plays such a central role in Moltmann's theology. It is the messianic compassion which brings him near to liberation theologies. It is what makes him as receptive to the great ecological dangers as to the mourning of a couple for a stillborn child.

3. Comrade and friend

There is a third element to think of in describing Moltmann's theology as a contemporary and a comrade of the kingdom. The word 'comrade' is by nature egalitarian, and was so long before it became the self-designation of members of socialist parties. Whether we think of comrades in alliances or guilds, battles or parties, the element of equality and equal standing always comes into play. Thus the term 'comrade of the kingdom' has a clear anti-hierarchical ring. Where Christians understand themselves as comrades of the kingdom they can imagine their life only on the basis of common and equal rights and duties. This emphasis is clearly anti-authoritarian, anti-episcopal and anti-monarchical. The community of the comrades of the kingdom understands itself as a community of men and women of equal status but of different gifts; it organizes its interest freely and in a comradely fashion. Their rights and duties concern all in the same way.

From this perspective we can understand the passion with which Moltmann understands the church of Christ as 'community', more precisely as 'community of the people and for the people'. Therefore he criticizes episcopal-hierarchical models of the church and fights for synodical structures of church government. This is the same perspective that supports his argument for democratic relations of partnership in politics and business and his commitment to human rights.

The term 'comradeship' therefore embraces the elements of freedom, justice and solidarity. So it is also understandable that these keep appearing together in Moltmann's ethical approaches.

But it is also these aspects which bring the concept of 'comradeship' near to another concept which plays a central role in Moltmann's theology, that of friendship. Precisely because for him the essence of friendship includes the aspect of reciprocal and public advocacy, it is related to his understanding of comradeship of the kingdom. *Comrades of the kingdom are friends of God* and as such advocates and witnesses of the oppressed and the disturbed, of people who are humiliated and deprived of their rights; for in them the suffering Lord of the kingdom is present.

Comrades of the kingdom see themselves not only as people who are loved by God. They also attempt to love God and accordingly long to be of one heart and one soul with God. This mystical perspective is unmistakable.

4. *Comradely theology*

No one can be a 'comrade of the kingdom' in isolation, any more than anyone can be a friend or a contemporary in solitude. The words 'comradeship' and 'friendship' presuppose community and are the basis of relationships of reciprocal responsibility and loyalty. Comrades and friends exist only in the plural. What does that mean for theology, or more precisely for the working out of theology?

Moltmann wants all his books to be regarded as 'contributions' to that theological work which he takes for granted as part of the 'communion of saints'. For him the 'priesthood of all believers' also means that all believers are theologians. This is true of his programmatic writings in a particular marked way. In them he wants to illuminate the whole of theology from a specific perspective. Therefore he also attempts to indicate the most important implications for politics, ethics, pastoral work or church reform. That is beyond doubt one of the reasons why Moltmann's books are so popular. He takes a position and shows the specific consequences of his theological considerations. But as so often, a person's strengths are also his weaknesses. Where Moltmann limits himself or has to limit himself to hints, readers would often like to read more, and more precise statements. In the previous chapters I myself have occasionally drawn attention to the fact that the detailed development of particular proposals leaves a great deal to be desired, so that they often persist in a certain proclamatory vagueness. The critical proposals for a reform of the church from the plan of a 'community church' leave many questions open. The preoccupation with Freud remains sporadic, and many aspects of pastoral theology really should have been discussed in more detail. As I have shown, the ethical remarks are fragmentary.

This may sound like censure of Moltmann's theology, but it is not meant in that way. My concern is rather different. In the case of each of Moltmann's three or four programmatic writings, and then again with the 'Contributions', I have asked myself the following questions: Why has no publishing house or other institution taken the initiative to bring together a team of theologians with the plan of developing the implications of each programmatic writing? Why is Moltmann left alone with his programmatic writings?

It may be objected that he has not been left at all 'alone' with his work. In the end there has been a committed discussion of his positions, as is shown by the two discussion volumes on *Theology of Hope* and *The Crucified God*. And there are reviews, letters and other reactions to his other books which fill whole filing cabinets. My question is about something different. The conditions for the production and reception of theological works which still prevail are out of date. Someone sits in a study and writes his or her work. If it is then published, often after laborious negotiations, the hope is that it will 'make its way'. Of course it is clear to me that there are effects of synergy both in working out theological books and also in using them publicly, but is not all too much left to the fashions, chance features and modes of the market? This may be a limited risk as long as a scholarly work is addressed to a small group of experts. But the broader the topics of a work and the more indefinite the audience to which it is addressed, the less chance there is that it will be really received. The more international and complex the reality which a work attempts to address, the greater will be the degree of selectivity.

Today there can be hardly an individual scholar, however learned, who can estimate and describe appropriately the scope of a programmatic scheme. That is also true of Moltmann. So why has no attempt been made to take one of his works as the basis of an international and interdisciplinary treatment and in this way to examine its scope and usefulness? In other scientific spheres, for example in ecology or in economics, work is being done with the hermeneutic model of the scenario. The 'Club of Rome' was one of the first group of authors to proceed in this way. They did not make the claim to be able to describe the problems of world-wide developments 'conclusively' or 'exhaustively', but worked with an experimental scenario in order in a provisional way to be able to deal with complex phenomena at many levels and arrive at tentative proposals for solutions. Why do we not proceed in a similar way in theology?

What would have been even more obvious than to use one of Moltmann's programmatic writings, shall we say *Theology of Hope*, as the basis for a scenario that would have given various experts the opportunity to develop specific aspects rather more precisely than is possible for an individual author in a single book? Then the problems for ethics, pastoral theology, the sociology of the churches, ecumenical work or philosophy could have been discussed in more detail than one can reasonably expect from an individual author, however learned and diligent.

So this work on a theological scenario would have to be regarded as a 'comradely' effort. It would need to be seen neither as a composite volume by pupils nor as a discussion volume by critical reviewers but as a communal attempt to examine the viability of a theological programme for various fields of theory and practice.

I still recall very clearly the helpless annoyance with which as a theological student I had to note how my professors withdrew into the fields of their expertise (as exegetes, systematic theologians, church historians or even as practical theologians) and left me all alone, expecting me to put together these varied approaches, methods and contents to form a theological picture with which I might confidently begin to work as a parish pastor. Since then I have been able to note that the trend towards forming an 'in-group language' has strengthened further. An awareness of increasing complexity encourages a retreat into the relatively limited field of a specific discipline, with the result that the theological experts withdraw into academic niches and the 'consumers', in so far as there still are some, act in an increasingly more selective way. Who will and can go to work to develop a coherent theology which is as understandable as possible without appearing to some as far too 'naïve' and 'journalistic' and to others still as far too 'intellectual'. In such circumstances does not the saying about the 'theology of all believers' become a farce?

It is not my view that the development of specific specialist languages can be revised, even if it has its doubtful side-effects. But I do think that it would be possible to work with scenarios within this theology which is split up into different disciplines. They would have the great advantage of making the hermeneutic communication between these 'professional languages' more intensive. In addition, applications and transferences by way of models could contribute towards reducing the distance between different fields of theory and praxis, between experts and 'lay' people. As Moltmann rightly keeps saying, it is not a matter of a *theologia perennis*, an eternally valid theology, but of a *theologia viatorum*, a theology for those who are on the way.

Therefore theologians too should have the courage to work with scenarios, not only to improve communication within theology, though this too is urgently necessary, but to contribute to the testimony of God's gracious kingdom in the spheres of life in our world.

There are examples of this mode of procedure in the ecumenical movement. One could consider the great study processes of the Faith and Order Commission which have led to declarations of convergence on baptism, the eucharist and ministry as such 'scenarios'.[172] However, what seems to me even more significant is the way in which feminist theology has formed and the modes of work it is developing. It is working in a really 'comradely' way, since it starts from the 'feminism of all women', i.e. it takes all interested conversation partners seriously and believes that they have relevant theological experience and insights. It organizes its way in partnership, and here academies and Kirchentage provide the basis for 'ambulant faculties'. It comes from the people (the women) and addresses the people (the women); it is not a sect of women but also addresses men. That most men act as if none of this concerned them is another matter. Granted, words like 'comrade' and 'comradely' are unfashionable; they lean too far to the left and are so dusty that even confessed Social Democrats are beginning to hesitate about addressing one another with these old honorific titles. But can that be sufficient reason for banishing the word from our vocabulary? Isn't the matter of which it speaks so important that we have every occasion to rehabilitate this age-old and venerable word?

The example of feminist theology shows what the contours of a new 'comradely' theology could look like. Where comradeship and involvement in contermporary affairs are combined, there comes into being *the kairos,* the messianic moment, which sets free charismatic forces. In other words, where the eschatological hope of God's gracious encounter meets the perception of our unredeemed circumstances, possibilities arise in which the Spirit is present. This insight can be read at many points in Moltmann's books, yet it is difficult to draw the practical consequences which arise from this.[173]

Basically, Moltmann's theological approach reaches beyond the theological faculties. Yet here he seems to have a blind spot. Indeed more recently it looks as if he wants to defend the system of theological faculties in German state universities, although this is really a legacy of the Constantinian association of throne and altar and therefore must be criticized as resolutely as the 'official church which looks after people'.[174] If it was really the case that the freedom of theology depends on its 'institutional independence'[175] then it would not be worth much. Important as a 'public theology'[176] is, it hardly needs the legal and financial support of state officialdom. This can also encourage academic eccentricity and political cowardice, just as church officialdom does not make pastors bold and courageous confessors of the liberating message of God.

The relevance of public theology emerges wherever people allow themselves to be kindled, set on fire and inspired by the messianic power of the advent God. It arises where people are led by this messianic fire to have compassion on all those who suffer in this world. And these people need comradely forms of collaboration, working groups and coalitions. To make this possible the faculties must make themselves available along with church officials. What public is involved where the kingdom of God is proclaimed? Moltmann writes: 'All Christian kingdom-of-God theology becomes for Christ's sake a theology of liberation for the poor, the sick, the sad and the outcasts. So kingdom-of-God theology doesn't just enter the already existing forum of its given society. It brings to light publicly the people whom society pushes into the underground or into private life.'[177] And because this must be so, the practical consequences need to go beyond what he himself has suggested thus far.

14

Discovering the Inviting Mystery –
Messianism and Mysticism
in Moltmann's Theology

1. The central theme: history in the advent of God

History is *the* theme of Jürgen Moltmann's theology. He is not interested in the question of being but with the question of becoming. What *happens* to us? What *becomes* of us and our world? They are questions which occupy him much more intensively than the classical questions of ontology.

It must immediately be added that 'history' is a *central theological category* for Moltmann. The way in which he speaks of history is deeply rooted in faith in the crucified and raised Jesus of Nazareth, the Christ of the world and the messiah of the peoples. That is evident at every point in his books.

The history of Jesus Christ is grounded in, and affirms, faith in the God who acts in history, of whom the Hebrew Bible is full. The experiences of Israel bear witness to God who 'makes' history in a surprising and contingent way. 'Yahweh' is not the transcendent ground of ever-recurring cosmic cycles but the God of the exodus, the God who inexhaustibly points forward, going before, guiding and accompanying. This Yahweh calls his people on a way and covenants mark the form of these wanderings in time. A common history comes into being; it deals with loyalty and apostasy, reliability and obedience, new starts and refusals. The prophetic and ultimately the apocalyptic testimonies show how the experiences with this history of God open up ever wider horizons until all peoples with their history, until finally history itself, and that means heaven and earth, are included.

Presumably Moltmann's early studies of Reformed covenant theology shaped his basic attitude to the theology of history, but it was substantially reinforced by the covenant theology of Old Testament exegetes like Gerhard von Rad and Ernst Bloch's philosophy of history. However, the resurrection of the crucified Christ remains the decisive point of reference, and it is here that hope gets its anchorage. What has happened to him can happen to all of us! If this one man has overcome death, death itself is overcome. Thus the transitory world is taken up in the undertow of the imperishable loyalty of God, and the experiences of transitoriness are put in the light of unhoped-for possibilities. And more than that: the resurrection of Christ symbolizes a divine power which does not just renew one or the other *in* history, but puts history itself on a new footing. The flow of time is reversed. Time flows from God's future. Where this advent God encounters us, all things appear in a new light. For the future is not already *passé*; on the contrary, even in the past there is much that is anything but *passé* and still has its future ahead of itself.

Thus eschatology becomes the determining quality of history. As we have seen in Moltmann's 'messianic christology', the 'way of Jesus Christ' opens up ever greater horizons. The eschatological expectation becomes cosmic and universal and is ultimately directed to the new creation of all things.

But the question arises, can the history of this one Jesus of Nazareth, which is two thousand years old and took place in a corner of this world, really serve as the starting point for such a universal eschatology? Does not this theology of history balance on the needle point of what is basically a very particular event? In his work Moltmann shows that his orientation on the cross and resurrection of Jesus Christ is by no means aberrant and particular, but leads into the centre of the Christian understanding of God. Therefore he thinks it important to state that the cross and resurrection of Christ form the substantive core of the theology of the Trinity. And therefore trinitarian theology is unfolded as one single great history of the love of God for his creation, which in turn is qualified again in such a way that it still has before it its consummation in the 'kingdom of glory'.

2. World history as 'anonymous' kingdom of God history?

The breadth of this universal eschatological theology of history is fascinating. It brings the whole world within the sphere of God's influence. It awakens hope, gives wings to expectation, encourages responsible work and strengthens powers of resistance against the forces that threaten to destroy God's creation. Precisely because the destructive capacities of human beings have become global, faith too must mobilize its universal vital force. Nevertheless, I ask myself, does not this theology of history assume too much? In the way in which it regards the whole history of the world as the history of God, does it not contain a claim which extends far beyond what the Christian religion may claim? Is there not here a disguised claim to domination?

This question occurred to me when I was reading Moltmann's critical account of the transcendental theology of Karl Rahner.[178] Rahner had started from the conviction that the human subject is intrinsically transcendental, since it is destined to receive God's self-communication. 'God's communication of himself to humankind through grace is matched by the fundamental inner self-transcendence of the human being.' [179] There is thus a correlation between theology and anthropology. God's communication of himself as incarnation therefore forms the mysterious nucleus of true humanity. Moltmann concludes: 'The immanence of God in humankind and the transcendence of humankind in God coincide in Christ.'[180] From here Rahner arrives at the reflection that to be a Christian is 'explicit' humanity and that true humanity amounts to being an 'anonymous' Christian.

Moltmann thinks that in talking about 'anonymous Christians' Rahner has built a bridge to modern men and women and overcome a picture of human beings which was narrowly defined by the church. In this way, Rahner can 'make clear the universal significance of being a Christian in particular', but would run the risk of not taking the pluralism of religions and the freedom of religion in the modern world seriously enough. 'Is not too much being asked of Christian existence if it is already meant to depict the universal truth to humanity? Is that not the old claim to absoluteness on which so many Christians have come to grief . . . ? Do we not also have Jewish existence and human existence in other religions alongside Christian existence, each its own way of being "expressly human"?'[181]

According to Moltmann, the strength of the thesis of the 'anonymous Christian' is that it 'mediates the whole Christian tradition by stressing the meaning of the mystical dimensions of Christian faith'. But in his view this is also its weakness, for it could also have 'the hidden purpose of laying claim to all that is truly human through the church'.[182]

Now this brief sketch of Rahner's position leads me to make the following observation: if we replace 'being human' by 'history' and 'being expressly human' by 'kingdom of God', then history becomes the 'anonymous' history of the kingdom of God. It is not as if Moltmann understood the kingdom of God as an abstract futurity which never intervenes in concrete history. On the contrary. For him the kingdom of God has a transforming, renewing, indeed revolutionary force, just as the history that really exists is receptive to the history of the kingdom of God. That is why eschatological chiliasm is so important to him. However, that means that all history, and not just Christian history, is 'transcendent' to the kingdom of God, and the hoped-for new creation of all things applies.

From the perspective of Christian theology that is certainly a universalizing which leaves behind a sectarian concept of 'salvation history' and certainly also an impressive way of describing the 'mystical depth dimension' of the Christian view of time and history. But as with Rahner, its weakness lies in the latent danger that it takes things over. What humanistic atheists would want to understand their view of history as an 'anonymous' history of 'God'? Nor could Muslims or Buddhists be content with subsuming their particular understanding of history under the universal-historical claim of Christianity. Why should their history of faith disappear in the 'kingdom' of a God in whom they do not believe? Ought they not to feel that this kind of universalism is a disguised form of a claim to domination?

I do not doubt that Moltmann would regard such an interpretation as a misunderstanding, yet I feel that the dilemma I have indicated is there. Is there a solution to it? I think that such misunderstandings could be reduced if Moltmann were to emphasize more clearly the *kerygmatic character* of his theology of history, and argue less by expounding theses. I understand the key word 'kerygmatic' to mean that we can attest the coming God most convincingly if we live and work in his Spirit. Moltmann himself has shown what that might look like in his critical consideration of Rahner's position: the more universal the messianic hope, the more partisan must be its messianic compassion for the poor and outcast: 'It is not the bourgeois liberalism in the First World which confronts theology with the fundamental problems of mediation and making present, but the liberation of the poor and needy in the Third World and among the displaced strata of modern society in the First World.'[183]

So really I am only recalling the hermeneutical principle that we keep finding in Moltmann's work, namely that faith must be recognized under its opposite. The eschatological universalism of kingdom of God theology is proved in the universalism of the partiality of the church for the victims of violence and destruction, wherever these may be. It proves itself also as the power of comfort for the many people who no longer see a meaning in their life and in the 'great' history fear only chaotic collapses.

In this connection we might recall Moltmann's interpretation of the honorific titles of the church of Christ at the end of *The Church in the Power of the Spirit*. There he says that the unity of the church consists in its freedom. Its catholicity is recognized in its partisanship, its holiness is proved in poverty and its apostolate shows its missionary power in suffering. By the key word 'kerygmatic', however, I mean something more, namely the very way in which theology presents itself. If the passionate hope of the coming kingdom of God proves itself in compassion for the poor and the helpless, then this should also be reflected in the language and style of the account. The 'higher' the subject, the more personal the conviction must be. The breadth of hope is not matched by the didactic and deductive style of the academic lectures but by a language which allows personal questions and tribulations to be expressed. To put it personally from my side, too: precisely because the subject is one which is 'higher than all reason', I do not want to be taught from a lofty standpoint, but I need comrades for the way who leave room for my aporias and doubts and openly indicate that sometimes they too are helpless.[184] Therefore I have always been able to use best those parts of Moltmann's books in which he is arguing personally. I do not believe that this is a matter of 'style' or personal temperament; it is part of the compassion and solidarity in which the expectation of the coming God takes form.

3. A speculative theology?

Anyone who describes Moltmann's theologies as 'speculative' must expect a cross reaction. For in his books the word 'speculative' always has derogatory connotations. What is remote from reality is called 'speculative'.[185] Now one could argue that there are passages in his works which by current notions are 'alien to reality'. I might recall, for example, the remarks on the cosmic Christ or the parousia of Christ.[186] The discussions of 'cosmic eschatology' and the 'divine eschatology'[187] also seem extraordinarily 'alien to reality'.

But that is not the point I am concerned with here. I think it necessary to overcome the derogatory use of the word 'speculative' so that the original meaning of this term can again be brought to bear. Since the days of the great Origen there have been venerable traditions of 'speculative theology'. It is no longer generally known that speculation played a great role in the Protestant theology of the nineteenth century. Richard Rothe, whom Moltmann esteems highly, also belongs in this context.[188]

Speculative thought is derived from the Latin word *speculum*, meaning mirror (the evocative terms *theoria* and *eidos* are the Greek equivalents). Thus it refers to something seen, to a 'vision' of things, and therefore starts from the perception of the senses.

And this sensual or historical experience becomes the ground (Greek *arche*) for the development of more complex connections.

For Thomas Aquinas, speculation is to be derived from meditation, and thus speculation means nothing other than the development in thought of a truth seen intuitively. To this degree speculative penetration of something grasped intuitively is a generally accepted process which is virtually indispensable for understanding between people. Only in modern times has interest shifted from speculative to practical science. However, we must ask whether Christian theology ever claimed to be a 'practical' discipline in this sense, i.e. a discipline which can be examined empirically. The resurrection of Jesus from the dead cannot be proved empirically, indeed were it to be proved as a historical datum it would forfeit its eschatological singularity. The same is true of the category of the covenant between God and Israel, and it applies lastly to the notion of God itself, since 'no one has seen God at any time', as aptly said in John 1.18. What we experience about God is based on the Logos, i.e. on what 'the only-begotten Son who is in the bosom of the Father' has 'proclaimed' to us. Thus this Logos is the *speculum* in which God's love is reflected, and we must keep looking in this mirror to assure ourselves of the ground of our faith.

So I think that theology as a reflective development of experiences of faith can essentially only be understood as speculative, unless it wants to allow itself to be reduced to the history of dogma or religious studies. Therefore I cannot see either why it should be a disadvantage to understand Moltmann's theology, especially the 'Systematic Contributions', as an example of 'speculative theology'. Such a perspective even makes it easier for me to follow him on his high flights of trinitarian theology or eschatology. Then I can understand far better his 'transcendental power of imagination'[189] as an expression of his 'curiosity' as a believer, than if I am asked to regard these as a logical development of allegedly self-evident 'truths of history'.

Earlier I have also described Moltmann's theology as a single great *exploratio liberationis dei*, as a discovery of the liberating action of God which has its *speculum* in the messianic history of

Christ. From this basis the speculative voyage of discovery extends into universal and cosmic breadths, but the kerygmatic and practical political reference can always be recognized. The issue is more than the salvation of the individual human soul and something very different from the invocation of an eternal salvation in the beyond; the issue is the understanding of God as a single energy embracing the world and drawing it into itself. Concepts like 'indwelling', 'perichoresis' and 'process' underline this dynamic concept. Thus Moltmann is not only pursuing the interests of enabling theology to enter into dialogue with scientific world-views, especially cosmological and evolutionary shcemes.[190] His theology of history is always also to be understood as an expression of his political commitment. 'In the biblical writings "the kingdom of God" is the broadest, *most comprehensive horizon of hope for the general well-being of the world.*'[191]

So that must not be overlooked. If Moltmann's theology is a 'speculative theology' it is at the same time *a theology of resistance*. Anyone who is seized by the one who is to come is not content with what is there. 'Delight in Christ's resurrection makes Christians what Christoph Blumhardt aptly called "protest people against death". And that includes the protest against the political and economic forces which have made a covenant with death.'[192]

4. *Talking about God is talking to God*

I have already pointed out that Moltmann also wants his theological talk about God to be understood as talking to God. 'It should also be possible to use theology for praying, lamenting or praising.'[193] I believe that the word 'use' is inadequate. When Moltmann goes on immediately to describe his theology as a 'journey of discovery of ideas in an inviting mystery',[194] prayer, lamentation and praise is more than a useful 'by-product' of theology; it is something like its inner dynamic. After all, prayer in all its forms is basically an exercise in receptiveness to the 'inviting mystery'; it is the daily effort towards an 'open heart' for the mystery of salvation. And this attracts our ideas, challenges them, even if time and again it defies all 'definitions'.

So I think it appropriate to read Moltmann's theology as an *explicatio orationis*, as an unfolding of prayer. Or to be more precise: his *exploratio liberationis* develops in the tremendous tension which exists between the petition 'Thy kingdom come' and the doxological affirmation 'Thine is the kingdom, the power and the glory, for ever and ever.' This tension contains both the experiences of abandonment and the darkness of God in which one cries out for the kingdom and laments its absence, and the inspiring experience of the radiance of the kingdom which in its power and glory already 'is' with us.

Here it is important that these two sentences from the Our Father have different forms. The 'come' in the first clause is an optative and an imperative at the same time. Thus it corresponds with the gesture of the petition and the imploring expectation. But the second sentence is governed by the indicative, the 'is'. Here nothing is any longer expected, but all is confirmed and reinforced. Here only the doxology, praise and thanksgiving, applies. Moltmann's theology is stretched out between expectation and trust, between impatient longing and cheerful relaxation.

So if I understand his theology as an explication of prayer, as a great convergence with the 'inviting mystery', the main indicative statements about the 'coming' of God, about the relationships within the Trinity, about Christ as the wisdom of the cosmos, and much more, take on another colouring. Then I no longer read them as the intimidating remarks of a religious divine, but perceive in them a tone of amazement and infinite awe. I begin to understand that the indicative statements have a doxological undertone. I learn no longer to read them as instruction but as an expression of joy and delight. Then I perceive in them not the teachings of an expert who knows 'better' about everything, but the invitation of a companion who gives me courage to attempt my own 'voyage of discovery into the inviting mystery'. Such voyages of discovery involve much imagination.

Therefore it is not by chance that Moltmann – alongside curiosity – has mentioned 'fantasy for the kingdom of God' as his most important theological virtue.[195] In the concluding volume of

his 'Contributions' he even uses the term 'theo-fantasy'.[196] But as
it is not a long way from fantasy to the fantastic, and Moltmann
is well aware of this, he aims at a theological explication which is
as ordered and logical as possible. Precisely because his theological trains of thought about God are to become a fanciful
'dance' of thought 'before' God, he wants to avoid intrinsic
contradictions and irrational leaps of thought. However, this does
not happen in order to present the ring dance of theo-fantasies as
a finished product, but to open it up to others. *Moltmann's
fantasy is intended to encourage the power of imagination* and
not to oppress others with an apparatus of learning.

So when I suggest reading Moltmann's books as an 'invitation
to an intellectual dance', I do not mean that this is a simple exercise.
This dance, too, has to be learned, and those who think it is done
with wild leaps are very wrong. It takes some patience to follow
the steps and figures which are performed and recommended in
this 'school' of dance. Moltmann would immediately concede
that this course is measured and adopts and varies some traditional moves. Indeed, I often have the impression that with his
'theo-fantasies' he persists far too much in the theological 'dance
school' which has developed over almost two thousand years, and
that therefore despite all the efforts to become a contemporary
he moves within a conceptuality which is comprehensible only
within the world of theologians with an academic training. That is
true of many of his central terms, I would mention only 'Trinity',
'kingdom of God', 'kingdom of glory', 'promise', 'rebirth',
'election in grace' or 'reconciliation of all things'. They all
require such an effort of lesser trained theologians and 'laity' in
particular that they might dampen down the delight in sharing
in the dance.

Is it illegitimate to describe Moltmann's theological work with
words from the world of the dance? In many pietistic circles,
dance was forbidden to the 'comrades of the kingdom'. So how
could the thoughts of believers learn to dance? And from this
perspective it must inevitably seem alien, if not frivolous, that
faith and theology have something to do with 'participation in
the delightful play of love of the divine Wisdom, which permeates

all that is created'.[197] What does this kind of erotic language look for in the world of theology?

5. *The mystical ground of theology*

Or when I describe Moltmann's work as an unfolding of prayer and at the same time as an erotically tuned dance of 'theo-fantasy', then I am approaching the mystical ground of his theologizing. Here I am aware that Moltmann would not describe himself as a mystic. Yet that is not out of order. On various occasions I have pointed out that Moltmann refers at length to the mystical traditions in Judaism and Christianity. It is even a characteristic of the 'classical' period of the 'Contributions' that the acceptance of mystical notions, images and forms of language increases.[198] In particular I would recall the Jewish Shekinah mysticism which has a significant place in Moltmann's trinitarian theology; Hildegard of Bingen has a normative status not only in 'Spirit theology'. Then there is also the long tradition of a speculative mysticism of history which extends from Jacob Böhme through Friedrich Oetinger and Benedict Baader to nineteenth-century philosophy. Without it Moltmann's eschatological process thought would be inconceivable. As I showed in the previous chapter, other mystical authors come into play. But it is in these three mystical currents that Moltmann's messianic theology of history is most clearly rooted.

So it is amazing that Moltmann does not make these mystical components of his work a more explicit theme. In the concluding volume of the 'Contributions', *Experiences in Theology,* which has already been mentioned on several occasions, there are extended hermeneutical reflections. But there is no chapter on the mystical ground of his thought in his theological epistemology. At best one could point to Chapter 3 in Part I ('What is Theology?'). There Moltmann discusses the question 'How does someone become a true theologian?'.[199] And the sub-title 'Suffering in God and delight in God' betrays that here mystical categories come into play. But this brief passage can hardly be regarded as a methodological treatment of the basic mystical features in Moltmann's theology.

Here we have a remarkable restraint. Part of the explanation is perhaps that academic (and male) theologians still react to mysticism with a certain inner reserve. For mystics were regarded – and still are – as weird outsiders, as irrational eccentrics and visionary fantasists. They are incalculable, their mode of expression evades a 'systematic' order, and cannot be conceptualized. Mystics know about falling silent in the 'dark night of the soul', just as they know about ecstatic jubilation in moments of visionary illumination. Therefore the mystics are regarded as aliens in the business of academic theologians, just as they have been suspect to church governments of all times as provocative disturbers of the peace.

Mystics are regarded as introverted aliens to the world and 'unpolitical'. How wrong this prejudice is becomes evident as soon as we look at their careers.[200] Precisely because they are so receptive to the 'inviting Spirit', they have developed radical alternatives to the course of the world. Poverty, lack of possessions, non-violence – the central themes of a political ethics come from mystical sources. 'Prophets are mystics in action' says the American mystic Matthew Fox. Liberating theology is at heart mystical theology.

It seems to me that with his theology Moltmann stands on precisely this threshold. He points to *the mystical basis of his messianic hope* without subjecting this, too, to a systematic analysis. His theology of history is based in messianic mysticism. I think it good that he acknowledges this basis without once again 'asking behind' it hermeneutically.

To make the point once again: for Moltmann, true theology is the expression of an 'intellectual love of God'.[201] But this 'love of God' is like any other love. We can say a great deal about it, but who knows what it is, where it comes from, how it is renewed and how it can be lost? Those who have never been in love cannot understand what others say about love. But those who are filled with love also know how poor the words are, how wretched and inadequate, so that the nearer we get to the inviting mystery, all that remains is the 'still cry', the eloquent silence. And the silent song of praise.

A century ago Rilke wrote the lines:

> I turn around God, the lover of old,
> and I circle again and again.
> And I wonder, am I a falcon, a storm
> or an unending refrain?

Here is the mystical movement of the incessant circling around the eternal centre. With Moltmann the mystical moment takes quite a different course. It is like a voyage on the open sea. What could distort the gaze on the horizon is left behind. There are no longer any markings for the way that the ship has to take. God's promises are the stars that govern the course. The breadth of the ocean seems infinite, but the messianic longing sees 'through the horizon'. It strives for the goal which comes to meet us; it does not seek refuge on any isle of the blessed but looks out for the new land, so to speak the 'Land of Good Hope'.

6. *Kingdom of God – kingdom of freedom*

For Moltmann the 'kingdom of God' is at the same time the 'kingdom of freedom'. His imagination for the kingdom is meant to be understood as imagination of liberation. Even if it is risky to put a label on a theologian, I think that it would be appropriate to regard Moltmann's life work as one great and varied work towards an applied or applicable theology of liberation.

Why do 'freedom' and 'liberation' have this central role for him? Because these two concepts are code words for modernity and at the same time in their theological qualification represent critical counter-concepts to the project of modernity.

When Moltmann's *Theology of Hope* appeared, questions relating to society and social politics were being widely discussed. 'Socialism' was by no means the non-word that it is today. 'Political theology' expressed the expectations and demands of many Christians. The impulses of renewal all over the world came from the beginnings of liberation theology. At that time Moltmann's theology was in fashion.

In the meantime it seems that many of us have lost faith that conditions can be improved. In other words, the everyday pressure of a 'world order' which is becoming increasingly global, which is increasingly dominated quite openly by the oppressive dualism of winners and losers, is numbing many people, making them perplexed, at a loss, disheartened, thoughtless. The claim of a public theology is falling victim to the manifold excursions into the new inwardness.

Is liberation theology *passé*? The base communities praised by many liberation theologians are in retreat, and not just in Latin America. By contrast evangelical communities and fundamentalist groups have entered on their triumphal course. Even if it were wrong to suspect these movements sweepingly of being 'apolitical', in their tremendous variety they reflect the varied range of our situations. Is 'liberation' still the key word for what humanity needs?

If we consider the forms of imprisonment in which humankind is bound, there can be only one answer. Liberation is needed as urgently as ever before. At the same time it is evident that liberation is all too often (mis)understood as permission to seize power. Indeed it is precisely here that the ambivalence of modernity lies, that it combines the undeniable gain in freedom with new forms of slavery.

Moltmann has associated the forms of liberation which humankind needs today with the key concept of 'indwelling'. I need not recall the manifold biblical echoes which are associated with this term. If liberation is understood as indwelling and indwelling as liberation, then a broad field of creative possibilities and challenges opens up. Will we learn to become human, to live in peace with one another, without allowing ourselves to be torn apart by economic discrepancies, battles over distribution and 'spheres of interest'? Will we learn to live with nature, as the various ecoregions allow, without asking of nature more than it can bear? Will we learn to preserve the world's capacity for life so that coming generations too can enjoy life?

The key words 'liberation' and 'indwelling' provoke a criticism of power. It is therefore important to intensify the 'comradely' qualities of freedom, for the narrower the spaces become in which humankind is concentrated, the sharper are the conflicts and the more merciless the forms of the misuse of power.

Earlier I quoted Matthew Fox's saying: 'prophets are mystics in action'. Having emphasized the mystical aspects in Moltmann's theology I must therefore now also emphasize its prophetic character. Moltmann may not be 'fashionable' in some quarters at present, but that does not matter. It is far more important that the prophetic protest remains alive, in season or out of season. His protest against all forms of imprisonment and his ethic of resistance to all forms of the misuses of power is needed as urgently as our daily bread. And only as we affirm this constant tension will we realize his passion for life and appreciate his deep joy in the blessed creation of God. In this constant contradiction his passion for life will be recognized and his deep joy in God's blessed creation understood.

A Select Bibliography of the Works of Jürgen Moltmann

In order of the dates of the original German publications. Dates of the English translations are given at the end of each entry.

1959 *Die Gemeinde im Horizont der Herrschaft Christi. Neue Perspektiven in der protestantischen Theologie*, Neukirchen

1959 *Herrschaft Christi und soziale Wirklichkeit nach Dietrich Bonhoeffer*, Theologische Existenz heute NF 71, Munich

1961 *Der verborgene Mensch. Zum Selbstverständnis des modernen Menschen*, Das Gespräch 35, Wuppertal-Barmen

1962/63 (as editor), *Anfänge der dialektischen Theologie* (2 vols), Theologische Bücherei, Munich

1964 *Theology of Hope. On the Ground and the Implications of a Christian Eschatology*, London 1967

1964 *Gottesbeweise und Gegenbeweise*, Das Gespräch 46, Wuppertal-Barmen

1968 *Perspectiven der Theologie, Gesammelte Aufsätze*, Munich and Mainz (the English translation, *Hope and Planning*, London 1971, contains just eight of these articles)

1970 *Umkehr zur Zukunft*, Siebenstern Taschenbuch 154, Munich and Hamburg

1971 '*Mensch. Christliche Anthropologie in den Konflikten der Gegenwart, Themen der Theologie*, ed. H. J. Schultz, 11, Stuttgart – Berlin

1971 'The First Liberated Men in Creation', in *Theology and Joy*, London 1973

1972 *The Crucified God. The Cross of Christ as the Foundation and Criticism of Christian Theology*, London and New York 1974

1972 *Die Sprache der Befreiung* (sermons and meditations), Munich

1977 *The Open Church, Invitation to a Messianic Life-Style*, Philadelphia and London 1978

1979 *Experiences of God*, London and Philadelphia 1980

1980 *The Trinity and the Kingdom of God*, London and New York 1981

1981 *Ohne Macht mächtig* (sermons), Munich

1985 *God in Creation. An Ecological Doctrine of Creation*, London and New York 1985

1988 *Theology Today. Two Contributions towards Making Theology Present*, London and Philadelphia 1988

1989 *The Way of Jesus Christ. Christology in Messianic Dimensions*, London and Philadelphia 1989

1989 *Creating a Just Future. The Politics of Peace and the Ethics of Creation in a Threatened World*, London and Philadelphia 1989

1991 *The History of the Triune God. Contributions to Trinitarian Theology*, London and Minneapolis 1991

1991 *The Spirit of Life. A Universal Affirmation*, London and Minneapolis 1992

1994 *Jesus Christ for Today's World*, London and Minneapolis 1994

1995 *The Coming of God. A Christian Eschatology*, London and Minneapolis 1996

1997 *The Source of Life. The Holy Spirit and the Theology of Life*, London and Minneapolis 1997

1997 *God for a Secular Society. The Public Relevance of Theology*, London and Minneapolis 1999

1997 (as editor) *How I Have Changed. Reflections on Thirty Years of Theology*, with contributions by N. Greinacher, E. Jüngel, H.Küng, J. B. Metz, E. Moltmann-Wendel, J. Moltmann, P. Potter, D. Sölle and J. Zink, London and Valley Forge 1997

1999 *Experiences in Theology*, London and Minneapolis 2000

D. Ising, G. Geisthardt, A. Schloz, *Bibliographie Jürgen Moltmann*, Munich 1987

W.-D. Marsch (ed.), *Diskussion über die 'Theologie der Hoffnung' von Jürgen Moltmann*, Munich 1967

M.Welker (ed.), *Diskussion über Jürgen Moltmanns Buch, 'Der gekreuzigte Gott'*, Munich 1979

H. Deuser, G.M. Martin, K. Stock and M. Welker (eds), *Gottes Zukunft – Zukunft der Welt, Festschrift für Jürgen Moltmann zum 60. Geburtstag*, Munich 1986

Notes

Full bibliographical details are given in the list of Moltmann's works contained in this book.

1. *The Source of Life*, 2. My italics.
2. Ibid., 4f. (author's italics).
3. Ibid., 6.
4. Moltmann has commented on various occasions on the charge of one-sidedness. In his answer to the criticism of *The Crucified God* he says: 'This "one-sidedness" is evidently a method in my theological work, perhaps more unconscious than conscious.' And he adds: 'One-sidedness has sometimes been claimed with a view to the greater fellowship of theology,' in Welker (ed.), *Diskussion über 'Der gekreuzigte Gott'*, 165f.
5. *The Trinity and the Kingdom of God*, xii.
6. In *How I Have Changed*, 20 (my italics).
7. *The Source of Life*, 5.
8. Ibid.
9. On the occasion of an international SCM conference at Swanwick in Summer 1947. Cf. ibid.
10. Ibid., 4.
11. Ibid., 6.
12. *How I Have Changed*, 15.
13. Elisabeth Moltmann-Wendel has given various pieces of information about her life and her career in theology. Most important is her *Autobiography*, London 1997. Her brief account in *How I Have Changed*, 37–44, is also illuminating.
14. Cf. Moltmann's article, 'Prädestination und Heilsgeschichte bei Moise Amyraut', *ZKG* 65, 1954, 270–303.
15. The Habilitation thesis appeared in 1961 under the title *Prädestination und Perseveranz. Geschichte und Bedeutung der reformierten Lehre de perseverantia sanctorum*, Beiträge zur Geschichte und Lehre der reformierten Kirche 12, Neukirchen 1961. It seems to me remarkable in this context that with Cocceius not only does a theologian come to the fore who had lived in Germany and Holland but that

he put the category of the covenant at the centre and grounded it in an approach with a markedly biblical orientation. This federal-theological dimension stamps Moltmann's understanding of covenant and history.
16. This is the German title of a successful book, published in English as *The Women around Jesus*, London and New York 1982, with which Elisabeth Moltmann-Wendel established herself as an independent theologian and as one of the leading representatives of feminist theology in Germany.
17. See especially Chapter 7, 131ff.
18. Moltmann, *Die Gemeinde im Horizont der Herrschaft Christi*, 7 (further references to this work will be cited with page references in the text).
19. The work of the Dutch theologian van Ruler had a liberating effect on Moltmann. There he recognized that after Barth it was still possible to work out an independent theology.
20. *Fundamenten en Perspectieven van Belijden* appeared under the title *Lebendiges Bekenntnis* in a translation by Otto Weber, who also wrote an introduction, ²1959.
21. In this connection it should be pointed out that in the very year in which his brief 'programmatic writing' appeared, Moltmann also published a study *Herrschaft Christi und soziale Wirklichkeit nach Dietrich Bonhoeffer*. This describes Bonhoeffer's doctrine of mandates at length (45ff.). It is illuminating that Bonhoeffer's influence on Moltmann steadily diminishes from the beginning of the 1960s.
22. Ibid., 61.
23. *How I Have Changed*, 15.
24. Cf. the reflections on a 'comradely theology' in Chapter 13, 224ff.
25. J.Moltmann (ed.), *Anfänge der dialektischen Theologie*.
26. Quotations are given by page numbers in the text.
27. *How I Have Changed*, 15.
28. Ibid.
29. Gerhard von Rad, *Old Testament Theology* II, London 1975, vii.
30. Ibid., viii.
31. Therefore it is remarkable that Moltmann has not published an ethics of hope. Certainly he has repeatedly given lectures on this theme, but he did not feel that the results he arrived at were sufficiently convincing to be published. That is hardly a good reason, since in his 'programmatic writings' Moltmann regularly adopts 'one-sided' positions which therefore need expansion. If in the death and resurrection of Christ God's history of promise opens up a new and unprecedented turning point in history, then must that not help not only the *docta spes* but also the *spes practica*? Or does it become evident in ethical reflec-

tion how ambivalent the concrete conclusions really are and how great the 'quota of errors' in concrete ethical judgements can be? But if that were the case, should it not then have been taken as an occasion to think through more precisely the ambivalence of any theology of hope? For Moltmann's ethical approaches see Chapter 6 (107–22).

32. It is impossible to trace the history of its effect. There is a first survey in W.D.Marsch (ed.), *Diskussion über die 'Theologie der Hoffnung' von Jürgen Moltmann*. This contains thirteen comments and an 'Answer to Criticism' by Moltmann. There is a list of further views on p.239.

33. Ibid., 233.

34. Ibid., 212.

35. Thus Marsch, ibid., 12. However, Marsch immediately adds that this 'lack of concretion' can also be indicated in all his critics. None of them 'has been able to indicate more precisely what God's "new world" really looks like – beyond fundamental democratic, social or socialist postulates'.

36. Ibid., 197, 198.

37. Ibid., 199f.

38. Ibid., 231.

39. Ibid., 237.

40. Ibid., 13.

41. Quotations are given by page numbers in the text.

42. *How I Have Changed*, 17.

43. Ibid.

44. The 'Cappadocians' include above all Basil the Great, Gregory of Nyssa and Gregory of Nazianzus, who were active in the second half of the fourth century and made an important contribution to the development of the doctrine of the Trinity which was stated in the creed of 381, the Niceno-Constantinopolitan Creed.

45. Cf. Chapter 8, where Moltmann's doctrine of the Trinity is described in more detail.

46. M.Welker (ed.), *Diskussion über Jürgen Moltmanns Buch, 'Der gekreuzigte Gott'*. This book has fifteen contributors in dialogue and in the appendix gives a far more extensive list of comments.

47. Ibid., 172.,

48. Ibid., 115.

49. *How I Have Changed*, 19.

50. M.Welker (ed.), *Diskussion über Jürgen Moltmanns Buch, 'Der gekreuzigte Gott'*, 113.

51. Quotations are given by page numbers in the text.

52. Dennis Meadows, *Limits to Growth. A Report for the Club of Rome's Project on the Predicament of Mankind*, London 1972.

53. Chapters V and V essentially form a unity. In Chapter V Moltmann discusses the 'means of salvation' and in Chapter VI the 'offices' or 'charisms' of the church. But both belong very closely together under the concept of the 'messianic community of service' (223).

54. Here it is worth referring, if only in a note, to a short book by Moltmann of only 79 pages in the German which was very important for him; it was published in English as 'The First Liberated Men in Creation' in a volume entitled *Theology and Joy*. This tract, which had been reprinted in Germany six times by 1981, was written in a direct critical discussion with the student protest movement and in conversation with the Dutch theologian Arnold A.van Ruler, the Czech philosopher Viteslav Gardavsky and the American theologian Harvey Cox. Explicit mention should also be made of the works of Gerhard Marcel Martin, Moltmann's assistant at the time. The concern of these 'attempts' is to reassert 'the value of aesthetic joy against the absolute claims of ethics' (thus in the introduction, 1). The leading question is: 'Have the old Pharisees and the new zealots with their conservative and revolutionary legalism scared us away from freedom from joy and spontaneity?' (ibid.). Of course the counter-questions immediately crop up: 'How can we laugh and enjoy ourselves when innocent people are being killed in Vietnam? How can we play when children are starving in India? How can we dance when human beings are being tortured in Brazil' (26f.). Moltmann maintains that in the face of the everyday torments of which the world is full, there are two kinds of game, the distracting games of the entertainment industry, which serves to veil and trivialize everyday pains, and on the other hand the prelude of liberation, which is seized by the joy of the coming kingdom in clear awareness of the suffering of this world. Moltmann sets over against the infantilization of the satisfaction and entertainment industry the Easter experience of being children of God. 'The images for the coming new world do not come from the world of struggle and victory, of work and achievement, of law and its enforcement, but from the world of primal childhood trust' (55). 'The rule of law spoils everything, even the revolution of freedom,' Moltmann states (64). This statement indicates what is at stake. Much as Moltmann makes the 'revolution of freedom' his cause, he also clearly recognizes the dangers which lie in an exclusive ethicizing and politicizing of freedom.

55. Moreover already in 1971 Moltmann had spoken on the theological understanding of human rights in a study by the Reformed World Alliance on the theological understanding of human rights: 'The Theological Basis of Human Rights and of the Liberation of Human Beings', in *The Experiment Hope*, 147–57.

56. Moltmann had already spoken on racism on various occasions since 1971. Here mention need only be made of 'Racism and the Right to Resist', in *The Experiment Hope*, 131–46.

57. Cf. Moltmann's article 'Die Rehabilitierung Behinderter in einer Segregationsgesellschaft', in *Sozialisation und Rehabilitation* 57, Stuttgart 1974, 73–82.

58. The term 'a church which looks after people' crops up in many places in *The Church in the Power of the Spirit* with polemical intent and serves as a criticism of the traditional practices of the church in the (West) German regional churches.

59. I ask myself whether this repudiation of the concept of sanctification is a happy one. Certainly sanctification has had an ambivalent history, but the same can also be said of the concept of rebirth. Moreover 'rebirth' at all events denotes the initial step into a relationship with God, whereas 'sanctification' reflects far more closely the process of this relationship. In his pneumatology of 1991, the notion of sanctification is discussed at length, see 161ff.

60. Since the famous 1950 'Toronto Declaration' of the Central Committee of the World Council of Churches, these ecclesiological problems have been on the agenda. Is the WCC merely an organ of its member churches or does it have its own ecclesiological validity? Can it be regarded only as an instrument of 'foreign policy' for churches which otherwise insist on their separate identity, or does it mark the beginning of something like a world-wide church in conciliar fellowship? Moltmann evidently opts for the latter perspective, but we should not overlook the fact that it is vigorously disputed in the WCC.

61. That is evident from the fact that in these sections almost always only Reformed theologians are quoted, above all Moltmann's teacher Otto Weber.

62. *How I Have Changed*, 27.

63. 'The separation of politics, economics, and the sciences from ethics has become intolerable and can no longer be tolerated,' stated Moltmann succinctly in 1989 (in *Creating a Just Future*, 47). How they could be brought together in practice remains an open problem even for Moltmann. The 'categorical imperative for the survival of humankind' (ibid.) alone will not do this. It could be that the death drive of humankind is stronger than its will to live.

64. From this perspective, yet further partners should really be introduced into the conversation, namely representatives of the various arts and cultures. If I see things rightly, Moltmann has not entered into this dialogue. Music and theatre, sculpture and painting hardly play any role.

65. *The Open Church*, 40.
66. Cf. Moltmann's programmatic article of 1967, 'Die Revolution der Freiheit', in *Perspektiven der Theologie*, 189–211. The first sentences of this text, which is based on a lecture at the conference of the Paulus Gesellschaft (April 1967), run: 'Christian faith understands itself authentically as a beginning of a freedom such as the world has not yet seen. It not only believes in freedom but is freedom. It not only hopes for freedom but is freedom' (189).
67. *Umkehr zur Zukunft*, 127f.
68. Ibid., 128.
69. Ibid., 121.
70. Ibid., 128ff.
71. Ibid., 130.
72. *Creating a Just Future*, 53.
73. Ibid., 66.
74. Ibid., 67.
75. Ibid., 69.
76. Cf. D.Ising, G.Geisthardt and A.Scholz, *Bibliographie Jürgen Moltmann*, and in it positions 157, 296, 297, 308, 319, 332, 357, 358, 415, 436. This reflects a preoccupation with the problem of human rights which extends continuously right into the 1980s.
77. *Creating a Just Future*, 13.
78. Ibid., 14.
79. Here too there is a diversity of shorter and longer comments. Cf. Ising et al., *Bibliographie* (n.76), positions 194, 305, 341.
80. Ibid., positions 425, 426, 444, 462, 463, 464, 495.
81. Cf. n.5. How radical the discovery of feminist questions was for E.Moltmann-Wendel was is evident from the first sentence of her autobiography', 'On an August morning in 1972 the world did a U-turn for me,' *Autobiography*, London 1997, ix.
82. *How I Have Changed*, 41.
83. *History and the Triune God*, 167.
84. At the closing consultation of this study in Sheffield the Moltmanns gave an address which was much noted, see Elisabeth Moltmann-Wendel and Jürgen Moltmann, *God – His and Hers*, London 1991, 1–16.
85. Cf. Ising et al., *Bibliographie* (n.76), positions 175, 176, 191, 241, 252, 265, 321, 401, 435, 476, 477.
86. *Mensch*, 163.
87. *The Open Church*, 59.
88. Ibid., 60.
89. Ibid., 62.

90. Ibid., 63.

91. Ibid., 90.

92. Ibid.

93. Ibid., 91.

94. Ibid., 89.

95. Ibid., 105. It is striking that here Moltmann works with the concept of 'brotherhood' (the inclusive language 'and sisters' in the published English translation has been added by the translator). He could have also spoken just as aptly of the 'friends of the Judge of the world'.

96. Ibid., 71.

97. Ibid., 72.

98. Ibid., 76.

99. Ibid., 117.

100. Ibid.

101. Ibid., 115.

102. Moltmann shares this approach with minjung theology.

103. *The Open Church*, 59.

104. Ibid., 107.

105. Ibid., 102: 'The only true socialism is democratic "socialism of the people" which is realized by the people.'

106. Cf. especially *Creating a Just Future*, and in it the chapters 'Does Modern Society Have a Future?' and 'The Nuclear Situation: The Theology and Politics of Peace', 1–50.

107. *Creating a Just Future*, 22.

108. Ibid., 4.

109. Ibid., 24.

110. *How I Have Changed*, 19f.

111. *History and the Triune God*, 180.

112. Ibid.

113. Ibid.

114. Ibid., 181.

115. Quotations are given by page numbers in the text.

116. By now in Germany it has already reached its eighth impression, 60,000 copies.

117. M.Bührig, *Spät habe ich gelernt, gerne Frau zu sein. Eine feministische Autobiographie*, Stuttgart 1987.

118. J.Moltmann, 'Die Theologie unserer Befreiung', review of I.Ellacuria and J Sobrino (eds), *Mysterium Liberationis, Orientierung* 19, 1996, 204ff.: 206.

119. Thus in the introductory chapter of *The Trinity and the Kingdom of God*, 1. Quotations from this book are given by page numbers in the text.

120. *The Church in the Power of the Spirit*, 61.

121. My italics.

122. My italics.

123. In 'I Believe in God the Father', in *History and the Triune God*, 7.

124. Cf. especially the second contribution in *History and the Triune God*, the title of which is 'The Motherly Father and the Power of His Mercy', 19ff. Starting from the background of motherly experience in the Hebrew understanding or mercy (the Hebrew word *raham* means both 'womb' and 'mercy'), Moltmann attempts to overcome the masculine content in the traditional concept of Father.

125. *History and the Triune God*, 6.

126. Ibid., 11.

127. Ibid.

128. Ibid., 14.

129. Ibid., 15.

130. Ibid., xviii.

131. These discussions take place in *History and the Triune God*, Part II, 91ff. We find another round of conversations in *The Trinity and the Kingdom of God*, 132ff., where the positions of Arius, Sabellius, Tertullian, Barth and Rahner are discussed.

132. *History and the Triune God*, xviii.

133. It is in keeping with this that Moltmann has dedicated his collection of articles *History and the Triune God* to Dumitru Staniloae. He calls this well-known Romanian theologian his 'fatherly friend', 'who encouraged and stimulated me in thinking about the Trinity'. It is important that Moltmann also concerned himself intensively with overcoming the *filioque* dispute, which is one of the essential reasons for the separation between the Eastern and Western church, and which has overshadowed the whole of the second Christian millennium. Cf. his proposals on this in *The Trinity and the Kingdom of God*, 178ff.

134. We can see from the Pauline conception that God is the head of Christ, that Christ is the head of the man, and that the man is the head of the woman, that this perspective is already used in the New Testament to characterize relationships between the sexes.

135. The doctrine of the Trinity as a critique of patriarchal forms of thought is impressively developed in the first two articles in *History and The Triune God*. The first text, 'I Believe in God the Father', from 1983, explicitly discusses patriarchal and non-patriarchal talk of God, 1ff.; the second article, written in 1981, is concerned with 'The Motherly Father and the Power of His Mercy', 19ff.

136. *Experiences of God*, 19–80.

137. *Gotteserfahrungen – Hoffnung, Angst, Mystik*, Munich 1979, 7f. (this passage is not included in the English edition, *Experiences of God*).

138. *Experiences of God*, 69.

139. Quotations are given by page numbers in the text.

140. From the generation before him, only Barth, Tillich and Bultmann were invited to give the Gifford Lectures.

141. However, the twelfth chapter is presented as an 'appendix' and is therefore not numbered.

142. Moltmann says: 'I have dropped the earlier divisions of theology, which followed the pattern of the three articles of the Apostles' Creed. Instead, I have interwoven these three articles together in a trinitarian sense so that I was able to develop a pneumatological doctrine of creation' (xii).

143. 'Creation is the term that describes the miracle of existence in general,' Moltmann notes in his discussion of theories of evolution (196).

144. That is discussed in more detail in Moltmann's eschatology, cf. Chapter 12, 201–4.

145. In a separate section in Chapter IX, Moltmann discusses the theme of the image of God in human beings. The trinitarian approach is evident from the fact that he develops the definition of the image in three ways. He distinguishes between the 'original determination of human beings', the *imago dei* and the 'messianic calling', the *imago Christi*, and then develops these further in the 'eschatological glorification of human beings', which he embraces with the term *gloria dei*. This 'social likeness' (234) is to be understood as a critical counter to the interpretations of the image of God which were accepted in Western Christianity, following Augustine, as theories of rule (of the spirit over the body, the man over the woman, human beings over nature). So this understanding of *imago* does not encourage any individualism, but emphasizes the social form of human relationships. In this connection Moltmann also speaks of the 'anthropological triangle' (241) which embraces the social and generative quality of the 'whole human being': 'everyone is a man or a woman, and the child of his or her parents . . . If the whole human being is designated the image of God, then true human community – the community of the sexes and the community of the generations – has the same designation' (241). It is important to note that here Moltmann adopts terms from gestalt therapy, because he sees this as a helpful parallel to the perichoretic structure of his anthropology (cf. 353 n.40).

146. In this connection I should mention reflections which Moltmann presented in different variants during the 1990s. Here I would single out the article 'Is There Life after Death?', which is about the following questions: 'Is everything all over with death? Is there a life after death?

What becomes of our life when we die?' In it he discusses the Catholic doctrine of purgatory, the Lutheran doctrine of the sleep of souls and theories of reincarnation. But above all he is concerned with the question of what will happen to the many forms of unlived, interrupted and squandered human life. If all really had to be up with death the 'whole world would plunge into absolute absurdity' (163). Against this he sets his belief in God, which is expressed in the following creed: 'I believe that God will also complete the work that he has begun in a human life. If God is God, even violent death cannot prevent him from this. Therefore I believe that the history of God will go on with our life after our death, until that consummation is achieved in which a soul finds rest' (163). Here we recognize the theocentric character of Moltmann's doctrine of creation and anthropology. As all creation is taken up into God's history of love, his love also 'lives' until this love reaches its consummation. So it is not our death which decides what becomes of our life; that is decided in and with God's love. See 'Gibt es ein Leben nach dem Tod?', in *Sterben und Tod. Studium generale der Ruprecht Karls-Universität Heidelberg*, Heidelberger Verlagsanstalt 1998, 151–64.

147. There are many themes in J.Böhme which are reminiscent of the Kabbala. But as he knew neither Latin nor Hebrew it is difficult to make out in what way he may have been influenced by them.

148. The English physicist and theologian A.R.Peacocke is quoted with approval, whereas the discussion with A.N.Whitehead and the process theology influenced by him could in my view have been longer.

149. Here I would mention the different understanding of time and eternity (112ff.) and the criticism of the 'psychological doctrine of the image of God' (235ff.).

150. Here particular mention should be made of Thomas's notion of the image of God in human beings (236ff.).

151. Among other things, Moltmann also criticizes in Barth the distinction between the creation as the *theatrum gloriae Dei* and the saving work of God as the 'drama' which is played out in this theatre (60ff.), the 'nominalistic' theory of God's freedom of choice (81ff.) or the subordinationist understanding of the 'ruling soul' and the 'ministering body' (252ff.).

152. *The Way of Jesus Christ*, 15. All subsequent quotations are given by page numbers in the text.

153. I should remark, by way of criticism, that I regard the term 'stages' as open to misunderstanding. It suggests a sequence of stopping points and thus a kind of mechanical straight line which involves particular phases or points. Thus notions are suggested which are liable to construct the eschatological character of the 'history of God'. The

term 'dimensions' used in the subtitle of the book seems to me to be more appropriate.

154. Chapters III and IV are close to the remarks which Moltmann has developed in *Theology of Hope* and *The Crucified God*, so that to sketch out these sections would lead to overlappings and duplications.

155. The English translation substitutes another hymn which is not quite so evocative. The notion of greening might go back to the mediaeval mystic Hildegard of Bingen, who had spoken of the 'greening' of the cosmos.

156. I am not sufficient of an exegete to decide whether it is admissible to understand the honorific titles of Jesus as messianic dimensions and use them to construct a kind of salvation-historical sequence. I begin from the assumption in form criticism and tradition criticism that the diversity of these 'titles' is conditioned contextually and historically, but that in the end they are always meant to express the same whole mystery of Christ. Thus for example the Gospel of John, by beginning quite emphatically with the Logos hymn, means that the whole life and activity of Jesus is that of the Christ of God, not just his activity as the risen One in the breadth and depth of the cosmos.

157. Cf. See pp. 213–15 below.

158. In the 1985 preface of the doctrine of creation Moltmann presents the overall plan. According to this the eschatology was to follow immediately after the christology. Cf. *God in Creation*, xv.

159. Quotations are given by page numbers in the text.

160. Here among other titles mention should be made of the contributions on pneumatology by Michael Welker, *Gottes Geist. Theologie des Heiligen Geistes*, Neukirchen 1992, and Geiko Müller-Fahrenholz, *God's Spirit Transforming a World in Crisis*, New York 1995.

161. Nevertheless Zinzendorf later expressed the insight that it was 'disorder' that he, a man, had proclaimed this office of mother and not a sister. By this he is indicating that he saw the emancipatory span of this Spirit theology, for example, in relation of the opening up of church leadership to women. That Moltmann emphasizes these aspects once again sheds light on his nearness to feminist theology. Cf. also E.Moltmann-Wendel (ed.), *Die Weiblichkeit des Heiligen Geistes. Studien zur feministischen Theologie*, Gütersloh 1995.

162. In this context he refers to his *Theology of Hope* and concludes that this overcomes the 'time-eternity scheme' of Karl and Heinrich Barth. It has been replaced by 'eschatology as the horizon of expectation for the historical experience of the divine Spirit' (7).

163. I have discussed the problem of forgiveness in more detail in *The Art of Forgiveness*, Geneva 1996.

164. The Joel revelation of the outpouring of the Spirit on all flesh plays a major role for Moltmann.

165. Quoted in J.Zink, *Dornen können Rosen tragen. Mystik – die Zukunft des Christentums*, Stuttgart 1997, 216.

166. Quotations are given by page numbers in the text.

167. Advent is the eschatological category and the category of the *novum* its historical equivalent.

168. That these reflections are directly rooted in Moltmann's biography is indicated in the middle of this eschatology. When he writes, 'Think of the life of those who were not permitted to live, and were unable to live', he is thinking of people in his own family. 'The beloved child, dying at birth' is the first child that was given to Elisabeth and Jürgen Moltmann and immediately taken away. 'The little boy run over by a car when he was four' is his brother's only son. 'The disabled brother who never lived consciously and never knew his parents' is Moltmann's brother, a year older than him, who died in 1940. 'The friend torn to pieces by a bomb at your side when he was sixteen' is his best friend who was killed alongside the sixteen-year-old Moltmann in 'Operation Gomorrah', which destroyed large parts of Hamburg. I refer to these biographical details because they can help to keep in view the existential urgency of Moltmann's eschatology, even if I find it difficult to follow where it moves in high and remote places.

169. He does not discuss the question of hell here but at the end of the 'historical eschatology', 250ff.

170. It is hard to see why Moltmann does not decide for one of the two terms throughout. Whereas in sections 3 and 4 he discusses two forms of 'political millenarianism', in 5 and 6 he speaks of 'ecclesiastical' and 'epochal' chiliasm.

171. *How I Have Changed*, 20.

172. I see the project *Mysterium Liberationis*, edited by I.Ellacuria and J.Sobrino, Maryknoll, NY 1995, as an illuminating example of a 'comradely' way of proceeding.

173. Even the most recent book, *Experiences in Theology*, offers no help here. Although he is discussing 'ways and forms of Christian theology' (to quote the sub-title) he does not go beyond the conditions of the construction of his theology.

174. Cf. 'Theology for the Church and the Kingdom of God in the Modern University', in *God for a Secular Society*, 245ff.

175. Ibid., 248.

176. Ibid., 1, 252.

177. Ibid., 253.

178. Cf. *Theology Today*, 67ff. In my view this little book is an excel-

lent introduction to the theology of the twentieth century. I find the individual accounts of Bultmann's 'existentialist theology', Rahner's 'transcendental theology' and Tillich's 'cultural theology' particularly illuminating.

179. Ibid., 69.

180. Ibid., 71.

181. Ibid., 73.

182. Ibid., 75.

183. Ibid., 78.

184. In her autobiography, Elisabeth Moltmann-Wendel sheds light on what I want to say here. She and Jürgen had expressed their readiness to give a dialogue lecture in the concluding consultation of the WCC study on 'The Community of Women and Men in the Church', which took place in Sheffield in 1981. In preparing the lecture 'there was the difficulty that our speaking styles were very different. In feminist theology I had learned to speak personally, to say "I", to make theological statements based on my own experience. Jürgen was used to the style of the theological lecturer, where the content was everything . . .' She continues: 'finally we found a tolerable style: Jürgen learned to say "I" and to connect this "I" with his theological insights and knowledge, and I learned that I could not make him a feminist,' in *Autobiography* (n.13), 103.

185. Cf. *The Spirit of Life*, 199. See also 126, where the concept of speculation is qualified with the adjectives 'obscure' and 'cloudy'. Cf. also the following sentence from *The Way of Jesus Christ*, in which Moltmann says, 'The vision of cosmic redemption through Christ is therefore not a speculation. It emerges logically from the christology and the anthropology' (183). Would that make speculation the opposite of logic?

186. In *The Way of Jesus Christ*, 274ff., 313ff.

187. In *The Coming of God*, 257ff., 321ff.

188. Cf. S.Ebbersmeyer, 'Spekulation', *HWPh* 9, 1355–72; E.Schott, 'Spekulative Theologie', *RGG*³, VI, 234–7.

189. This is an expression of Kant's which Moltmann reclaims for his theology. Cf. his retort to the review by C.Link of *The Way of Jesus Christ*, *EvTheol* 1, 1987, 93.

190. As I have demonstrated, Moltmann discussed Teilhard de Chardin at some length, but did not get beyond occasional references to Alfred North Whitehead. Here it would have been stimulating had Moltmann gone more intensively than he did into Whitehead's approach to a 'speculative philosophy' given in Edinburgh in his 1927/28 Gifford Lectures, almost sixty years before Moltmann's. Cf.

Process and Reality. An Essay in Cosmology, New York 1960, especially Part I, 'The Speculative Scheme'.

191. *God for a Secular Society*, 252.
192. *Experiences in Theology*, 26f.
193. *How I Have Changed*, 30. Cf. also 'How does someone become a true theologian? Suffering from God and delight in God', in *Experiences in Theology*, 23ff.
194. Ibid., 19.
195. *How I Have Changed*, 20.
196. *Experiences in Theology*, 25.
197. Ibid.
198. However, we should not overlook the fact that Moltmann had already done work on Protestant mysticism in the 1950s, 'Grundzüge mystischer Theologie bei Gerhard Tersteegen', *EvTheol* 16, 1956, 205ff.
199. *Experiences in Theology*, 23ff.
200. D.Sölle, *Mystik und Widerstand. 'Du stilles Geschrei'*, Hamburg 1997, and J.Zink, *Dornen können Rosen tragen* (n.165), are illuminating in this context.
201. *Experiences in Theology*, 25.